# CHARACTER AS FORM

D0815139

# CHARACTER AS FORM

## Aaron Kunin

### With illustrations by David Scher

BLOOMSBURY ACADEMIC
LONDON • NEW YORK • OXFORD • NEW DELHI • SYDNEY

BLOOMSBURY ACADEMIC
Bloomsbury Publishing Plc
50 Bedford Square, London, WC1B 3DP, UK
1385 Broadway, New York, NY 10018, USA

BLOOMSBURY, BLOOMSBURY ACADEMIC and the Diana logo are
trademarks of Bloomsbury Publishing Plc

First published in Great Britain 2019

Copyright © Aaron Kunin, 2019

Aaron Kunin has asserted his right under the Copyright, Designs and Patents Act, 1988, to
be identified as Author of this work.

For legal purposes the Acknowledgments on p. 215 constitute an extension
of this copyright page.

Cover design: Alice Marwick

All rights reserved. No part of this publication may be reproduced
or transmitted in any form or by any means, electronic or mechanical, including
photocopying, recording, or any information storage or retrieval system,
without prior permission in writing from the publishers.

Bloomsbury Publishing Plc does not have any control over, or responsibility
for, any third-party websites referred to or in this book. All internet addresses
given in this book were correct at the time of going to press. The author and publisher
regret any inconvenience caused if addresses have changed or sites have
ceased to exist, but can accept no responsibility for any such changes.

A catalogue record for this book is available from the British Library.

Library of Congress Cataloging-in-Publication Data

Names: Kunin, Aaron B., author.
Title: Character as form / Aaron Kunin.
Description: London, UK; New York, NY: Bloomsbury Academic, 2019. |
Series: Beyond criticism | Includes bibliographical references and index.
Identifiers: LCCN 2018030389 (print) | LCCN 2018050545 (ebook) |
ISBN 9781474222686 (ePub) | ISBN 9781474222693 (ePDF) |
ISBN 9781474222716 (hardback) | ISBN 9781474222723 (paperback)
Subjects: LCSH: Characters and characteristics in literature. | Literary form–History.
Classification: LCC PN56.4 (ebook) | LCC PN56.4 .K86 2019 (print) | DDC 809/.927–dc23
LC record available at https://lccn.loc.gov/2018030389

ISBN: HB: 978-1-4742-2271-6
PB: 978-1-4742-2272-3
ePDF: 978-1-4742-2269-3
eBook: 978-1-4742-2268-6

Typeset by Deanta Global Publishing Services, Chennai, India
Printed and bound in Great Britain

To find out more about our authors and books visit www.bloomsbury.com
and sign up for our newsletters.

# CONTENTS

# INTRODUCTION

## Confession

Part of what one does in a job is pretending to do the job. Pretending to be a teacher or a cop or an assistant in an office or a store. Pretending to be busy. Pretending to listen. I suppose it is an element of play in work. It explains why workers need evidence "that they are still in the trade they were trained for," as Erving Goffman observes (Goffman 1961, 145). Stacking chairs, moving pianos—is this part of my job? Goofing off—is this how I spend my time? Everything that I do without caring demoralizes me, and I look for evidence that I care about something.

Sometimes the answer is yes. This pretending can be good for me. Pretending to know something or to be interested in something. I rely on imagination for my intellectual development. If I stopped pretending, I might never learn anything new. Much of what I do as a teacher boils down to inventing reasons for my students to care about something they may never previously have imagined as a valuable thing. The Shakespeare survey that I teach comes as a relief because it is a rare occasion when I do not have to create the value of the book we are reading. My students bring their own reasons for thinking that Shakespeare is important. In fact the value of teaching Shakespeare does not have to be explained to anyone outside of the profession of literary studies.

Part of my job exists only to convince me that I am actually doing my job. To remind me that "I am in the trade I was trained for." This is the worst kind of pretending. In school, where I work, this pretending takes the special form of question and answer. My students ask a question and I invent an answer. I ask my students a question and they invent an answer. I listen to an interesting lecture, ask a question about something vaguely relevant, and get a brilliant improvised answer. I listen to a boring lecture, invent a question out of pure spite, and ignore the speaker's response.

Some of these questions are sincere and productive of knowledge. Others, without intending to produce knowledge, may do so inadvertently. They are all seemingly designed to produce false issues. School is always creating situations where talk is required, and these situations are a breeding ground for intellectual dishonesty. Because saying something is automatically superior to saying nothing, because no one takes my protestations of uncertainty or ignorance seriously, because it is never acceptable to refuse to answer, because the continuation of the form of question and answer is the only thing about which anyone reliably cares, I invent false issues. Then, because what I say is coercive—it seduces me more than it seduces my audience—because anything that exists tries to convince me to adjust to what is already there, because what I imagine saying but keep to myself has its own dark coercions, I pretend to care about the false issues. I add to them. They become my life's work.

It is possible to dedicate your entire working life to false issues. Things that (you would think) no one could possibly care about.

The same problem may be observed in writing. I once knew a writer whose entire style, on the level of the sentence, was about multiplying false issues, moving them into view, and pretending to care about them. Always at the center of what he wrote, he narrated the production of his own narration until he somehow managed to dress the needless in the clothes of the fundamental and crucial—describing this attention to the needless as, finally, an ethics.

Something that is not well understood about writing is that when you write something, you have to inhabit it. I was about to say that I don't mean that in a magical thinking way, but I do sort of mean it in a magical thinking way. Everyone knows how it happens when you read a book. If you read a book about bees, for instance, you start to notice the bees in your life. It can feel as though bees are following you. They appear before you as though in crazy synchronicity with the content of the book you are carrying. Suddenly they are everywhere. And their presence is easily explainable, because the book is simply pointing out the bees that were always in the background of your life.

And the same process occurs, in magical and non-magical ways, when you write a book. If you write a biography of Paulette Goddard, and the book comes out, someone might ask you to give a lecture about her. Someone organizes a symposium on movie stars from the 1930s and invites you to give a paper. That happens a couple of times, and pretty soon, before you know it, you have written enough material for a second book about Paulette Goddard. Then you read about a conference on women in classical Hollywood film and start grumbling because they *didn't* invite you to participate. Someone just mentions Goddard, and you say, "Yes, here I am, present!" Meanwhile you have been doing research, spending all your days in the Goddard archive, and members of her family and the Remarque family and the Meredith family have been sending you stuff, old letters, clothes, photos, all the stuff they don't want and can't fit in their closets, and it piles up in your house until, really, the subject of your book has taken over your entire life, and you may truthfully say, "I am Paulette Goddard."

When you write something, you have to inhabit it. An ethics for writers should start here. Thus I am opposed to the idea that the relationship between writer and reader models a better kind of social relationship. That from studying books I learn to read people better. That in reading I encounter something other than myself and learn to recognize it, respect it, empathize with it. And the related idea that writers should prepare for the activity of readers. That I should empathize with readers, anticipate what they will care about, and reward them for their attention.

These ideas are not only wrong but harmful. Wrong because how you feel about other people is not a reliable foundation for an ethics. It isn't possible to have a personal relationship with everything. It isn't even true that my actions would be better if I learned to empathize with my victims. No. Better to treat people well regardless of how I felt about them. Regardless of whether I cared. Even if I couldn't stand them.

Harmful because everything I write without caring demoralizes me. There is nothing worse than writing, trying to write, what I do not care about. At these times my imagination of how readers are likely to respond, sheer paranoia and projection irrelevant to my own pleasure and conscience, torments me.

One of the first things you learn about poetry is that it is an address to something that does not appear. Writing that professes to accommodate readers, to reward them for their attention, has already given up on this possibility. Accommodating readers is not ethics at all; it is rhetoric. About which I am skeptical, and, like everyone, suspicious.

# How I wrote this book

The ethics of writing, I am saying, is to write well. To be honest and have good style. Writing well is a problem for literary criticism. You know, we live in a world in which there is a lot of great art. We are blessed to live in a world where there is so much great poetry and music and painting and film. But there isn't a lot of great criticism. There is a certain amount of good criticism, and that's better than nothing. When criticism is good, it produces useful knowledge. Great criticism is as great as anything. Criticism, really great criticism, like in essays by Empson or Auerbach or Poulet or Colie, can be just as great as music or the movies.

Reading Michael Clune's essay on Orwell's *1984*, I see the novel in a new way. Reading Anne-Lise François's essay on Hardy's *Poems of 1912-1913*, I see the poems in a new way. The critics show you things that were always in the works of literature that they are studying, but that no one saw before. Reading great criticism, you are reading a work of literature through someone else's eyes. That experience is unfortunately a rare one.

I want to write better criticism. At least I want to do better than what I have done so far.

I started writing this book in 2007. Two things happened to me that year, two responses to my writing, that made me want to write differently. The first was something a few readers said in response to my style. Three different people, Robert, Peter, and Sawako, had asked what I was writing about. Then they got interested in what I told them and asked to see what I was writing. And when I gave them some writing, they couldn't read it. These were all highly educated people. All three were writers. The first two had appointments in English departments at schools with a lot of prestige. They were familiar with idioms of academic writing in literary studies. They read a lot of literary criticism. But they couldn't read my writing. Even when they were excited about my ideas and wanted to read about them.

Their responses felt like a sign of a serious problem. The problem isn't only mine. Part of the problem may be professional jargon. And it may be unfair to complain about the use of jargon in academic writing. I mean, if academic writing is going to produce useful knowledge, it has to be allowed to develop its own precise language. And maybe part of the problem is overspecialization. Maybe academics like Robert and Peter are uncomfortable reading outside of the small area of their expertise. But the biggest part of the problem, and the only part I can address, is my style. At a minimum I would like to write criticism that can be understood by someone who is genuinely motivated to read it.

Since then I have been trying to improve my style. My greatest success came a few years ago when I was invited to give a talk to an audience of mainly visual artists at the Mandrake Bar in Culver City. I talked about the character of the misanthrope in Shakespeare, and I gave basically the same talk that I had given a couple of times to audiences at schools and academic conferences. Somehow it went better than usual. Later I saw a transcript of the talk and it really was better than most of my other writing. In my effort to accommodate an audience of nonprofessionals, I struck a vein of clear thought and speech.

In this book I am trying to write the way I spoke that night at the Mandrake Bar. This means giving up some of the precise diction and dense cross-references of academic criticism and replacing them with a personal idiom that may be more vague but should also be more clear and energetic. I intend to talk to you in this book like an unreliable narrator, casually revealing personal information in arguments about literary history. The goal is to give you a sense of where criticism comes from.

Actually I dislike the idea of an unreliable narrator. It's a serious mistake not to rely on what a narrator tells you. Even if you don't trust the narrator, do you really think that you are getting information from someplace that isn't narration? Aren't you still relying on the narrator for all of your information?

# Another way I wrote this book

The other thing that happened in 2007 is that I had written an essay on Aphra Behn's novel *The Fair Jilt* and I was having trouble finding a publisher. Several academic journals had rejected my manuscript, and the readers had submitted reports that seemed completely Martian. I am not complaining about the process of peer review, which is one of my favorite things about the profession of literary studies. You can always learn something interesting from a reader's report, whether the reader is sympathetic or hostile. Maybe you learn more from a hostile reader's report. Whereas, when you send a poem to a literary journal, it can feel as though no one reads it. The editors might accept or reject your poem, but they rarely tell you more than that. The process of peer review in literary studies feels much healthier. When you submit a manuscript to an academic journal, you know that someone is going to read it. They are going to read the hell out of it.

What I finally learned from the readers' reports is that I thought something about literary character that other people did not think. One of the reports said that I did not know what a character was. In other words, the reader's report was telling me that I had a new idea. Something that seemed obvious to me was not obvious to the rest of the world. So I decided to write about my newly discovered idea. I wanted to put everything that I thought about character in one place, so that I wouldn't have to keep explaining myself.

What I think about character is pretty simple. I think that a character is a collection of every example of a kind.

Have you ever seen a Fred Astaire movie? Picture Astaire dancing. In a scene from *Blue Skies* he dances, flanked by six other male dancers who perform the same movements. Astaire is at the center of the frame, spinning. To one side there are three other dancers, also spinning, moving as he moves, wearing the same costume. Evening clothes. Same gender. Same height. Same build. They probably take the same size in a suit. On the other side of the frame, three other dancers who look pretty much the same, and they are doing the same thing.

What is the role of the extra dancers? What does the film gain by their presence?

This isn't like Astaire dancing with Ginger Rogers. A partner dance articulates a series of relationships between the bodies of two dancers. Those relationships tell a story. One of the bodies might submit to the other. Or one might challenge the other. They might be having a contest to see which one is stronger. In Astaire's movies the partner dances often indicate plot developments. Sometimes the plot develops through the dances.

Something else is happening in the scene from *Blue Skies*. There's no story here. There's no relationship between the different dancers. The dance appears to be a solo performed simultaneously by seven men. The contribution of the other dancers is purely formal. They help to balance the composition of the frame, and they aggressively underline the shapes that Astaire's body assumes and the sequence of his movements. They are extras, but they are not playing minor characters. They play the central character, Jed, also played by Astaire, one of the film's stars.

This scene, this kind of dance, puts on display an obvious but overlooked truth about character in performance. Different performers act as the same character. Isn't this configuration equally common in the history of serious drama, although perhaps not as easy to spot? In the 1943 film version of *Jane Eyre*, Jane the girl is played by Margaret O'Brien, and Jane the woman by Joan Fontaine; in the 1996 version, Charlotte Gainsbourg plays Jane. The difference between musical comedy and serious drama is that no film version of *Jane Eyre* includes the unthinkable scene where multiple Janes appear dancing in parallel.

The character of Jane does not originate in 1944. Jane grows out of Brontë's novel, first published in 1847, and extends into earlier and later epochs in literary history. One important later example of the same character is the unnamed protagonist of du Maurier's *Rebecca*. (A role also played by Joan Fontaine in a film directed by Hitchcock.) Other examples might include many of the heroines of modern historical romance novels. Following Brontë's sources I would say that an important earlier example is the title character in Richardson's novel *Pamela*. Richardson's Mr. B is probably a model for Brontë's character Rochester, and Brontë may also have studied Burnet's biography *Passages in the Life of John Wilmot, Earl of Rochester*. The character of the reformed rake collects both historical and fictional examples.

If you read criticism of *Jane Eyre* you will notice a certain conceptual resistance to the tendency of the character of Jane to collect examples in an open sequence of revisions and remakes. Most readers think that the job of a character is to individuate. A character ensures that a person is a self, precisely one, neither more nor less. This understanding is shared by critics who celebrate the ethos of individualism and those who use characters to critique the ideology of liberalism.

My definition is different. A character collects examples. In fact a character collects every example. "Who is Sylvia?" sing Proteus's musicians in Shakespeare's *Two Gentlemen of Verona*. "What is she?" (4.2.38). "Who" asks for the portrait of a unique individual. "What" asks for the qualities, characteristics, that associate a person with a group. In Sylvia's case, these qualities are holiness, fairness, wisdom (4.2.40). The "what" of Sylvia is her character "in the old meaning of the word," as Hannah Arendt puts it (Arendt 1958, 181). Not personal identity but a grouping based on a shared characteristic. Only the old meaning of character accounts for the ability of characters to transport materials across contexts, as in the history of the character of Jane Eyre. Only the old meaning accounts for the ability of multiple examples of a character to inhabit the same unthinkable space, as in the scene from *Blue Skies*.

Characters have to be able to do these things. Otherwise literature and criticism would not function as they do.

# How to use this book

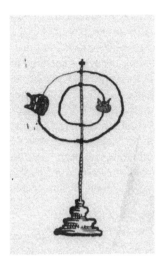

This book is going to be fairly short. The shortness is part of the argument. I am arguing that literary characters allow you to hold something that seems bigger than your hand, in your hand. Characters funnel whole societies of beings into shapes that are compact, elegant, manipulable, and portable.

I have read numerous books on the subject of literary character, and I can tell you that many of them begin by apologizing for not being "comprehensive," as Deidre Shauna Lynch puts it. Her influential book *The Economy of Character* does not "pretend to offer a comprehensive history" of all characters in all novels. Lynch's real expertise is in the study of the eighteenth-century novel. Her knowledge of this field is incredible—I think she has read more junk fiction from the eighteenth century than any other living person. But even when it comes to the period in the history of the novel that she knows better, probably, than anybody else, she still doesn't want to say that she is writing a comprehensive account. "One book cannot enumerate the full range of discourses that eighteenth-century writers mobilized" to talk about characters (Lynch 1998, 12).

What she is saying makes a kind of sense. The history of the novel in the eighteenth century includes a large number of books. Lynch is only writing one book. How can one book account for many books? Lynch writes as though to preempt the criticism of a hostile reader who expects a precise numerical correspondence between a book and its subjects.

Not surprisingly, in other circumstances, she is that very reader. In her review of Alex Woloch's study *The One vs. the Many*, she criticizes Woloch for not following a program of strict induction. She complains that Woloch generalizes about minor characters in novels without considering any epistolary novels, that he neglects the eighteenth century, that there are not enough "surprises" in his archive, and that "he prompts readers to reread, rather than sending them to something new" (Lynch 2005, 281–82). Woloch anticipates this criticism when he prefaces his book with an apology of his own for not including "a wider range of materials," for not being "exhaustive" (Woloch 2003, 33, 36).

Lynch's method is basically historicism and Woloch's is basically formalism. However, in my view, they have the same problem. Following Frances Ferguson, I would call it antiformalism. They think that character individuates. What's more, they seek a method that emulates individual characterization. At least they want to show some respect to characters as individuals.

Lynch and Woloch feel an obligation to be comprehensive in their accounts of character. At the same time they believe that to be fully comprehensive is impossible. What can they do? An extravagant solution would be to expand the dimensions of their monographs so that Lynch could discuss "the full range of discourses" of eighteenth-century literary theory and so that Woloch could discuss every character in every realist novel. Every single thing that characterizes, in the sense of individuates, "should have a case," its own case, in the motto that Woloch takes from Henry James. A practical solution would be to limit the argument so that a monograph would be responsible only for the novels and characters that appear in its pages and no others.

The problem of comprehensiveness does not end there. Taken seriously, the complaint that Woloch "prompts readers to reread" would undermine the practice of close reading by which knowledge in literary studies is generated. What can "one book" do? If one book can't generalize about the novels written in the eighteenth century, how can it treat a three-volume novel in a chapter of fifty pages? Consider how close reading deforms, empties, and disperses the heavy object that was once a novel. Consider how close reading takes parts for wholes. How can a single book of criticism hope to treat another book comprehensively?

I make no apology for not dealing specifically with all characters in all novels, poems, plays, films, and comics. Nonetheless I assert that this book is intended to be comprehensive. My argument applies to everything called a character in all the contexts in which they appear. How can this be?

George Meredith proposes the formalist solution to the problem in the prelude to his novel *The Egoist*.

> Now the world is possessed of a certain big book, the biggest book on earth; that might indeed be called the Book of Earth; whose title is the Book of Egoism, and it is a book full of the world's wisdom. So full of it, and of such dimensions is this book, in which the generations have written since they took to writing, that to be profitable to us the book needs a powerful compression.

**(MEREDITH 1979, 3)**

Before *The Egoist* became a novel, it was another, longer book about egoism. Meredith likes to make this move, I've noticed. He likes to begin a novel by imagining another book that he proposes to excerpt or epitomize. In *The Ordeal of Richard Feverel* the imagined source book is an anthology of moral maxims, "The Pilgrim's Scrip," which Feverel inherits from his father. "The Pilgrim's Scrip" influences Feverel's life and some of its language is quoted in the novel, but the text of the novel is not the same as the imaginary book of maxims. Basically the imaginary book shapes Feverel's opinions of women but not his impulses toward them. In *Diana of the Crossways* the narrator charts a course through a vast archive consisting of all the private letters and diaries of London society in the nineteenth century. In *The Amazing Marriage* there are two narrators who in the frame of the novel enact their own subplot wherein they compete for narrative authority. One of the narrators, Dame Gossip, is a modern instantiation of the classical god of fame, whose being extends to the limits of discourse. She is a compendium of all that is spoken and written in history.

Now Meredith could have written some of the imaginary books. He could have written "The Pilgrim's Scrip." Every quotation from "The Pilgrim's Scrip" sounds like something he would say, one of his obscure epigrams that turn out to be very funny if you pause to work out the joke. He could not have written the book of all gossip. Without better technologies for capturing information, human civilization still could not produce a compendium of all gossip. In any case such imaginary books do not have to apologize for not being comprehensive. If they had to make an apology it would be because they *are* comprehensive. They are libraries of Babel, containing all knowledge exactly as it appears in the given world. They are so thorough in their coverage that they disable any effort at understanding or communication.

It is for this reason, and not because he lacks access to the right database, that Meredith eschews the attempt to transcribe the "Book of Egoism." The problem is that the "Book of Egoism" is really the "Book of Earth," which is to say that it is a new celestial body as vast and forbidding as the planet Earth. The combined surfaces of its pages are equal in area to the planet's land masses. In duplicating the given world the great book adds nothing useful to it. The exact correspondence between egoism and earth means that the book will not be an effective key to unlock the mysteries of earth. The book introduces its own obscurities in place of nature's. Those who look into the unwieldy, unprofitably long book would be just as likely to discover the wisdom they seek by examining the massive, confusing planet that the book translates. Or just as unlikely. Egoism, which explains nature, is no easier to understand than nature itself.

Meredith is an obscure writer but his books are easier to understand than nature. His aid to understanding is art. He says, "Art is the specific" (4). I think he is using "specific" primarily in a medical sense: art cures the disease of nature, which is overparticularity. "Specific" also means the problem of the relationship between the universal and the particular. If I am right, "specific" refers both to the disease and to the cure.

Meredith's novels are not redundant for the given world like the imagined great books. He obliquely refers to Darwin's *Origin of Species* as a representative of the kind of world-covering book of the ego that he is not interested in writing. (I don't think he is fair to Darwin.) An evolutionary biologist might want to depict the world in all its inexhaustible particularity "by the watchmaker's eye in luminous rings eruptive of the infinitesimal," whereas the artist reads the book of the world "pointed with examples and types under the broad Alpine survey of the spirit born of our united social intelligence" (4). Art creates a society by connecting examples to types. Meredith, an artist in communication with the Comic Spirit—the name of the spiritual offspring "of our united social intelligence" is comedy— "condenses whole sections of the book [of Egoism] into a sentence, volumes into a character; so that a fair part of the book outstripping thousands of leaves when unrolled, may be compassed in one comic sitting" (5). Character (playing on the different senses of letter and figure) is a form of art by which examples are drawn into types.

This novel is a character sketch; not the quality, egoism, but the character who is defined by this quality, the egoist. The character of the egoist helps to make the wisdom of the big Book of Egoism portable.

# Another way to use this book

I love Meredith's novels. His place in my book and in literary history is a bit of a problem. For one thing he has a gummy style. At the level of the sentence it is never easy to say what is going on. Just now, in discussing a short passage from the prelude to *The Egoist*, I felt compelled to argue that secondary meanings of words were more important than primary meanings. When you start reading one of Meredith's novels there is always a period of adjustment where you keep gagging on the complex sentences. You feel shocked and outraged. Really? I have to do all this work just to understand the plot and the jokes? After a couple of chapters you grow accustomed to the work and don't notice that you are still doing it.

I also feel that Meredith is a weak example because he agrees with me. I mean, I do really believe that Meredith understood character in terms that are similar to mine. I think he came to that understanding by studying Molière, another writer who matters to me. But I am not making an argument about what character meant to Meredith. I am not even trying to make an argument about what character meant in an old tradition of comic writing that includes Molière and Meredith. I am trying to do what Meredith did. I want to use characters to generalize. I want to make an argument about all characters.

My second example is a stronger one. The example I have in mind is a book as full of the world's wisdom as *The Egoist* although it participates in literary tradition vicariously. Daisy Ashford, the author of *The Young Visiters*, was a young contemporary of Meredith's. At the age of nine years, "somehow," in Edward Gorey's succinct description, she "penetrated to the heart of all the clichés of social behavior and presentation" (Gorey 1978, 27).

The plot of *The Young Visiters* concerns class mobility. Ashford is interested in how classes are open, how status can change, and how classes are limiting. Mr. Salteena, who is admittedly "not quite a gentleman" (15), goes to the Crystal Palace, where impoverished nobles support themselves in their sumptuous "compartments" by giving lessons in the manners of high life. For the price of 42 pounds Salteena is able to "rub himself up" (34) to a position at Buckingham Palace, although he never becomes a sufficiently desirable suitor to Ethel Monticue, the other young visitor.

The subtlety of this analysis of social class is remarkable. It may even be accurate. It could be true that the European nobility of the nineteenth century used enigmas of polite behavior to absorb some of the wealth of the middle class and to protect ancient kinship bonds. I am tempted to call Ashford's invention of living compartments in the Crystal Palace a brilliant historical hypothesis. Maybe institutions of political rule become places of entertainment open to different classes while continuing to house the ruling class. Maybe the graces of nobility become transparent but remain intact and unbudging. A glass ceiling for Victorian social mobility.

How did Ashford figure it out? She sees into the heart of society, and yet, in the absence of a discernible path of access, what can she know about society? The word itself frequently appears in her novel as she heard it pronounced: "socierty."

Ashford knows something, but what she knows is not terribly contentful and does not depend on library research or intelligence gathering in guest rooms. She doesn't know things, but she knows how to do things. She knows how to write a novel. She has the practical knowledge of "how it should be done," as Katherine Mansfield, also a practitioner, recognizes (Mansfield 1930, 31). Ashford's knowledge of "how it should be done" makes empirical knowledge of people irrelevant. Literary devices such as character make it possible for Ashford to write a book that knows more than she does.

When Gorey says that she "penetrates to the heart of all the clichés of social behavior" he does not mean that she sees past the clichés into some primary matter behind them. He means that clichés are the beating heart of her vision of society. His comment correctly identifies the basic mode of social interaction in *The Young Visiters*. Ashford's characters speak in clichés. They use dreadful, barely appropriate proverbs:

> They traveled 2nd class in the train and Ethel was longing to go first but thought perhaps least said soonest mended.
>
> **(19)**

> Well half a loaf is better than no bread responded Mr Salteena in a gloomy voice.
>
> **(53)**

Yes, that's what Mr. Salteena says when Ethel rejects his proposal of marriage! Or else the characters use a purple literary language:

> I love you so intensely that if you say no I shall perforce dash my body to the brink of yon muddy river.
>
> . . .
>
> Oh Bernard she sighed fervently I certainly love you madly you are to me like a heathen god.
>
> **(57)**

Or else the characters use banal phatic expressions:

> Could you direct me to the Crystale Palace if you please said Mr Salteena nervously.
>
> Well said the genial policeman my advice would be to take a cab sir.
>
> Oh would it said Mr Salteena then I will do so.
>
> **(30)**

The whole exchange culminating in the vague promise, "I will do so," is gratuitous and could be replaced by a line of narrative: "Mr. Salteena went to the Crystale Palace in a cab."

Clichés are the raw material for *The Young Visiters*. To put it another way, they are Ashford's Scrip. The novel selects from a universal chronicle of social conventions, a book of nature that transcribes all instances of polite conversation. Ashford's exposure to this chronicle is limited by her short life; she can only have read a few pages of clichés in her preliminary research. Still, the vastness of the chronicle does not put her at a special disadvantage as a reader since no one can read the entire thing. Anyone who proposes to do what Ashford does, to mold this compendium of separate instances into a single work of art, would be faced with the same problem. Ashford has some kind of trick, a key, an index, a map, that allows her to move rapidly through the chronicle, finding and selecting the material that she wants and rejecting the rest.

Her positive, original contribution to the raw material is tone. Gorey understood this too. The value of the novel, he says, its unique, inimitable quality, has to do with its "funny tone," its "loony tone which no other fiction I've ever read quite has" (27). Ashford declares her interest in analyzing tone on every page of her book. One short passage distinguishes between "rarther a socierty tone," "a loud tone as someone was playing a very difficult piece on the piano," "a somewhat showing off tone," and "a peevish tone" (51–2). Everything spoken in the novel has an identifiable tone.

These different tones comprise the knowledge that Ashford brings to the novel. She might not have more than a vague sense of the meaning of the clichés she transcribes. For example, she seems to use the expression "born on the wrong side of the blanket" to express a class distinction between tradespeople and high society. She might or might not know that this expression denotes illegitimacy in Scott's novels. She probably doesn't know that the phrase "Sinister son of Queen Victoria" means the same thing in heraldry. Either that, or she is having a "nastily precocious" joke at the expense of her characters:

Not really cried Ethel in excited tones but what does that mean.

Well I don't know said Bernard it puzzles me very much but ancestors do turn quear at times.

Peraps it means godson said Mr Salteena in an intelligent voice.

Well I don't think so said Bernard but I mean to find out.

(24)

The meaning of the phrase never gets any clearer. Meanwhile the positive content of the scene is tone: the excitement in Ethel's voice when she puzzles over the meaning, the intelligence in Mr. Salteena's voice when he offers his unintelligent answer. Tone is what happens when Ashford runs a cliché through the voices of her characters. The character's voice filters the cliché to color its meaning with one quality, or, in some cases, the layering of several qualities. The peculiar tone that Gorey enjoys is the effect of sounding several notes at once. The gloom that Mr. Salteena can't keep out of his voice sounds a dissonant note as he produces the cheery reflection that he still has "half a loaf," an inadequate and barely appropriate response to Ethel's rejection of his marriage proposal with the inadequate but thoroughly conventional consolation that "I shall always think of you in a warm manner."

Ashford starts with something that she doesn't know completely, cliché, and ends with something that she does know, tone. The conduit that connects them is character. Mr. Salteena's character does not depend on what he does. In his attempt to draw his own character, his convoluted statement that he is "not quite a gentleman but you would hardly notice it but cant be helped anyhow" (16), the independence of character from "notice" is precise and accurate. Character allows Ashford to give shape to her material regardless of what she knows. Character converts cliché into tone, social convention into society. Or, if you prefer, socierty. That, Ashford knows, and Mansfield affirms, is how it's done.

I don't want to underestimate Ashford's literary knowledge. Barrie was probably right to say that she was a serious reader of "everything that came her way," including "the grown-up novels of the period" (8). It is just possible that she could have encountered *The Egoist*. Barrie himself, who published appreciations of both Ashford and Meredith, is one slender thread linking the two authors.

But please keep in mind the difference between Meredith's literary knowledge and Ashford's! *The Egoist* is the culmination of a lifetime of reading. The exemplary egoist Patterne is carefully modeled on Molière's misanthrope Alceste. Ashford invents her hero Mr. Salteena out of a much shorter lifetime of reading. She had only a few years and one household in which to encounter the world and its literatures. Mr. Salteena might be compared favorably with Molière's bourgeois gentleman Monsieur Jourdain, but not because the author studied French neoclassical comedy. Her writing must have had some models, but Molière's play was not one of them.

Meredith explains the genesis of Patterne from Alceste in the opening pages of his novel. Ashford uses character for the same purpose but offers no explanation. In different ways, both authors avail themselves of the power of character to generalize.

This is the power that antiformalist criticism would relinquish. Antiformalist criticism sets itself the task of comprehending character, which it can do only by treating each instance separately. Formalist criticism affirms that we already have devices that funnel examples into types, and character is one of them.

Why is form a concern for criticism? Because we do not need only accounts of things that do not translate. We also need accounts of what parts of things translate, what devices translate them, and where it happens.

# The riddle of form and style

This book is called *Character as Form*. The meaning of form is an embarrassing problem for formalist critics. Marjorie Levinson has observed that critics associated with formalism not only do not share a definition of form but in fact have no such definition (Levinson 2007, 561). Henry Turner, with another twist of the knife, has shown that some of the definitions of form that formalist critics do not share actually contradict one another (Turner 2010, 579–81).

What is form supposed to mean in this book? By form I mean what I take Frances Ferguson to mean in *Solitude and the Sublime*. According to Ferguson, form makes it possible for there to be "more than one of something" (Ferguson 1992, viii, 20–21, 31). Ferguson's formalism is a kind of abstraction, remote from the sensuous particulars of aesthetic experience. Nonetheless form is involved in acts of making. Imposing form is how things are made.

Ferguson's sense of form is the one that makes both Lynch and Woloch, for all their differences, antiformalists. Sometimes I think that Ferguson is the only true formalist critic. The rest of us wallow more or less sordidly in subjective experience. Well, I'm exaggerating. Related understandings of literary form inspire Franco Moretti's efforts to reduce literary history to abstract patterns and Wai Chee Dimock's work connecting American literature to movements in "deep time."

Some of the work I want to do in this book depends on a fine distinction that Ferguson makes between form and style. This is also a tricky problem. Have you ever read Tristan Tzara's recipe "To Make a Dadaist Poem"? At the end he says, "The poem will resemble you" (Tzara 1977, 39). That would be a good way to think about style: the image of the author in the work.

How does the poem come to resemble you? In Tzara's piece, the poet's image miraculously emerges from a series of chance operations. The poet cuts words out of a newspaper, places them in a bag, gives the bag a "gentle shake" to scramble the syntax of the newspaper article, removes the words, and transcribes them as they come up. At almost no point in the process does the poet make a decision. The selection of the words, the order in which they appear, the divisions between them—Tzara takes every important decision out of the hands of the poet. The determination of length seems to be the one responsibility that Tzara is willing to delegate: "Choose from this paper an article of the length that you want to make your poem." Don't use your judgment, in other words. Don't choose a piece of writing that you like, or whose subject appeals to you, as your source. You only get to decide whether you want to write a short poem, a medium-sized one, or a long one.

And yet the claim of iconic resemblance is not mere bravado. Other artists who employ chance operations and collage in their work have observed the same miraculous effect. Rosmarie Waldrop once told me that she started making collages of texts by other writers as a way to avoid writing her autobiography in every poem; however, she said, her personal experience and family history have a funny way of reasserting themselves even in poems filtered through pieces of language quoted from Beethoven, Humboldt, Duncan, and Wittgenstein. Jackson Mac Low, supremely inventive and various in deploying complicated procedures to baffle his intentions, admits that his writing nonetheless represents him accurately because "the ego is implicit in everything you do" (Mac Low 1993, 110).

The humanists of the European Renaissance made a similar discovery. Montaigne and Burton wrote long books that were essentially patchworks of quotations from classical poetry and philosophy. Nonetheless Montaigne writes at the outset of his essays that he is the same as "the subject of his book," and Burton calls the words of *The Anatomy of Melancholy* "all mine and none mine" (Montaigne 2003, lxiii; Burton 2001, 24). Collage seems to be an ideal medium for self-expression.

Why will the poem resemble you? The traditional answer would be that anything you write, anything you make, will necessarily look like you.

Language most shows a man; speak, that I may see thee.

**(JONSON 1985, 574)**

Jonson's motto from *Timber, or Discoveries* suggests an incredible confidence in talk. There is no more perfect image of me than the sound of my voice, which "most shows" me. Every word that I pronounce could be a lie, but my voice can't help telling the truth about me.

Somewhat less confident in the value of images, Milton nonetheless seems to agree that images approximate their makers if not their subjects:

Friends, since you cannot recognize the man depicted, laugh at the wretched picture of a wretched artist.

**(MILTON 1991, 162)**

Supposedly what happened is that Milton didn't like the engraving that the printer wanted to use for the 1645 edition of *Poems of Mr. John Milton*. He thought the engraving didn't look like him. So he insisted that the engraver had to add a motto saying, "This doesn't look like me." Only he wrote the motto in Greek so that the engraver wouldn't see the insult. I wonder about the last part. It seems to me that if you spend your working life handling Greek letters, eventually you will learn the meaning of some Greek words. I have learned a few Greek words myself from reading poems from the English Renaissance. Isn't that what would happen to anybody?

I can believe that Milton might not have wanted the printer to be able to understand the motto. There is an elitist aspect to Milton's thinking, a sense that some people are unredeemable, worthless, and you shouldn't even waste your time talking to them. It's his least attractive side, and I think even he knew that it was a bad attitude and tried to move away from it. There are other, similar stories told about him. He is supposed to have taught his daughters how to read Greek and Hebrew texts so that they could pronounce the words but not so that they knew what they were saying. And maybe that was what Milton wanted, but I still think that if Milton's children were reading to him in Greek and Hebrew every day, then eventually they would learn some Greek and Hebrew.

Whatever the engraver knew and whatever Milton wanted him to know, the engraving affixed to the frontispiece of *Poems of Mr. John Milton* is a "wretched picture" of Milton since his friends do not recognize him in it. Still, this murky image of Milton is not a bad image of the engraver's bad technique. Not even a lousy artist can escape the ironclad law of mimesis. We recreate our own images in everything we do.

Tzara might not agree that the reproduction of personal style is inevitable. If you *tried* to describe yourself, the result might not look like you. Yet neither does he seem to think that the Dadaist poem takes the impression of the poet's unconscious desires. You might expect to hear a psychoanalytic explanation from a modern artist. Something like, we are most ourselves when we are least aware of ourselves. Carlo Ginzburg has a great essay on the connoisseurship of Giovanni Morelli, who wrote a series of essays reattributing some of the masterpieces of Italian Renaissance painting to different masters. Morelli's principle was that painters reveal their signatures not in obvious motifs or technical innovations but in insignificant, sordid details, such as habits of depicting fingernails or earlobes (Ginzburg 1989, 87–112). The details are most telling for connoisseurs because the master painters and their followers put little thought into them.

The riddle of style, in Tzara's formula, is that it emerges apart from a diminishing series of creation (where I resemble the thing that made me with a slight diminishment, and the thing I make resembles me but looks more diminished, and if that thing generates another thing it will be a further diminishment) and apart from the accidental revelation of unconscious motives. "The poem will resemble you." So it does. But it really shouldn't.

The whole point of this exercise is that the poem becomes a vehicle for your personal style without your being able to have an impact on its form.

# Form mistaken for style

One way of differentiating form and style emerges out of an exchange between Ferguson and D. A. Miller. I see this exchange as an event in the history of criticism, the "Ferguson-Miller debate," and for several years I have been encouraging other critics to call it by this name, but other critics, maybe including the two critics directly involved in the exchange, do not seem to see the disagreement as anything so intense or stark.

The background of the exchange is an account of the realist novel that was popular in works of criticism published in the 1980s and 1990s. You see it in Nancy Armstrong's book *Desire and Domestic Fiction*, in Miller's *The Novel and the Police*, and in books by other literary critics who were having a conversation with Michael Foucault's intellectual history. Foucauldian arguments make novels simultaneously the most significant and least powerful objects in a culture. Significant because they appear to introduce new modes of subjectivity and social organization. Powerless because they add to a culture only what is already in the culture.

In his Foucauldian period, Miller views novelistic conventions such as omniscient narration as invasions of the privacy of characters. He argues that these conventions are homologous to the practices of surveillance by which states police individuals and by which individuals learn to police their own behavior. This account makes police an important presence even in novels where no characters work for the police either as detectives or as informants. Pursuing this homology, Miller is able to make Trollope's *Barchester Towers*, a novel in which there is no mention of police, the endpoint of his history of the novel rather than an exception.

This kind of argument never sat easily with formalist critics. Here I am not talking about abstract thinkers like Ferguson but rather the kind of reader who approaches the form of a novel as an accumulation of decisions at the level of the sentence and the word. Someone like Dorrit Cohn, who remarks that the problem with such accounts of power in novels is that "no matter how unequal their power status, fictional characters are all equally inhabitants of the same conflicted fictional world" (Cohn 1999, 171). There is no reason to care about inequalities if they are not, Cohn says, "potentially reversible." A people can depose a monarch and establish a different form of government, but a cast of characters can't depose a narrator. You can tell a story about deposing a narrator—something like that happens in a novel by Flann O'Brien, *At Swim-Two-Birds*—but you will need another narrator to do that.

In her article "Austen, *Emma*, and the Impact of Form," Ferguson codifies the problem. She calls it the confusion of form for style. Here is a simple example of this confusion. If you are writing a synopsis of the plot of the opera *Tristan and Isolde* and include the fact that Tristan is a tenor, then you are treating the musical form of the opera as a stylistic decision. "This is the story of an obese tenor who accidentally drank a magic potion, and the doomed love he shared with the obese soprano who plotted to kill him until she drank some of the same potion." The fact that Tristan and Isolde are always singing is a principle by which they are constituted in performance. It has nothing to do with their story. They might use their voices expressively, but their musical expressions are directed to an audience, not to each other. Their highly trained signing voices are not part of their relationship. Their community offers no incentives for exceptional musical ability or for public expressions of innermost feelings.

Ferguson has a more complicated example of the confusion of form for style. She questions Miller's homology between the narrative technique called free indirect discourse and the ideological regimes by which citizens ostensibly internalize the work of state surveillance. In passages of free indirect discourse, which Miller describes in an evocative phrase as "close writing," narrator and character approach each other closely but in principle never touch (Miller 2003, 58). Despite their closeness, Ferguson argues, they do not pertain to "the deeply conceptual link between individuals and discursive regimes" (Ferguson 2000, 160). Miller is mistaking a personal stylistic preference for a formal principle. (According to Ferguson, the only genuine "formal contribution" of the novel is free indirect discourse.)

Miller's ingenious response is to say that Ferguson is fundamentally right about his method in every way except that she calls it a mistake. He takes her objection and turns it into a method, brandishing as a banner the technique of treating form as style. In Austen's novels he finds "the secret of style": that it really wants to be form. The narrator is a person who does not want to be a person:

> Whereas the somewhat naïve narrator of *Northanger Abbey* effectively declares, "I am not Woman," "I do not submit to female social necessity," "I do not need to get married," the mature narration encourages us to think of it in truncated intransitives: "it is not," "it does not submit," "it does not need," period. . . . No one who writes with such possession can be in want of *anything*.

**(MILLER 2003, 34)**

The narrator is the idealized image, happily shucked of the trappings of personhood, that Austen really wanted to be.

If Ferguson is right, treating form as style may be a mistake. Miller proves that this mistake can be productive. It produces his compelling reading of Austen, and, if he is right, the same move originally produced Austen's novels. It also seems to have produced the disappointing movie *Stranger Than Fiction*. As a rule I try not to talk about bad art, but I'm going to make an exception because *Stranger Than Fiction* fails as a movie but helps to clarify the terms of the Ferguson-Miller debate. It draws a picture of what happens when the form of character is stylized.

The conceit of the film is that its voice-over narration is part of the plot. Harold, played by the comedian Will Ferrell, experiences the narrator of the story as a voice in his head. His awareness of the third-person narration still leaves room for dramatic irony. What the character knows is not quite the same as what the audience know. The audience both hear the voice in Harold's head and see the voice attached to the body of the actor Emma Thompson, playing the character Kay, who is struggling to write a novel about Harold.

I guess the reason for the existence of this movie is to test Ferrell's range as a serious actor. It allegorizes Ferrell's ambition to play dramatic roles by substituting Thompson's attempt to legitimate herself as a serious author. Thompson herself, not just the character she plays, has pretensions to the literary style of Jane Austen. These pretensions are documented in Ang Lee's film version of *Sense and Sensibility*, for which she wrote the screenplay and played Elinor, and rewarded by an Academy Award for "best adapted screenplay." *Stranger Than Fiction* stylizes the form of omniscient narration as though D. A. Miller himself wrote the screenplay. Here the narrator's impersonal voice is not the personal idealization of Austen, but that of a performer, Thompson, for whom Austen is a consciously chosen personal ideal.

What happens to form when it is treated as style? The obvious effect here is that it breaks out of the frame of the movie into the plot. This effect may be incidental. The important point illustrated by *Stranger Than Fiction* is that the formal principle acquires a human face. Thompson's human face. The narrator becomes a person.

—I'm afraid what you're describing is schizophrenia.
—No, no. It's not schizophrenia. It's just a voice in my head. I mean, the voice isn't telling me to do anything. It's telling me what I've already done . . . accurately, and with a better vocabulary.

The shrink is probably right to dismiss the trivial difference between a voice that speaks to you and one that speaks about you. In literary analysis that would be a significant difference. It might be the difference between lyric and narrative. If you have a voice in your head, then your problem is a medical pathology rather than a literary genre. From a psychological point of view the lyric and narrative voices are both recognizable paranoid fantasies. They translate universalizing modes of discourse into coded messages, and take these messages personally in the sense that they address precisely one person. Harold must share at least a suspicion of this pathology since he has sought the advice of a doctor. However, if his problem is truly a literary one, he would be better off consulting a critic.

Up to this point the screenplay has followed Miller's reading of Austen so closely that it could almost be an adaptation. Unfortunately the critic Harold consults is a structuralist narratologist, played by Dustin Hoffman, who is interested only in identifying the genre of the narrative in which Harold is a character. If instead Harold approached Ferguson, she might tell him that he is making the common mistake of treating form as style. Or, better, if he talked to Miller, he might learn that he is a "stylothete" who hears the alluring voice of Style and experiences the embarrassment of not being that voice. Harold isn't sick; he's right. He knows something that even the "cleverest character," according to Miller, rarely if ever knows. He knows that he is a character, that he is "being narrated" (Miller 2003, 17). His apparent problem is a kind of realism.

# Style mistaken for form

If treating form as style produces a condition easily misrecognized as schizophrenia, then the reverse, treating style as form, tends to look like a different problem. With his usual tartness Molière explores the consequences of this move in the final scene of *Tartuffe*, where, in an unexpected deus ex machina, the king returns Orgon's property to him as a gift.

What should happen at the end of the play is the triumph of the hypocrite Tartuffe. As the legitimate owner of Orgon's property Tartuffe has won. He has won everything. Orgon has signed his entire estate over to him just to spite his family, to show that he does not believe them when they accuse Tartuffe of hypocrisy, impiety, and disloyalty. Along with the rest of the property Tartuffe also now possesses documents detailing the secret history of Orgon's treachery. (Once, years ago, Orgon harbored an enemy of Louis XIV.) The cherry on top of owning everything that Orgon used to own is that Tartuffe can at any time remove him from society by bringing these documents to the attention of agents of the king who, if they follow the law, will arrest him and probably put him to death. Tartuffe does exactly that. But the agent of the king doesn't follow the law. In a surprise move he restores the property to Orgon and arrests Tartuffe.

The play ends by congratulating the king for the godlike discernment that inspires him to switch the positions of Orgon and Tartuffe. The agent explains:

> We live under a prince who does not tolerate fraud, a monarch who can read the hearts of men, and who is not taken in by the wiles of hypocrites. The keen discernment of that lofty mind at all times sees things in their true perspective; nothing can get past the firm constancy of his judgment nor lead him into error. . . . In short, the king, filled with horror for his [Tartuffe's] base ingratitude and treachery towards you [Orgon], added this to his other terrible crimes, and only put me under orders to see to what lengths his effrontery would go and to make him give you full satisfaction. All the documents of yours he says are his I am to take from him and return to you. His majesty, by an act of sovereign prerogative, annuls the deed which gives him title to all your possessions. Furthermore, he pardons you that clandestine offense in which the flight of a friend involved you.
>
> **(MOLIÈRE 2000, 5.7)**

Isn't this an admission that the king's justice is completely arbitrary? His decision has no justification and is based on no evidence. All the evidence points in the other direction. A document signed by both parties gives Orgon's property to Tartuffe, and another document confirms Orgon's actual treachery. Meanwhile Tartuffe's "crimes" (meaning his hypocrisies?) are rather difficult to trace since their quality depends on an appearance of upholding the law. And hypocrisy, the pretense of piety, is not a crime! But in any case Louis XIV doesn't criminalize hypocrisy, only one instance of it. Another name for his "keen discernment" would be caprice.

The unreason of the king's decision casts a retrospective glow of reasonableness on Orgon's actions, which throughout the play have been made to look ridiculous. Wasn't Orgon right, after all, to trust his friend Tartuffe, to defend him against the spiteful accusations of the rest of the household? The rest of his family are universally petty and selfish, with the possible exception of the servant Dorine. At least, wasn't Orgon right to trust his friend until the moment when he witnessed him propositioning his wife?

Molière might intend this speech as praise of the political institution that supported and protected him, or, as in the *Versailles impromptu*, he might want to channel his voice through the king, imagining himself as a power behind the throne. In either case he describes a sovereign power without legal restrictions that can suspend the rights of property, imprison subjects, and condemn them to death for no reason. A king who famously took care to remind his subjects that he alone was the state might not argue with such an unfair constitution. Orgon gratefully receives his property through the king's breaking of form because the property, like all properties, was originally an undeserved gift from the king. This is tyranny. And this is what happens when you mistake style for form, as Molière's critics seem to have done for centuries, since none of them has noted the implications of this chilling scene.

# Perfection assailed by repetition

I have a better example of the difference between form and style. In Jørgen Leth's short film *The Perfect Human* there is a slight lag between the voice-over narration and the image. You are looking at an image of a man slowly unlacing and pulling off one of his shoes; meanwhile the voice-over describes a woman taking off a pair of boots. What the voice-over describes is what you are about to see in the next shot. Lars von Trier, a keen observer of Leth's films, identifies the modernist stylistic trait of which this lag is a single instance: Leth does not like to use images to illustrate words. Each element of the film should make its own contribution and be independent of the others. Thus you are always looking at something that differs slightly from what the voice-over is saying.

There is also a big lag. The voice-over keeps talking about "*the* perfect human," singular, while you are looking at images of two distinct beings whose perfection is at least debatable.

The voice-over says: "There is a bed in the room. The bed on which the perfect human sleeps, and makes love." Meanwhile you are looking at a bed with two human bodies, a man's and a woman's, in the bed. Which one is supposed to be the perfect human?

In another scene, the voice-over says: "How does the perfect human eat? We will see its eyes and its mouth, eating." "Its eyes," says the voice-over, "its mouth," referring, I guess, to the parts of one body. Onscreen, meanwhile, two bodies are seated at a table. Which "it" is supposed to be perfect, the man or the woman? Can the voice-over tell the difference? Can the voice-over count as high as two?

The voice-over does not draw attention to any details that you or another viewer might regard as imperfections, but he does register some of the physical signs that differentiate this man from this woman. "This is how an ear looks. Another ear." "Then a mouth. A mouth and another mouth." Two mouths, in other words, not two views of one mouth. "Look: now he falls. How does he fall? This is how he falls. . . . Look: now she lies down. How does she lie down? This is how she lies down. Like this." A man and a woman, in other words. Not the same human body. The voice-over can tell the difference.

Well, this is open to doubt. The voice-over uses the pronouns "he" and "she" only in those two lines. In every other instance the voice-over prefers the neutral pronoun "it," as though lacking information, as though gender were an alien concept. Again: "How does the perfect human eat? We will see its eyes and its mouth, eating." Here the voice-over forgets part of the meaning of the insistently repeated word "human." To be human is not to be an "it." How can the perfect human be both singular and plural? How can the perfect human be both he and she, and it and they?

There are a number of possibilities. The film could be staging a contest between two champions. Which one will deserve to be called the perfect human? The one who achieves the highest degree of perfection will take the prize. Gender difference could turn out to be crucial. Although both humans are perfect, one might subordinate to the other by virtue of gender, or in the performance of traditional gender roles. The moral of the story could be the fairness or unfairness of this social order. Or maybe the perfect human is not an individual human being but at least two. A heterosexual couple? Or the reverse: each human is perfect in isolation but regresses when coupled with another?

I prefer a typological account. *The Perfect Human* is a character sketch. It represents a type. Like all characters this one posits an ideal. What makes this character special is that its ideal is not just any quality but the perfection of qualities. Because there are many ways of being human, there are also many ways of being perfect. "Plurality is the condition of human action," Arendt writes in *The Human Condition*, "because we are all the same, that is, human, in such a way that nobody is ever the same as any human who has ever lived, lives, or will live" (Arendt 1958, 8). "There is no one type for man," Oscar Wilde writes in *The Soul of Man Under Socialism*. "There are as many perfections as there are imperfect men" (Wilde 1905, 22). *The Perfect Human* puts two examples of perfection on display. Two actors, Claus Nissen and Majken Algren Nielssen, play the role of the perfect human.

Character types might help to explain how the man and the woman act together without quite interacting. Typology makes sense of the strange, neutral space they inhabit. When they undress, for instance, they undress together, even though each one is isolated in a separate shot. The edits connect their acts of undressing. Implicitly you are asked to compare how they undress. Later you are asked to compare how they move, walk, smoke, and dance. The voice-over obligingly lists the points of comparison: "Moving. Walking. Jumping. Falling."

The set design gives no context for comparing them. Are they related as actors in a plot? Are they competitors? The voice-over denies that the space in which they act has any context: "Look: the perfect human moving in a room. . . . Here are no boundaries. Here is nothing." The voice-over calls the space a "room," which means that it is indoors, but this room has "no boundaries," which means that there are no doors or walls. What sort of architecture is this?

You might say that this room is the cutting room. It's the room made by cutting. I would say that this room is the unthinkable space of character. It's the same space that Fred Astaire and the chorus use for their dance in *Blue Skies*. In this space several examples of the same character gather.

The collection of examples of perfection is not the only image you see in *The Perfect Human*. In the two shots where both man and woman appear in the frame, they are interacting. On one occasion they sit at opposite ends of a dinner table, eating. On another occasion they mount and caress each other in bed. Two pieces of furniture, bed and table, bring them together and constitute the bones of a plot. "The room is no longer empty," the voice-over says with a tone of surprise although not quite dismay. "There is a bed in the room." The edits and the voice-over are not involved in setting the plot in motion. Their job is to establish the typology of character by identifying the qualities that the actors share. That is why, when the man and the woman appear together in the frame, the voice-over continues to refer to both of them as "the perfect human," singular.

My typological interpretation finds some support in the five remakes that Leth produced under the tutelage of Lars von Trier in the film *The Five Obstructions*. In the original short film Claus Nissen may not be the only actor who represents the perfect human, but he is the only man. In the remakes other actors play both the man and the woman. In *Obstruction #2* Leth himself plays both the man and the woman. In *Obstruction #3* Patrick Bauchau and Pascal Perez play the man and Marie Dejaer and Meschell Perez play the woman. Finally, in *Obstruction #4*, the cartoon segment, different examples of the perfect human appear in a single frame.

In interview segments in *The Five Obstructions* Leth singles out apparent imperfections, the marks of experience on the bodies of the actors, for praise. He is interested in casting Bauchau as the perfect human because he does not have the perfect body that he had in his youth, because his face shows "experience of life," and because one of his youthful roles was Adrien, the seductive male lead in Rohmer's moral tale *La collectionneuse*.

The title character of Rohmer's film is the collector, so you know from the title that the film sees itself as a character sketch. The film is trying to do what a character does, to collect examples of something. If you have seen the film you might remember a surprising scene where Haydée, the collector, argues with the title of the film and the trait that defines her character. She insists that she does not collect people. "I'm not a collector. I'm looking . . . I'm looking for something." The motive for her promiscuity is that she is searching for a specific sexual partner whom she has not yet found. Like Kafka's hunger artist she is a bad example of her type. The hunger artist is not hungry for any actual food, and the collector does not collect the people she sleeps with. They resemble each other in that they lack the appetite essential to their characters but they express this lack in opposite ways. The hunger artist does not eat because he has never found the food that he would like to eat; the collector sleeps with everyone because she has never found the one person she would like to sleep with.

(The performer Haydée Politoff understood this fact about her character before the director did. She first asserted that Haydée was not a collector in an improvisation. Rohmer objected to this interpretation of the character at first. His unease is understandable since her interpretation seemed at odds with his original concept and the title of the film. Later he assented to her wisdom and incorporated the improvisation into the screenplay.)

The five remakes of *The Perfect Human* might be offered as counterexamples to Whitehead's observation that "not even perfection can endure the tedium of indefinite repetition. . . . Adventure is essential, namely, the search for new perfections" (Whitehead 1933, 332). I think

Whitehead is basically right. Adventure is an important value in ideas and art. Not just pleasure but danger. Not just novelty but challenge and risk. In the absence of other values, the lure of adventure can lead one to put value in strange places and make foolish decisions.

On the other hand, if you think about it, you can do a lot in the way of building civilizations without valuing adventure. Note that Whitehead does not say that perfection is impossible to achieve. Nor does he say that the achievement may not be repeated or that the repetitions would not be highly desirable. Whitehead's examples, Confucian China and the Byzantine empire, suggest that a civilization can sustain itself by repeating its perfect achievements, and, as Whitehead says with some understatement, these civilizations are "worthy of admiration." If you heard a perfect song, you would want to hear it again. You might want to listen to it even if you knew it by heart and could anticipate each stage of its progress. You might find yourself humming its tune occasionally. It might become your soundtrack.

(The truth is that you don't need more than one song. A civilization, too, although it needs a lot of people, could get along well enough with just one song. The song, however, needs another song. It needed a lot of other songs in order to exist at all.)

I see *The Perfect Human* and its remakes in *The Five Obstructions* as a confirmation of Whitehead's observation. Once is not enough for this perfect film. Something so beautiful should be viewed and remade again and again. But repetition is not enough either, so von Trier provides an element of adventure with his obstructions. In the process, I will argue, he makes a clean separation between form and style.

# Style defended against form

Why did von Trier commission Leth to remake *The Perfect Human* five times?

The project of *The Five Obstructions* is to ruin Leth's style. Von Trier does not use these exact words. Instead he says that he would like to "ruin" *The Perfect Human*. Or, he says more than once, the real object of his hostility is not the film but Leth himself. He wants, he says, to "trip up" Leth. To "banalize" him. To "hurt" him. To "mark" him. He wants to leave him feeling "like a tortoise on its back," free to move, but helpless.

Then, once or twice, von Trier seems to say the opposite. His seeming hostility is meant for Leth's well-being. All of his tricks and traps are, in reality, therapeutic exercises. His project? "Help Jørgen Leth!"

I am tempted to say that von Trier treats Leth like one of the sacrificial victims who are usually the heroines of his fiction films, like Bess in *Breaking the Waves* or Selma in *Dancer in the Dark* or Grace in *Dogville* and *Manderlay*. If you asked von Trier he might say that he views these heroines as versions of himself. He might say the same thing about Leth. Von Trier identifies with the sacrificial victim. Maybe, although he devises different ways for Leth to suffer, he, not Leth, is the suffering martyr. In fact, he tells Leth, "All your guilt I have taken on me."

I don't trust that line. The imitation of Christ feels like a dodge. You would be more on the right track if you said that von Trier's method in his melodramas and in his collaboration with Leth was infernal. You would be right, for one thing, to notice that Hell is the kind of concept that appeals to von Trier. The second assignment in *The Five Obstructions* is to remake *The Perfect Human* in "a miserable place." For example, von Trier suggests, what if you were to synchronize the voice-over narration from *The Perfect Human* with footage of a dying child in a refugee camp? Leth interprets this suggestion, reasonably, as an approximation of Hell. When one of von Trier's obstructions hits home, like the imposition of a maximum shot length of twelve frames (*Obstruction #1*) or "complete freedom" (*Obstruction #3*), when Leth is feeling the total obstruction of his creative powers, he admires the intelligence behind the test. To express his admiration he calls that intelligence "Satanic" or "Infernal."

Von Trier's method is Satanic in more ways than one. If the obstruction succeeds, if it genuinely obstructs (trips, banalizes, hurts, marks), then it is Satanic; and the master plan for the project, encompassing the many translations that occur between Denmark, Cuba, India, Belgium, Texas, and Haiti, is to shoot the film on location in Hell. Von Trier's role in the scenario might be compared with that of the accuser who tests the faith of God's creatures or with the ruler of Hell who oversees the punishments of the damned.

Both comparisons reveal a surprising parallel. Satan shares with Job a tendency to question the divine instructions. He also has damnation in common with all of the damned. Satan doesn't just want to make other souls suffer; he wants to widen the scope of his personal suffering, even though, as he says in *Paradise Regained*, "Fellowship in pain divides not smart, / Nor lightens aught each man's peculiar load" (1.401–02), since pain can't be divided, and when you try to divide it you spread it around.

The method addresses style by personalizing Hell. That is why, in defining the goal of his obstructions, von Trier does not distinguish between therapy and punishment. That is why, in defining the object that he wants to obstruct, he does not bother to separate Leth from *The Perfect Human*: because his project would succeed only at the point where artist and work separate. His obstructions target the part of the film that resembles Leth, the style, and aspire to blunt the resemblance.

They are ingenious. Leth has never been to Cuba? Then "obviously" the film has to be remade on location in Cuba, with a maximum shot length of twelve frames. Leth tends to detach himself emotionally from the subjects of his films? Then the film has to be remade in "a miserable place," a place of intense suffering, but without showing the suffering people directly. Leth resists taking orders from von Trier? Then let him have "complete freedom" to make his own decisions. Leth "hates cartoons"? Then he must make one. (The two filmmakers are united in their disdain for animation. Together they repeat the statement, "I hate cartoons," four times. "I can't imagine that it will be anything but crap," von Trier predicts.)

These obstructions, covering shot length, narration, location, and medium, are brilliant. They are truly worthy of a diabolical adversary. The obstructions are so good because von Trier understands Leth so well. Although he does not pretend expertise in any academic field of study, he does claim to be "an expert" on the subject of Leth, having watched *The Perfect Human* "more than twenty times." With each assignment he identifies an element of Leth's style and attempts to curb the development of the style by making the exclusion of that element the single condition of production.

And he fails. His failure makes the film inspiring, even exhilarating. Every time he watches a new remake, he gnashes his teeth and marvels at the resilience of Leth's style. "It was like watching an old Leth film." "There is not a mark on you." Why doesn't it work? Why can't von Trier mark Leth? Why can he not engineer a procedure for Leth to make a version of the film that does not look just like himself?

(1) *Artistry*. The first lesson of the film is that Leth is a great artist. He is also something of an escape artist. You could blindfold him, tie his hands behind his back, and throw him down a well, and he would emerge alive, breathing, and victorious, bearing yet another perfect short film.

His activity has a definite pattern. First, Leth learns how von Trier is going to interfere with his work. He despairs. An edit at least every twelve frames? Von Trier has already won. The film is "ruined" before shooting. Nonetheless Leth goes to work, draws sketches, auditions actors, scouts locations, gathers his forces. A few scenes later, swimming in a hotel pool in Havana, Leth smiles and jokes that "the twelve frames are a paper tiger." By running together brief takes of a single action, the finished film creates an impression of fluidity to relieve the sharpness of the jump cuts. "The twelve frames were a gift," von Trier comments, his tone mixing wonder with regret.

He should have known better. He should have known that Leth would be enough of an artist to solve the problem, and he should have known that the existence of the problem would be enough to activate Leth's artistry. All artists know that *technical problems are generative.* I am not able to improve on William Morris's statement:

> [Such limitations] are as far as possible from being hindrances to beauty in the several crafts. On the contrary, they are incitements and helps to its attainment. . . .
>
> Now this must be clear to you, if you come to think of it. Give an artist a piece of paper, and say to him, "I want a design," and he must ask you, "What for? What is to be done with it?" And if you can't tell him, well, I dare not venture to mention the name which his irritation will give you. But if you say, I want this queer space covered with ornament, I want you to make such and such a thing out of these intractable materials, straightway his invention will be quickened, and he will set to work with a will; for, indeed, delight in skill lies at the root of all art.
>
> **(MORRIS 1993, 263)**

"Delight in skill." This might be the motto of artistry. Or the motto might be Leth's remark that, faced with a problem, "we can't help becoming involved and looking for an idea that satisfies us." When von Trier complains, "That's not the film I asked for," Leth replies, "One always tries to make a better film." Von Trier, far from obstructing Leth, has given him the gift of a resistant material on which to exercise his skill. That is why the requirement to make a cut after twelve frames (at most) have elapsed was, in fact, "a gift," and that is why the most difficult obstruction is "complete freedom." That is why, finally, the basic premise of the film is the most diabolical trick of all. To remake one's own early work eternally could be Hell for an artist.

(According to Diderot's dialogue in *Paradox of the Actor*, most people can express an emotion only once; the feeling diminishes with each retelling. Part of the art of the actor is a perfection that can endure indefinite repetition: to sustain an emotion across numerous rehearsals and performances at the level of intensity of its first expression. Good actors learn this art by examining their feelings with an attitude of intellectual curiosity, and this attitude makes them better philosophers than most philosophers. Because if the philosophers were really smart, then they would be cool, like the actors. But they are not cool; they are nerds. They barely know how to express what they feel when they feel it the first time [Diderot 1994, 120–25].)

Artistry only explains so much. It explains how Leth is able to make a film under difficult conditions, and how he is able to make a beautiful film. It does not explain why the result resembles him.

(2) *Modernism*. It is sometimes said that modernism is no longer viable as a method. The modernist project of critique, which purifies nature and society so as to use each one to undermine the other, has "run out of steam," Bruno Latour tells us, but that is all right, because, after all, "we have never been modern" (Latour 2004, 237–41). The problem with critique, Graham Harman tells us, is that it has neither a project nor a position of its own; it only wants to ruin everyone else's fun (Harman 2009, 110). The problem with critique, Eve Kosofsky Sedgwick tells us, is that it is paranoid, views every surprise with suspicion as potentially a "bad surprise," and consequently wants to eliminate surprise from the world (Sedgwick 2003, 130).

I am hardly the person to scoff at these stories. I nod in approval when they are told; I sometimes tell them myself. However, I fear they may be wishful thinking. Worse, I fear that they may be asking me to surrender some wonderful tools that have not outlasted their utility.

These fears may carry more conviction coming from someone like Jørgen Leth. He is a champion of modernism. He declares his allegiance to modernism in opposition to what he identifies as von Trier's romanticism. This is a significant moment in the film, when von Trier and Leth give opposite verdicts on Leth's response to the second obstruction. The assignment, you will recall, is to remake *The Perfect Human* in "a miserable place," but not to show misery directly. Leth responds by building a set in the middle of a street in the red light district in Calcutta and mounting a transparent screen between the set and the citizens on the street, who can be glimpsed through the screen as vague colorful shapes. The use of the screen is where the judgments of the two directors conflict. Leth is pleased with his solution, which he pronounces, "simple," "playful," and "elegant." Von Trier deems it out of bounds. Instead of following instructions Leth has made a "better" film than he was supposed to.

The sources of the conflict are as follows. Von Trier devises the second obstruction to address Leth's practice of detaching himself from his subjects. As usual he does not err in his diagnosis. Detachment is an obvious tendency in Leth's work. A minor dispute erupts regarding the depth at which this element of style survives. Von Trier thinks it is nothing but a "pose," a surface behavior, acquired, and easily dispensed with. Leth insists that he is not posing; detachment is his deeply ingrained and ineradicable "instinct."

Maybe Leth's modernism is instinctive. He juxtaposes images to heighten tensions between them, preferring montage to illustration. He purifies, formalizes. Above all, he seeks to distance himself from his objects so as to regard them critically. When you listen to the voice-over for *The Perfect Human* you hear the manifesto for an artistic practice that does not imagine itself as creative. "We will look into that." "We will investigate that." Leth does not have to create the perfect human. His task is to criticize it.

According to Leth, von Trier's impulses are romantic in origin. The whole premise of the second obstruction is "pure romanticism," he says with what sounds like disgust. Von Trier has a simple faith in the incapacity of the human subject to remain whole when confronted by the misery of other people, as though "you can only witness so much before you break down."

This diagnosis is insightful, although slightly confusing. My sense is that von Trier's instincts are romantic insofar as the romantic movement is a reaction against enlightenment rationalism. Von Trier's most deeply held value is a negative one: an abhorrence of enlightenment. The hospital in *Kingdom* was founded by a bad doctor, but that is not the problem; that does not explain why it is haunted. The problem is that it is a hospital. The doctors, good and bad, who staff the hospital get into trouble because they believe that modern medicine can cure illnesses. Those of us who fantasize about living in a postcritical age should take a good look at von Trier, because he consistently allies himself with forces in society that critique has tried to keep in check: superstition, ignorance, brutality, magic, Hell, misogyny, and Nazism.

The dramaturgy of a film such as *Dogville* is flagrantly Brechtian. It is probably the most Brechtian staging of any story captured on film since Godard's *Weekend*. But von Trier works his way back to tragic theater from epic theater, putting Brechtian devices to Aristotelian uses. The violent outburst that concludes the film, where Grace superintends the destruction of the town and the massacre of the citizens, both gives the audience what they want and makes them feel guilty for wanting it. A form of catharsis: purging the desire for violence in the act of satisfying it.

Leth's triumphs over von Trier demonstrate the viability and vitality of modernist critique. They do more. They show that *critique is generative*. For Leth, as for Brecht, critique is "our great productive method" (Brecht 1964, 187). Brecht exemplifies the critical attitude by "that detached eye with which the great Galileo observed a swinging chandelier. He was amazed by this pendulum motion, as if he had not expected it and could not understand its occurring, and this enabled him to come by the rules by which it was governed" (192).

The eye of the critic looks at the chandelier not with cynicism but with wonder. As though it had never seen a chandelier before. Critique is not satisfied with what is given and wants to try something else. To create something else.

This means that positionlessness, the bugbear of the postcritical movement, is not the dream of critique. The distance from its objects that critique intuitively cultivates does not place the object somewhere and the critic nowhere. The critic just has to be somewhere the object is not. Even hypercritique, the universal refutation of all positive statements (which, I am inclined to say, even in its most knee-jerk manifestations, remains always a pose, never an instinct) can't help being somewhere, and, contrary to all its declarations, making some things.

(3) *The difference between form and style*. Why is von Trier able to dissect a style but not murder it? When he excludes elements of style, when he obstructs them, he thereby gives Leth something positive. Earlier, paraphrasing Morris, I said that he gives technical problems, which are generative. Although I can't improve on the eloquence of Morris's statement, I can be more precise. Von Trier inadvertently assigns the gift of form.

What he initially identifies as stylistic traits turn, as if by magic, into formal features. To prohibit the use of an element of style has the effect of objectifying that element. The prohibition also closes the film formally, and, in so doing, creates a new vehicle for the Leth style. Although von Trier fails to take the image of Leth out of his product, he succeeds in the task of differentiating style from form.

Style alone is hard to instantiate. Harman has done some fascinating experiments on the style of H. P. Lovecraft, the author of weird tales, by subjecting Lovecraft's sentences to various adjustments until the style mutates from impure to ruined to a different style (Harman 2012, 38–51). In this way he exposes some of the elements of Lovecraft's original style.

Von Trier goes further. Harman is testing Lovecraft's sentences to see how much they can take before the style has been ruined. At the same time, he is testing himself to see if he can write in a style different from Lovecraft's, which, of course, he can. Similarly, Von Trier is testing Leth's film to see how much it can take before the style has been ruined. But, at the same time, he is testing Leth to see if he can make a film in a style different from his own, and Leth resists mightily.

Von Trier might have found the perfect formula for dividing form from style. He correctly identifies the elements of Leth's style. But they are not the style. Each element is detachable. The element of critical distance could be taught, imitated, parodied; and it could be discarded. All of the elements could be discarded. The obstructions ascend toward ultimate emptiness, gradually decreasing Leth's participation, and, in the final sequence, where Leth reads a text for voice-over written by von Trier, minimizing it. At last, in the recording studio, von Trier worries that Leth is evading his instructions by reading with a funny accent, stressing the wrong syllables. "You're doing everything you can to evade the text! . . . You are really wriggling."

My colleague Colleen Rosenfeld writes to remind me that von Trier is discovering something that George Puttenham knew in the late sixteenth century. In *The Art of English Poesy*, Puttenham observes that style pertains "to the whole tale or process of the poem or history, and not properly to any piece or member of the tale" (Puttenham 2007, 233). Good style, then, should be able to absorb contradictory elements. I have always been suspicious of interpretations of the "consistent inconsistency" that Aristotle allows to tragic personae (Aristotle 1982, 26–28). But maybe this is what he meant. The deep consistency of the character as a whole can include inconsistencies, qualities that contradict the defining characteristic.

Think of the formulaic reversals in situation comedy. According to Scott Sedita's manual for acting in television, a good actor in a sitcom has to master the technique of making a statement, waiting a beat, then making the opposite statement with equal conviction (Sedita 2005, 22).

Or think of the effect that Barbara Herrnstein Smith calls "terminal closure": the breaking of the poem's pattern in its final iteration gives a signal that the poem is done (Smith 2007, 158–65). It may even be the case that styles naturally include their contradictions. Thus von Trier reinforces Leth's style with each intended obstruction. The fact that Leth hates cartoons is a fact about him. A cartoon that he makes can hardly avoid communicating this fact.

A style depends neither on the presence of one key ingredient nor on a checklist of ingredients. It does not require a majority of its elements; nor is this a case of family resemblance in that it does not require any common elements. Style does not have to express itself in a manner (style putting itself on display as style) or in unconscious tics (as in Morelli's connoisseurship). As long as you give Leth some things to work with, he is going to put the things together in his way. Style is the relationship between the elements, whatever they are.

# 1 MANY IS NOT MORE THAN ONE

## What a character is

I define character as a device that collects every example of a kind. This is not an original definition. It is based on accounts of character by Thomas Overbury, John Earle, Jean de la Bruyère, and other writers of the late Renaissance whose books rework a classical genre pioneered by Theophrastus. Thus La Bruyère writes of the character Ménalque, the distracted man, that he is "a collection of examples of distraction" (La Bruyère 1951, 311).

Reading usually happens backward. A critic reconstructs the context in which a work of literature was produced and places it in that context. Another critic, also working back from the modern world, uses a modern theoretical framework as a lens for reading an older work. I'm doing something different. This book reads forward insofar as it derives a theory from seventeenth-century books of characters, then applies the theory to later works, such as realist novels, and other genres in which characters appear, such as poems, comics, and performances in film and theater. Reading backward, Roland Barthes writes that we in the modern world can't "name" La Bruyère (Barthes 1972, 222); reading forward, I contend that La Bruyère has no trouble naming us.

The oldest use of character is in a book called *Characters* by Theophrastus, a follower of Aristotle. Theophrastus analyzed thirty different types of men and women. English and French writers of the seventeenth century revived Theophrastus's experiment in their own collections of what they called "characteristic writing." The seventeenth-century writers are the center of my study, and the center of the center is the character of the misanthrope.

Although I will look at many examples of characters produced in recent years, my book is, at heart, a work of Renaissance studies in that it champions what character meant in the Renaissance. The poets of the Renaissance had the right idea about character. They did not invent it but they made it the basis of an entire literature.

My first example is a work of literature from the Renaissance that does not use the word character in the ancient sense.

# "Let me play the fool"

Shakespeare's comedy *The Merchant of Venice* is a good example for me just because it's a comedy. In a pure comedy, with all its energy and bustle, nothing happens, or nothing that has lasting consequences.

In *The Merchant of Venice*, events are possible, approached, threatened. But they never quite occur. Think of the casket game. What you're seeing in this scene, repeated three times, is an actor vocalizing interpretations, reasons, and finally a preference. In other scenes, revenge, justice, mercy, and infidelity are discussed, but they are not part of the action. Shylock thinks about revenge. Portia makes Bassanio think that she has been unfaithful to him. And they talk about these things.

The play may have tragic premises. That's a tendency in Shakespeare's plays, the tendency to mix genres. But if *The Merchant of Venice* has tragic premises, it never develops them. Tragedy is a theory, not a sequence of actions.

What is the theory? The overlooked character Gratiano represents the theory in its purest form. Zdravko Planinc observes that Gratiano is "grace itself" without being graceful or gracious: "He only says 'grossly' (5.1.266) what others say with more sophistication" (Planinc 2007, 3). That's the kind of character I like to study, the one who says what everyone else is already saying, only more clearly. Or, as Bassanio says, "Gratiano speaks an infinite deal of nothing (more than any man in all Venice)" (1.1.114–15).

Maybe the word for theory in Venice is "nothing." Like theory, nothing is a way of talking that avoids tragic consequences. It lets you have ideas without having to die or kill for them. This description of Gratiano recalls the complaint against Mercutio in *Romeo and Juliet*: "Peace, peace, Mercutio, peace. / Thou talk'st of nothing" (1.4.95–96). Mercutio's way of talking, unlike Gratiano's, ultimately requires his death. Even before the tragic implications of his talk are allowed to develop, his talk already performs violence in that there will be "peace" only when he shuts up.

"Nothing" means poetry in Verona, whereas in Venice it means theory. "Talk" also has different meanings in different dialects. Mercutio's performance confirms his reputation as a guy who "talks of nothing." His talk appears to be talk, draws attention to itself as talk. But this description doesn't quite match Gratiano, who, in performance, turns out to be not much of a talker. If Gratiano is a type of Mercutio he is a Mercutio on a tight leash. Shakespeare is not going to give him an opportunity to recite fifty lines about Queen Mab while the plot grinds to a halt.

Lorenzo complains that "Gratiano never lets me speak" (1.1.107), but that is obviously false. In that moment Lorenzo is speaking, not Gratiano. Dialogue in Shakespeare's plays is usually serialized. Only one character speaks at a time. (There are exceptions, like the witches in *Macbeth*, who speak together.) Here the serial form of the dialogue isn't letting Gratiano speak.

When he gets a chance to talk, this is what he says.

—I hold the world but as the world Gratiano,
    A stage, where every man must play a part,
    And mine a sad one.

—Let me play the fool,
    With mirth and laughter let old wrinkles come,
    And let my liver rather heat with wine
    Than my heart cool with mortifying groans.
    Why should a man whose blood is warm within
    Sit like his grandsire, cut in alabaster?
    Sleep when he wakes? and creep into the jaundice
    By being peevish? I tell thee what Antonio
    (I love thee, and 'tis my love that speaks):
    There are a sort of men whose visages
    Do cream and mantle like a standing pond,

And do a wilful stillness entertain,
With purpose to be dress'd in an opinion
Of wisdom, gravity, profound conceit,
As who should say, "I am Sir Oracle,
And when I ope my lips, let no dog bark."
O my Antonio, I do know of these
That therefore only are reputed wise
For saying nothing; when I am very sure
If they should speak, would almost damn those ears
Which (hearing them) would call their brothers fools.

                                                                    (1.1.77–99)

I believe this is his longest speech. It's a speech of self-definition. Gratiano's question is not, who am I? But rather, what kind am I? His psychology is social rather than personal. He sorts people into types and considers which type would best describe him. The next move, you might think, would be to perform as that type. Only that never occurs in the play. Instead he theorizes: these behaviors (talking, laughing, making faces) are characteristic of me. He doesn't devote a lot of energy to laughing and talking. He has a lot of stage time—more, probably, than Mercutio—but he doesn't have many lines. It's almost as though he belongs to a third type, the Antonio-type ("these / That therefore only are reputed wise / For saying nothing" [1.1.95–97]), for whom "saying nothing" means silence.

Detached from the environment, detached from himself, Gratiano does not define himself by performing but by talking about how he wishes he could perform. He does not even say that he is the fool but instead, tentatively, "Let me play the fool," as though he did not yet have a part. As though auditioning for the role of the fool.

The part that he clearly wants is something like Mercutio, but the one he finally settles for is that of a sub-Bassanio. What happens in the second half of the play is that Bassanio sees, loves, and receives a ring from Portia. Gratiano does the same thing with Nerissa. Bassanio gives his ring to Balthasar, who is actually Portia in disguise, and Gratiano gives his ring to the clerk, who is actually Nerissa. It looks as though Gratiano is watching Bassanio's every move so that he can scale it down to his position and copy it.

To me, then, it's all the more interesting that Gratiano insists he is *not* observing and imitating Bassanio. He tells Bassanio, "My eyes my lord can look as swift as yours" (3.2.197). If Gratiano is telling the truth, his vision is simultaneous with Bassanio's, not derivative from it. Gratiano's vision seems to come after Bassanio's for the trivial reason that dialogue serializes simultaneous actions.

(There is also a brief exchange during the trial scene where Gratiano becomes an echo for Shylock. In these lines, where he is repeating another character's lines, Gratiano is admittedly derivative. He admits it himself: "A Daniel still say I, a second Daniel!—/ I thank thee Jew for teaching me that word" [4.1.338–39]. Understandably Gratiano seems grateful for the change. He enjoys repeating Shylock's lines after he has been following Bassanio's script in so many of his scenes.)

Gratiano is typical of a Venetian commitment to a social theory that proceeds by sorting persons into types on the basis of shared characteristics. There are some exceptions to this rule. The first lines of the play describe Antonio's failure to provide an account of himself: "In sooth I know not why I am so sad" (1.1.1). His sadness is idiopathic, without cause and incommunicable: "But how I caught it, found it, or came by it, / What stuff what stuff 'tis made of, whereof it is born, / I am to learn" (1.1.3–5). He will say only that he is sad and doesn't know why. He can describe what he feels in the present ("It wearies me" [1.1.2]) but will not use his feeling to assign himself a group.

His skepticism about the usefulness of the social theory is magnified when he considers applying it to others. "You say it wearies you" (1.1.2) implies that he is reluctant to make any statement about the feelings of other people. He takes the sayings of others as evidence of the fact that they are saying it. What other people say doesn't tell him what they are feeling or what kinds of people they might be.

The second scene begins just like the first. Portia is sad for no reason: "My little body is aweary of this great world" (1.2.1). Or, as Nerissa points out, Portia is sad despite the fact that she has an abundance of reasons for being happy. Similarly, in the trial scene, Shylock's hatred of Antonio is idiopathic. He both fails and refuses to give a reason for his actions against Antonio: "So can I give no reason, nor I will not" (4.1.59). Instead, in response to the question, he asks a different question: "Is it answer'd?" (4.1.43). And repeats the question: "What, are you answer'd yet?" (4.1.46). Shylock's question is, what would an answer look like?

In these important moments, Antonio, Portia, and Shylock speak lines that are ostensibly not part of the script. Society rejects them. They have not been assigned a type. Still, as exceptional as these moments are, even if the social theory fails to assign these characters a type, they seem to have no other language for talking about themselves.

Finally all of these scenes resolve in the renewal of characterological thinking. Solario and Solanio attempt to give Antonio a character by suggesting the two conventional reasons for sadness in Venice, money and love. Portia and Nerissa run through the list of Portia's suitors and assign each one a type based on his national characteristics. Shylock produces new, as yet unnamed social groupings: "some men" who hate roast pork, "some men" who hate cats, "some men" who hate bagpipes (4.1.46–57).

# What a character is

In these scenes, Shylock, Portia, Nerissa, Solario, and Solanio are working in the genre later called characteristic writing. So is Gratiano, but contrary to convention he is trying to assign a character to himself, not to others.

The problem of characteristic writing can be described historically. Although Theophrastus provides a classical precedent for the genre, and although characterological thinking persists in later prose fiction, the pure form of the genre, the book of characters, appears to be specific to the seventeenth century. What were readers in the seventeenth century getting out of these books that earlier and later readers didn't need or want?

The problem is not historically specific in that the books of characters had no obvious use even in the time of their primary production and reception. The question of "what a character is" is posed in the final entry of the influential collection of characteristic writings *Overbury His Wife* (Overbury 1936, 92). (I use the name Overbury for convenience. Editors agree that Thomas Overbury wrote only a few of the entries.) Isn't it strange that Overbury asks what a character is at the very end of the collection? He seems confused. As though one could read the entire book and not know exactly what a character is. Or as though one could compose such a book without being sure.

The book is organized like a reference book with a short entry on each type of person. For example, the title "A Pedant" is followed by a list of horrible clichés about pedants. The fact that the book includes only clichés makes it inessential, to put it mildly, for the purpose of reference. If you are part of the culture, the book can only tell you what you already know and say and hear every day about pedants. If you aren't part of the culture, then the book appears to present slabs of raw ideology. A view of ideology might be a useful resource for social history or cultural criticism, but the rawness makes it less compelling as material for ideological critique. Social historians tend to prefer their own categories (from the point of view of sociology, a coquette is not a kind of person), and critics like to look for symptoms of ideology in places where they are hidden. For those who live inside the culture and for those who study it, the books appear to have the redundant function of making visible those aspects of persons, their characters, which are already their most visible aspects.

What are characters for? I'm not interested in what readers do with them. Instead I want to propose an answer to this question by looking at what other characters do with them. In Dickens's novel *Our Mutual Friend* the character Mr. Boffin collects instances of another character called "the miser":

> Size, price, quality, were of no account. Any book that seemed to promise a chance of miserly biography, Mr. Boffin purchased without a moment's delay and carried home. Happening to be informed by a bookseller that a portion of the Annual Register was devoted to "Characters," Mr. Boffin at once bought a whole set of that ingenious compilation, and began to carry it home piecemeal. . . . It was curious that Bella never saw the books about the house, nor did she ever hear from Mr. Boffin one word of reference as to their contents. He seemed to save up his misers as they had saved up their money.

**(DICKENS 1960, 486)**

This episode may provide evidence for the durability of character as an aesthetic institution. Centuries after their composition, the characters acquire new value as rare objects that can be collected like antiques. Or maybe this is the value they have always had. What does Boffin do with characters? He buys and saves them. That is all he does with them. He doesn't display them or talk about them. He doesn't even use them for "reference" since he is not capable of "reading at sight." (For Dickens, literacy is a way of seeing: "No one who can read, ever looks at a book, like one who cannot" [19].)

Illiteracy does not always prevent him from reading books. He employs Wegg to read to him from Gibbon's *Decline and Fall*, and he uses Bella, who can "read at sight," to identify possible "lives of odd characters" that might include misers in a bookseller's window. My point is that Boffin doesn't need to "reference" the characters of misers himself or have someone else read them out loud. His education in this regard is complete. He already knows what the books are about, what a miser is, just as he already knows what a character is. Simply by buying and hoarding the books, and without doing any more reading, Boffin gradually becomes, not a miser, but the miser. A representative figure who collects other examples of misers.

(If you have read *Our Mutual Friend*, you probably remember that Boffin is playing the role of the miser. That is, he wants to make Bella think that he has miserly tendencies. What Shklovsky calls "Boffin's secret," the question of Boffin's affinity with misers, the question of whether Boffin is merely pretending to be like the other misers or really has some qualities in common with them, is not relevant to the process of collection [Shklovsky 1990, 122–23].)

Character is the device that makes it possible for the members of this collective to assemble. Character makes it possible for the miser to be not just one miser but all misers. Character makes a seam between Dickens's novel and other books, so that Boffin can collect examples from earlier, obsolete forms of imaginative writing; and between the novel and history, so that he can collect biographical as well as fictional examples. Gratiano does the same thing, or tries to, when he attaches himself first to Mercutio—a character from another play—then to Bassanio. He and Antonio do the same thing when they attach the "world" to the "stage" in which everyone acts as a character. A sad "part" of a single collective subject (1.1.77–79).

Character is the fixed point that allows Antonio and Gratiano to "hold the world . . . as the world" and to leverage it. When Gratiano sketches the character of the fool, he becomes a spokesperson; he speaks for all fools. When Portia gives characters to her suitors based on their patrilineal inheritances and places of origin, she organizes societies, and, in some cases, nations. When she says of Monsieur Le Bon that he is "every man in no man" (1.2.58), she assimilates him to a society called France. She does so without having to bring all France, or even Le Bon, onstage. She is right to say that in marrying him she would "marry twenty husbands" (1.2.60–61). Marriage with Le Bon would put her in relation to the entire society that she characterizes through him.

# Company

This account of character as a collection of examples is a paraphrase of seventeenth-century characteristic writings. As such it should be uncontroversial. You probably won't disagree with me when I say that Overbury and his colleagues think that a character is a collection of examples, although you might not agree with me that they have the right idea about what a character is.

What I'm saying so far is not different from what Leo Spitzer says in a beautiful essay on Saint-Simon:

> Character is the structure which arches over all the facts of history; it is the totality which embraces historical personalities in their full extent and substance. Character is like some Trojan Horse concealing historical acts, events, and customs, which can climb out of its belly and yet leave a clear visible skeleton. . . . Character here is the unmoved mover, the essence or Being from which the Becoming of history springs: individual historical events flow from individual aspects of Being as honey, so to speak, may flow from the separate cells of a single honeycomb.

> **(SPITZER 1983, 117)**

Spitzer and I agree on this interpretation but not what to do with it. The difference between us shows up vividly in the phrase, elided above, that introduces these sentences. "*For Saint-Simon*, character is the structure which arches over all the facts of history." Because Spitzer is committed to the primacy of style and the integrity of the work of art, he allows this definition of character to be true only for one historical epoch, and only for Saint-Simon, and really only for the "Caractère de Louis XIV." My reading follows this definition of character everywhere it goes. I take seriously the idealism of characteristic writing in order to rewrite subsequent literary history and include everything that we call a character in the same way that the realist concept of character rewrites earlier literary history so that what used to be called character has to be renamed caricature or stereotype.

To explain what characters are for, Spitzer needs the mechanism of French neoclassical style. More recently, to explain what characters are for, Elizabeth Fowler has invented the mechanism of a "social person" a projection of the self that mediates interactions between individual and society. Blakey Vermeule refers to the mechanism of the human brain, which has evolved to want to know what is going on inside other human heads.

In order to explain the ability of a character to collect examples, I don't need to add a mechanism to character. I don't need literary influence. I don't need a reader. I don't need society. I don't need the brain. The only mechanism that the form of character requires is meaning. The collection of examples is simply the meaning of the character. A character collects every example in the same way that an entry in a dictionary collects different definitions of a word. Or in the way that the encyclopedia entry on anvils is about every anvil.

Boffin's use of characters is illuminating because his illiteracy precludes mechanisms such as the influence of literature on a reader. For him the process of collection has to occur before reading. Recognition, identification, and influence never have a chance to become issues. It doesn't matter whether Boffin only pretends to be the miser without actually being miserly, or whether, as some critics think, he consciously or unconsciously identifies as a miser, or, as others think, Dickens changed his mind about this question in the process of composing the novel. This is "Boffin's secret," in Shklovsky's precise phrase. We don't know whether he is a Stanislavsky method actor or a commedia dell'arte actor or somehow both. We do know that he is part of the community of misers. The word Dickens uses is "company." Boffin is in the company of misers.

Note that the acts of collection and reading occur as distinct strata of sociability. When Boffin collects the misers, he is in "bad company," and when Wegg reads to him he is in "worse company" (498–505). Two different social relationships.

# Many is not more than one

Gratiano does not need more stage time than he is given to build a collection of examples. He does not have to recite as many lines as Mercutio in order to define a character type based on Mercutio.

Similarly, for Boffin, "size, price, quality, were of no account." Boffin doesn't need more space in the novel to store his books or to include every example of the miser. He represents the entire society of misers without the tedious labor of reading through the books of characters page by page, and without Dickens's having to transcribe them even more tediously.

Two people are more people than one person, but not necessarily more of a society insofar as one person can be a character such as the miser, the coquette, the pedant, or the old maid. Molière puts his finger on this aspect of character in a line from *Dom Juan* about hypocrites: by playing the hypocrite, Dom Juan says, by making faces, by putting on the hypocrite's mask, "one forms a solid pact with others of the same persuasion" (Molière 2008, 5.2). Dom Juan does not mean that the hypocrites schedule meetings, conspire, or act in concert. He does not mean that their grimaces are a secret code, like a wink, by which they communicate their plans. The faces they make are only a sign of the form of their character. By making the face of the hypocrite, one instantly collects every example of hypocrisy.

Many is not more than one. There is a paradox here. To see it clearly, let's go back to Aristotle. His treatise on poetics identifies three "unities" that determine the dimensions, the boundedness, and the formal closure of a poem. Neoclassical critics of the seventeenth century codified "the three unities" as prescriptive rules. A dramatic poem should represent a single action, a single location, and a unit of time no longer than a day. But there has never been any notion of unity of person.

Aristotle is clear on this point. A person is incapable of determining the formal closure of a work of art because a person is never a unity. In Hutton's translation:

> Many things, indeed an endless number of things, happen to any one man some of which do not go together to form a unity, and similarly among the actions one man performs there are many that do not go together to produce a single unified action.
>
> **(ARISTOTLE 1982, 53)**

According to Aristotle, an object has unity if its wholeness is remarkable in perception and retained in memory. Can you remember everything you do, everything done to you? I don't even remember the paper I wrote on *Poetics* in my last year of college. I am not a unity.

Aristotle thought that a person could never be a unity. Theophrastus and his followers went in another direction. They discovered a unity in character that did not correspond to action, place, or time. Because it's a paradox. Both multiplicity and unity. Many is not more than one.

Here's how it works in a seventeenth-century character sketch, Samuel Butler's "Character of a Small Poet":

> There was one, that lined a Hat-Case with a Paper of *Benlowse's* poetry— Prynne bought it by Chance, and put a new Demi-Castor [beaver hat] into it. The first Time he wore it he felt only a singing in his Head, which within two Days turned to a Vertigo—He was let Blood in the Ear by one of the State-Physicians, and recovered; but before he went abroad he writ a Poem of Rocks and Seas, in a Stile so proper and natural, that it was hard to determine, which was ruggeder.
>
> **(BUTLER 1908, 53)**

This sketch includes all known characteristics of small poets. Here is one piece of knowledge. Small poetry, the writing produced by small poets, is a dangerous material. It's a contagion running from the lining of a hatbox to the lining of a hat to the inside of your head. Something that touches small poetry, and then touches something else that touches your head, could hurt your head.

Small poetry is a physical danger. It could lead to head injury. Its influence does not end there. Vicarious contact with one sheet of Benlowes's poetry causes Prynne to start writing his own small poetry. The chain of influence runs from poem to hatbox to hat to head to new poem. Possibly each new medium amplifies the signal. You might say this is a story about a society in which poetry has more writers than readers. Or a story about the power that poetry can have when you *don't* read it.

The "character of a small poet" is a relationship between individual and society. The small poet is powerful enough to create an army of small poets and thus a danger to society. This social problem is also the form of the character sketch. Benlowes, an actual bad seventeenth-century poet, is a representative figure in whom facts that are true of all small poets may be viewed. The hat is used as a medium. Anyone who wears the small poet's hat is in danger of becoming a small poet. Out of Prynne's hat, Butler produces the entire community of small poets.

When the speaker in Overbury's collection finally explains "what a character is," he literalizes and classicizes it.

> If I must speake the Schoole-masters language I will confesse that Character comes of this infinitive moode [kharassein] which signifieth to ingrave, or make a deepe Impression. And for that cause, a letter (as A.B.) is called a character.
>
> **(92)**

Many readers have been struck by the role of writing in this definition. "A letter is called a character" seems to externalize the most basic facts about the person. In the words of my teacher Jonathan Goldberg, "The depth of a character is the result of an inscription, what others read on the surface" (32). It has not previously been remarked that these lines are spoken in character too: "If I must speake the Schoole-masters language." Unlike the other entries in the book, the character of character is written in the first person, and it doesn't begin with "is," it begins with "if." He speaks the language but he isn't the schoolmaster. Even as he assigns himself a character, the schoolmaster, he reserves a neutral part of himself that does not conform to the script.

The writer in the Overbury collection asks us to notice something else about the relationship between character and writing:

Those elements which we learn first, leaving a strong seal in our memories.

In a sentence fragment set apart as a single paragraph, character shares with writing a priority in education. That is the entire basis for the comparison. The first meaning of character is the impression it leaves not in conduct but in memory.

The writer then ventures another etymology and two more definitions. This is a wonderful passage and I don't know why it has been neglected:

Character is also taken from an Egyptian hieroglyphic, for an impress, in little comprehending much.

To square out a character by our English level, it is a picture (real or personal) quaintly drawn, in various colors, all of them heightened by one shadowing.

It is a quick and soft touch of many strings, all shutting up in one musical close; it is wit's descant on any plain song.

**(OVERBURY 1936, 92)**

What is character? First it's writing, then it's a few other things that are not writing. Different colors arranged together to make a picture. Different musical notes played simultaneously to make a chord. This is a relationship between part and whole. A special relationship where the meaning of each part includes the whole, "in little comprehending much."

Frances Ferguson writes eloquently of a solitude at the heart of "character itself, the extension of individual action through narrative until it has become romance, the impossibility of action" (Ferguson 1992, 102). This solitude belongs to all characters. It is a feature of the unthinkable space where different examples of the same character collect. When he asks to play the fool, Gratiano reveals that he is not yet the fool. His character is not given and must be earned. He uses the role of the fool to establish another part of himself offstage, neither part of the plot of the play nor a member of the collective of fools. When Portia lists her suitors, she assigns a character to everyone but herself. Not only is her weariness not determined by her personal traits, it appears somehow to contradict them. It's as though she's saying, all of my suitors are characters, but I'm something else. Not a character.

Milton has an unusual exercise in characteristic writing, the pair of poems "L'Allegro" and "Il Penseroso." The pensive one, "Il Penseroso," prefers solitude to company. But curiously he never seems to be alone. Like the happy one, he is accompanied by a "crew" of personified abstractions— Peace, Quiet, Fast, Leisure, Contemplation, Silence, and Melancholy (45–55). Already that crew sounds typical of Milton's poetry. There's a similar moment in the garden in *Paradise Lost* where a bird's song accompanies silence without negating silence, and "Silence was pleased."

The pensive one might be alone in relation to other people. But in the unthinkable space of character, the pensive one belongs to a society of pensive ones. And then each character trait, even silence, comes with a whole other collection of examples. Like Gratiano's, the assignment of character to the pensive one happens in the first person. The whole experience of melancholy is imagined not merely as membership in a collective but as a relation to another person who turns out to be genealogically related to a number of others who are called the "crew."

The pairing of the two opposite characters is anomalous in the history of literary character, but typical of Milton's sensibility. The anomaly that makes Milton really sound like Milton is the use of a contract. Milton presents a life "with" Melancholy as a temptation scene, or, as he less intensely puts it, a choice between two companions. "These pleasures *Melancholy* give / And I with thee will choose to live" (175–76). The happy one in "L'Allegro" ends by offering to formalize the relationship to Mirth in a similar contract: "These delights, if thou canst give, / Mirth, with thee I mean to live" (151–52). The important part is "if." The implication is that Mirth's gifts have yet to arrive; the speaker has not yet entered into the relationship. "If" is the first principle of characteristic writing. The real space of character.

# Proper names belong to everyone

Mirth, says Rosemond Tuve in her great essay on Milton's pair of poems, "is a way of talking about the absolutely not the contingently real" (45). Or, Ferguson might say, Mirth is a way of making more than one of something. I believe that Tuve's distinction between levels of reality, absolute and contingent, corresponds to the distinction in Overbury between "real" and "personal."

Tuve limits the use of her own description because she does not allow it to read forward. On the contrary she carefully opposes Milton's allegory to modern conceptions of character. With deep regret, she says, "such images" as Mirth "no longer surround us" (32). Her distaste for modernity elsewhere finds expression in the heretical statements that "an eminent singleness of meaning characterizes symbols" (33), and, even more bracing, that satisfaction is preferable to desire. "We do not tire of pleasures or of thought but of the pursuing without taking possession" (15–16).

Dorothy Van Ghent and Ian Watt agree with Tuve that modern characters in realist novels are individuals, and the novel is the genre of contingent reality. According to Van Ghent, "For fiction the particular body that a thing has is of the very greatest importance. . . . Does it squeak, is it brown, is it round, is it chilly, does it think, does it smash?" (4). Even Bunyan's allegory *The Pilgrim's Progress* succeeds as a novel "only because Bunyan founds his allegory of human qualities in the objective reality of human manners"; in other words, because characters such as Christian are not "abstract personifications" (29). She further differentiates novels from works of history in this way: history generalizes, whereas the novel individuates (4). Watt, who agrees with her, notes that the philosopher Shaftesbury made the opposite distinction: "The mere Historian . . . traces every feature and odd mark" (16).

There appears to be a consensus among these literary historians of the mid-twentieth century that would partition the nature of reality by genre and by epoch. Absolute reality pertains to premodern poetry, contingent reality to the modern novel. The fact that these two conceptions of reality, the philosophical and literary, are both called "realism" is, in Watt's words, "a paradox that will surprise only the neophyte" (11).

Is it true that abstract personifications do not surround us in modern civilizations? Do characters in novels no longer act as figures of absolute reality? The reversibility of the formulas about history and fiction suggests that the distinction may be a false one. At least the two genres are linked by their use of characters.

One alternative to this seeming consensus is suggested by research by Naomi Schor, Sharon Marcus, and Toril Moi on the idealist tradition in the novel. Schor argues that criticism that identifies situations in novels with a recognizable historical reality is inadequate to protocols of interpretation in nineteenth-century French novels in which anything that happens on the level of representation must posit an ideal, understood both as "the heightening of the essential and the promotion of the higher good" (40). Schor quotes from a conversation between Sand and Balzac.

> [Balzac tells Sand,] You are looking for man as he should be; I take him as he is. . . . But the ordinary human beings interest me more than they do you. I make them larger than life; I idealize them in the opposite sense, in their ugliness or in their stupidity.
>
> **(40–41)**

Most critics of realism, following Van Ghent and Watt, see a crucial difference between Balzac's "man as he is" and Sand's "man as he should be." But if idealism is the paradigm, then there is no way to separate the two modalities. Make no mistake: Balzac wants his characters to express an ideal. That is why he includes the "magnificent images of integrity" Jeanie Deans (from Scott's *Heart of Mid-lothian*) and Alceste (from Molière's *Misanthrope*) in *Père Goriot* (165). That is why he considers the women in his novels to be superior to Jeanie Deans: because his characters have the Virgin Mary as an exemplar, whereas "the Protestant woman has no ideal" (15).

Tracing the reception of French literature in England, Marcus finds that Victorian critics share their French contemporaries' assumptions about idealized representations. She also discovers that Victorian critics use "realism" mainly in a pejorative sense. "What realists would call an objective and encyclopedic grasp of the world, idealists called 'granting a bill of indemnity to all that is perverse and ungovernable in our nature'" (271). For the nineteenth-century critic Leslie Stephen, the canon of realism is confined mainly to French Sapphism, sensational stories about sex between women. It includes just a few books by Balzac and Zola, not their entire output, and a number of poems by Baudelaire and Swinburne. (Baudelaire, whose art criticism champions imagination against historical reality, is a realist in this literary formation!)

I want to push this argument a little further. Where Marcus elegantly remarks that "contemporary critics have idealized realism," I would argue that they are right to do so, because realism itself idealizes realism. In other words, the neophyte is right to think that realism means realism, and Watt is wrong to exclude philosophical realism from literary realism.

One of Watt's first examples, the name protocols in the novels of Henry Fielding, fails to support his argument to an almost comic extent.

According to Watt, the early English novel uses "proper names that were characteristic, and nonparticular and unrealistic in some other way" such as Mr. Badman and Euphues (19). In later novels, like Fielding's, a character's name is used "to symbolise the fact that he is to be regarded as though he were a particular person and not a type" (20). Watt immediately has to make exceptions for Heartfree, Allworthy, and Square. It does not occur to him to make an exception for Joseph Andrews, whose name is purely literary, a back-formation based on Richardson's *Pamela*. Even the name Tom Jones is a placeholder whose function is to suggest an idealized ordinariness, an exaggeratedly ordinary English name. In any case Jones is not the character's family name, which is Allworthy.

Finally Watt regroups and suggests that Fielding had reformed his name protocols "by the time he came to write his last novel, *Amelia*." The shift from significant names to ordinary names, which was originally supposed to take place over the early history of the novel, is now recapitulated within Fielding's career. Even in *Amelia* Watt has to make exceptions for "Justice Thrasher and Bondum the Bailiff." The evidence of Fielding's new attitude toward naming is that the names of other characters (Booth, Matthews, Harrison, and so forth) are apparently copied from "the list of subscribers to the 1724 edition of Gilbert Burnet's *History of His Own Time*," a practice that suggests, if anything, that the characters are designed to collect both historical and fictional examples, just like generic types.

If the English novel does not give up on significant names in Fielding, when does it happen? In Trollope, who gives his characters names such as Quiverful and titles such as Duke of Omnium? In Joyce, who calls his youthful surrogate Stephen Dedalus? Maybe it happens in Helen Fielding, who writes about a character named Bridget Jones. Again I am convinced that the uses to which characters put one another are more illuminating than the uses to which historical readers put them. Consider the inclusion of characters from Austen's *Pride and Prejudice* in *Bridget Jones's Diary*. The latter is an adaptation of the former, but the relationship is strangely oblique in that Fielding adapts not the novel but the BBC television serial. She acknowledges this genealogy by having Bridget watch the series during the time of its original broadcast, remarking on the social phenomenon of England sitting down as a nation to watch the same program.

> Love the nation being so addicted. The basis of my own addiction, I know, is my simple human need for Darcy to get off with Elizabeth. . . . They are my chosen representatives in the field of shagging, or, rather, courtship.

(215)

Despite her election of Darcy and Elizabeth as her representatives, Bridget has nothing to say about the obvious resemblance of her story to theirs. Unlike Boffin, Bridget is hardly illiterate—she keeps a diary and works at a publishing house—but she seems not to recognize the fact that she is living the plot of an old novel. (Fielding does gently suggest that Bridget may be, if not illiterate, then a poor reader. Her colleague Perpetua—another significant name!—complains that "a whole generation of people only get to know the great works of literature—Austen, Dickens, Shakespeare, and so on—through the television. . . . And you do realize *Middlemarch* was originally a book, Bridget, don't you, not a soap?" [86–87].) Even the fact that one of her lovers is named Darcy goes unremarked. In the film adaptation this blindness is compounded by casting Colin Firth, the actor from the BBC series, as Darcy.

The example of Bridget shows that a character collects every example without effort or consciousness. Bridget can play the part of Elizabeth without trying to, without realizing what she is doing. Her status as a type of Elizabeth does not depend on her identification with Elizabeth or recognition of Darcy—neither of which occurs.

History may not follow a straight line from *Tom Jones* to *Bridget Jones*, but the novels are linked not only through name protocols that announce the characters as figures of absolute reality, and not only through the shared surnames of the protagonists (Jones), but also through those of their authors (Fielding). That is because proper names belong to everyone. (Just as much as common names do.)

# There is no zero

The association of Bridget Jones with Elizabeth Bennett, and of Mark Darcy with Fitzwilliam Darcy, should be distinguished from the idea of "character migration" or "character extension" that David Brewer develops in *The Afterlife of Character*. Brewer documents the later existences of characters from Shakespeare, Richardson, Sterne, and Scott, in the form of continuations, revisions, and adaptations. "Migration" is an aspect of what Brewer calls "social canonicity," a term he takes from Franco Moretti. The social canon depends on what readers do with characters. Unlike the "academic canon," which is based on prestige, the social canon is a popularity contest determined by numbers of readers. Brewer uses migration to gauge social canonicity. "Character migration, one might say," he says, "not only speaks the unspoken presumptions surrounding social canonicity, it turns them up to eleven" (Brewer 2005, 18). A character succeeds, on his account, by attracting more readers and provoking more revisions.

Partly to avoid confusing character types with migrating characters, I have not been discussing individual historical readers such as those who populate Brewer's archive. I concentrate instead on fictional characters using other fictional characters, and I especially like characters who are either illiterate (like Boffin) or insensitive (like Bridget) with respect to their source texts. The association of Boffin and Bridget with archaic characterologies can't be understood as an effect of influence. Boffin and Bridget are part of their collections along with all the other examples. The process of collection is separate from the psychological identification of readers or audience members with particular characters, or the recognition of kinds of persons in art and in the world.

Try instead to think of character as a container that gives shape to the materials it contains. That is what Robert Walpole does when he insults William Yonge: "Nothing but such a character could keep down such parts" (Butler 1966, 417). Or think of character as a hive, as Meredith does when he describes the character of the egoist as "a body of insects perpetually erecting and repairing a structure of extraordinary prettiness" (Meredith 1979, 289).

These are facts about characters that everyone knows. In film and theater it is taken for granted that a character is portrayed by an actor, and can be portrayed by other actors in other performances or remakes. "An Excellent Actor," in the words of the Overbury collection, "fortifies morall precepts with examples" (77). Actors sometimes specialize in a character type, making a career out of playing different examples of the same character. It also frequently happens in a single production that one actor will play several characters. For reasons of economy it happens less frequently that several actors play one character, but it does happen.

In *That Obscure Object of Desire*, both Carole Bouquet and Angela Molina play the character Conchita, who alternately seduces and rejects Mathieu. There is no confusion about this double performance either in the community of the film or in the history of viewing the film. Although viewers, unlike Mathieu, notice differences between the two women, everyone agrees that they are playing the same character.

Then there are actors who do not play to type or have no consistent type in their performances. In *An Actor Prepares*, Stanislavski uses a universal "emotional memory" to account for the ability of actors to play different characters whose life experiences may be totally unlike their own. Any actor can play a killer because anyone who has killed an insect remembers emotionally how to commit murder. Stanislavski's exercises ask actors to find an emotional path to the absolute reality that Tuve sees in Milton's mirth, who is "every man's Mirth, our mirth, the very grace herself with all she can include" (Tuve, 20).

A character does not succeed by accumulating more examples than another character with which it is competing. In communities of characters, many is not more than one. Brewer's accounts of migrating characters are fascinating, but his attempt to extrapolate social canonicity from migration is based on the mistaken idea that many is always more. The mistake is ultimately Moretti's. It is implicit in Moretti's fear that "a canon of two hundred novels . . . is still less than one percent of the novels that were actually published" and the odd idea that a piece of writing "becomes extinct" if it doesn't have a lot of readers, and particularly evident in the evangelical passages in his work, in proclamations that "if comparative literature is not this, it's nothing. Nothing" (Moretti 2005, 4, 72; Moretti 2000, 68).

Moretti thinks that critics, like books, are significant only when there are more of them. But why should there have to be more than one counter for that one to count? Moretti's work is just as significant in its singularity as it will be when he converts his colleagues by the thousands, and quantitative critics are in the majority position.

Moretti and Brewer could learn something from Scott Carey, the hero of Richard Matheson's novel *The Shrinking Man*. For most of the novel, Scott, who is shrinking daily at a constant rate, assumes that he will eventually cease to exist. He predicts when it will happen. After a certain time, shrinking at a certain rate, he will be zero inches tall. In the last chapter, on the day of his projected disappearance, he surprises himself by coming to consciousness in a new landscape in which the scale has changed. He quickly understands that the facts of his previous existence, his concerns (his giant wife and daughter) and terrors (bullies, cats, and spiders), are no longer relevant. He must adjust to a new set of concerns and terrors on a cellular level, and, if he keeps shrinking, on an atomic level, and a subatomic level, and every level below that.

Scott's new formula is, "To nature, there is no zero" (204). (In the film *The Incredible Shrinking Man*, this line becomes, "To God, there is no zero," as though Matheson, who also wrote the screenplay, wanted to equivocate like Spinoza on the identity of God or Nature.) Or, as they say at the Actors Studio, there are no small parts.

# The wealth of characters

What are characters for? When I ask a novel what characters are for, I am not interested in what readers do with characters. Instead I focus on what other characters do with them. This is a basic point of methodology. I make no discoveries about readers by studying passages from a novel, but I might learn something about characters that way. Similarly, I maintain that the best way to understand character in theatrical performance is not by tracking the responses of an audience but rather by studying scenes where performance reveals itself as performance. For example, the Maurice Chevalier scene in the Marx Brothers' film *Monkey Business*. I am going to talk about this scene at some length.

For reference, here is a brief summary, inevitably false to the dream-logic of the scene. The four Marx Brothers are stowed away on an ocean liner crossing the Atlantic. As the boat comes into port they are stumped as to how they are going to disembark without attracting the notice of the unsympathetic captain and his crew. When Zeppo acquires a passport belonging to Maurice Chevalier, they concoct a mad plan to act as the international movie star. Working as a group, they rudely insert themselves at the front of the line of travelers going through customs. In quick succession, each brother, wearing a straw hat, presents a passport identifying the bearer as Chevalier, and confirms his identity by belting the first two bars of "You Brought a New Kind of Love to Me," a song that Chevalier made famous in his movie about a transatlantic romance *The Big Pond*. The same skeptical but surprisingly patient customs official endures all four performances before ordering them to the back of the line.

I think you should watch the scene. You should be able to follow my argument even if you don't. This book doesn't include any clips or even any film stills. I don't ordinarily use stills when I talk about scenes from films, and that is deliberate. One advantage of writing literary criticism is that you are working in the same medium that you are studying. When I write about a poem the proof of my argument is a quotation from the poem. I can take a piece of the poem and put it into my book. I can't do that with a film. The film has to be created from scratch in my book. If I'm doing a decent job you shouldn't have trouble following my argument even if you haven't watched the scene. You should watch the scene anyway because it is such a great work of art and a delight.

This scene is a performance of a performance. An absurd command, given for reasons that are not remotely adequate even to the incoherent, arbitrary plot, requires the same performance of Zeppo, Chico, Groucho, and Harpo: "You've got to sing one of Chevalier's songs to get off this boat." Four bodies pass through the same conduit. Hat, passport, and song. With what result? What message is this scene trying so insistently to convey?

Before taking a look at some technical aspects of the performances I want to approach these questions by observing that Chevalier must be one of the easiest impressions in the entire history of performance. If called upon, any actor, professional or amateur, no matter how insensitive, no matter how limited in range, should be able to produce a recognizable impression of Chevalier. It's like how any comedian is able to summon Arnold Schwarzenegger by drawling, "I'll be back." It isn't even necessary to get the vowel sounds right. That's how easy it is. In 1931 merely singing a phrase from "You Brought a New Kind of Love to Me" is enough to make Chevalier present.

> If the nightingale could sing like you,
> They'd sing much better than they do,
> For you brought a new kind of love to me.

How easy is it to do Chevalier? Think of Pépé le Pew. Compare Pépé in the Warner Brothers cartoon *For Scent-imental Reasons* with Chevalier's performance of "Mimi" in *Love Me Tonight*. You are looking at two performances of the same character, and something more is going on. Pépé is influenced by and deliberately built out of the materials of Chevalier. Look at the sparkling eyes and the big smile. The passion that overflows in shooting, grabbing hand gestures. The stream of asides that deteriorate into unintelligible subvocalizations punctuated by long, drawn out vowel sounds. The murmur of Chevalier's exaggeratedly accented English is remarkably close to the stream of French-like sounds that Mel Blanc produces for Pépé's "vocal characterization."

Is Pépé a parody of Chevalier? I'm not sure. The question is surprisingly hard to answer. The script of *For Scent-imental Reasons* is parodic. For example, Pépé's line, "Oh! . . . my little peanut of brittle," parodies exclamations that you might hear from Chevalier's characters such as, "Oh! . . . you funny little good for nothing . . . you sunny little honey of a Mimi." On the whole, though, it's hard to see how anyone could parody Chevalier, since the level of his commitment to his performance goes so far beyond parody. Would it be possible to put more arousal into the syllable "Oh"? To exaggerate a sigh more than he does?

Now it's one thing to say that Zeppo, Chico, and Groucho do not resemble Chevalier. The customs agent says it three times: "Say, this picture doesn't look like you!" Still, they do look a little bit like Chevalier, and so does Harpo. They have certain basic features in common with Chevalier. They are all humanoid, their sex is male, and they are roughly the same age. It's something else altogether to point out that Pépé looks nothing like Chevalier. He may be anthropomorphic and masculine, but the resemblance ends there. His face and body do not even caricature Chevalier.

The only telling point of physical resemblance is the straw boater that Pépé sometimes wears.

Pépé demonstrates how easy it is to do an impression of Chevalier. You can be a skunk. A cartoon. Without looking remotely like Chevalier you can still do an effective impression. I do not mean that making an animated short subject is easy. I would not discount the visual inventiveness of Chuck Jones, the vocal range of Mel Blanc, or the painstaking labor of the other artists and writers. I am saying that Pépé looks even less like Chevalier than Zeppo does. Unlike Zeppo, Pépé is not even trying to look like Chevalier. And yet he is Chevalier, unmistakably, just because of the voice and the hat. (The hat, I will argue, is all you need!)

Can I be certain that Pépé is Chevalier? His name suggests something else, I admit. The name refers to the character Pépé le Moko, first played by Jean Gabin in the film of the same name, and later by Charles Boyer in the Hollywood remake *Algiers*. To be sure, Pépé le Moko represents a different type of masculinity. Where Chevalier expresses his desires in every look, every wild gesture, and in the accented, exaggerated articulation of every vowel, Pépé le Moko keeps all his feelings inside. He is not susceptible to human feelings. (Well, he really is, as he demonstrates when he makes a final, pointless sacrifice.)

Pépé le Pew's short subjects regularly cite the mise en scène of these two films. Some episodes, such as "Little Beau Pépé" and "The Cat's Bah," take place in North Africa, and in one of the less aggressive moments in *For Scent-imental Reasons*, Pépé tries to make a date "in the Casbah" with the cat whose unluckily striped back makes her look enough like a skunk to arouse his interest.

Can a skunk play both Chevalier and Boyer (and, behind Boyer, Gabin as well)? Think of it this way. Maurice Chevalier's character, the one that he plays in nearly all of his films, is a magnet for misconceptions about France. That is his use. (*Folies Bergères*, where he plays two roles from two distinct social classes, may be the only exception.) When he appears on screen, smiling and cooing and gesticulating, all France is contained within the frame. The same is true for Pépé le Moko and for his lover Gaby. (Pépé le Moko falls in love with Gaby because she has a quality that reminds him of the Paris Metro.) Pépé le Moko and Chevalier project ideas about France but the two ideas do not include each other. Pépé le Pew includes them both—not because his character is somehow more general than the others, but because he participates in two different characters at the same time.

This braiding of distinct masculine types teaches a valuable lesson in the nature of performance. From Pépé we might learn how it is that Chico, Groucho, Harpo, and Zeppo are able to perform as Chevalier without relinquishing their own iconic status.

# Hats are emotional

How important is the hat?

The straw hat is not important to Pépé le Pew. He almost never wears it. Only one characteristic consistently associates him with Maurice Chevalier, and that is the changeable voice of Mel Blanc speaking something resembling French. The hat is just an extra touch; it adds character.

Zeppo, Chico, and Groucho wear straw hats in *Monkey Business*. The hats appear identical and are in the same style as Chevalier's, with a black band. Only Groucho angles the hat over his face as Chevalier does. It isn't clear whether Groucho does so in homage to the movie star who provides the pattern for his performance, or whether the brim of the hat is supposed to protect his face from the inspection of the customs official. The moustache painted over his lip might raise suspicions that he is not Chevalier.

The hat gives Groucho a different character, Chevalier's, without giving him a new face. It leaves untouched the detachable facial features (greasepaint eyebrows and mustache, spectacles) that you or I would put on in order to play the part of Groucho. These features, along with the cigar (which does not appear in this scene), are signatures of the type in which he is cast. They turn the unpredictable human face into a mask, diminishing its mobility and muting its expressivity. What Groucho may be feeling at any moment is uncertain.

(On the first page of *Seize the Day*, Saul Bellow observes the usefulness of hats not for obscuring the face but for restricting its expressive capabilities; hats are thus "emotional" in the Steinian sense that they limit or regulate emotion.)

Harpo is an exception. He eschews the straw boater in the Chevalier style for his own familiar battered top hat. For much of the scene he gives no indication that he is trying to impersonate Chevalier. He might not even be trying to get through customs. Other objects draw his attention: the piles of papers on the customs table he crumples and flings into the air; the rubber stamp and inkpad at first he applies haphazardly, not seeming to care whether he marks the papers or not, later targeting the bald head of the customs official; and the pens protruding from the inkstand he grabs and pumps as though they were the controls for an engine, or perhaps a drill. When asked to "come on with that passport," he responds with two weak plays on words, "pasteboard" and "washboard."

Isn't that funny? Although a silent actor, Harpo can make puns. He does it frequently. They aren't exactly visual puns. They are verbal puns, and they are spoken eventually, just not immediately, and never by Harpo. The technique is for Harpo to present the pun in a dormant mode for another actor to vocalize. Here the customs official has the job of speaking the pun: "I said passport, not pasteboard." A few scenes later, when Harpo mishears the command to "take the pulse" of a fainting woman as "take her purse," Chico narrates, turning a silent action into a verbal quibble.

So far Harpo seems to be playing himself rather than Chevalier. He only strengthens this impression when, between the quibble over the piece of pasteboard and the quibble over the washboard, he performs his signature move. I think of it as the legshake. He places the crook of his knee in the customs official's waiting hand and swings his foot in a pendulum motion. Like the passport, like Chevalier's song, "You Brought a New Kind of Love to Me," like Groucho's eyebrows and glasses, like Chico's Italian accent, the legshake is a mark of identification. Who is this? The one who, when you are introduced to him, puts his leg in your hand instead of his hand.

This interpretation doesn't feel right to me. It misses the flexibility of Harpo's performances.

What is Harpo doing? Mostly he plays, in every sense of the word. Wayne Koestenbaum has written about this aspect of Harpo's performances with wonderful sympathy (Koestenbaum, 106). Two impulses express themselves in Harpo's play. One is intimacy with objective reality. In his presence all the tools of the trade on the customs table become active as toys rather than tools. He is not using them to get something or go somewhere; he is making them active and mobile. The second impulse, closely linked to the first, is mirroring. Harpo follows in a track that others have created.

The celebrated mirror scene from *Duck Soup*, where Harpo puts on Groucho's face as a mask, is paradigmatic. Harpo has no objective in the mirror scene, only an identification with an object, Groucho. He isn't trying to fool Groucho or take something from him. He only wants to replace Groucho with an image, so his reflection does not have to be perfect. A Panama hat reflects another Panama hat but a top hat will do just as well. By the same logic he does not concern himself with getting off the boat in *Monkey Business*. If you want to get off the boat you are going to need a state-issued passport or a decent forgery, but if you are interested only in representing the passport—or, which seems more likely, if you are interested only in suggesting the sound of the word "passport"—pasteboard and washboard become interesting possibilities.

It is a matter of indifference to Harpo whether he passes as Chevalier or not. He puts some care into acting as Chevalier but he cares just as much about portraying his brothers, the customs official, the papers, and the stamps. At first Harpo is wholly committed to mirroring his brothers. Following in the footsteps of Zeppo, Chico, and Groucho, he takes his place in line. He deviates from and expands on their patterns only because he is distracted by other intriguing patterns in the environment. He wants to be all the objects and persons on and around the table.

I think that what finally inspires him to show a passport is the sound of the customs official's knuckles rapping the table. This sound is so interesting that Harpo wants to hear it again. He looks for an instrument to make the same sound. His hands find a passport; he stamps it twice. By handing it over he is claiming Chevalier's rights as a citizen. By stamping it he is doing the official's job and imitating his noise. In that moment he is not playing Chevalier any longer. Now he is playing the part of the official!

Harpo's passport, unlike the others, appears in close-up. It includes a still photograph of Chevalier's head. I believe this is the only photograph of Chevalier in the film, although there are many other images that represent him. This is not, I assume, a shot of Chevalier's actual passport photo but rather a headshot provided by the studio for purposes of publicity.

The decision to show an image of Chevalier wearing a cap as opposed to a straw boater must be deliberate. The significance of this decision is to confirm what Harpo has already proved by entering with a top hat. From his entrance we know that the straw hat is not necessary for a performance of Chevalier. The hat can be detached from the head and replaced by another kind of hat, a top hat or cap.

In a scene from the later film *Love Me Tonight*, Chevalier crushes his own hat under a carriage wheel. Is he still Chevalier? One may doubt it:

—Ha! Ha! Your hat! Look at it! What will you do without your straw hat, Maurice? And where's that smile of yours? No straw hat, no smile. It's all over, Maurice; you can't go on.

[Maurice raises index finger, looks intently for a beat, goes to suitcase, removes spare hat, puts it on his head, smiles.]

—Now we can go on, Pierre.

Pierre believes that the hat is important. It is some kind of talisman of performance. The character depends on the smile and the smile depends on the hat. The hat is truly the actor; in framing the face and limiting its mobility, it imposes a single expression as a mask on the actor's face. The consequence of removing and destroying the hat is to remove and destroy the character too.

Maurice is indifferent to the hat. He must be. He's the one who casts it into the road where it can be lost under a wheel while he supports Jeanette Macdonald's injured body. The character is not exhausted by the loss of the hat. For Maurice the resources of the character are inexhaustible; he has as many hats as he has smiles.

Don't get me wrong. The hat really is important. In fact the hat is sufficient. Chevalier's first entrance in *Love Me Tonight* is in the form of a hat. This scene is an example of the genre of the urban symphony, and it includes many interesting features that exceed the concerns of my argument. Its main purpose is to demonstrate the interpenetration of sounds and actions in the city. Its secondary purpose is to demonstrate the range of the soundtrack, from silence to maximum density of tracks.

The resolution of the scene, which occurs as the background music rises and drowns out the street noise, is the discovery of the hero of the film. In this shot the hero is not played by the international movie star but rather by the hat that he is going to wear. To make the point as clear as possible, the hat unnecessarily emphasizes its function as synecdoche by casting its shadow on an outline of a human figure drawn on the wall. The hat, the object by itself, is one example of the character of Chevalier, and its meaning is the entire collection of examples. It includes all the others.

The hat is important in that it has import. It is sufficient but not necessary. If Maurice were separated from his hat, stranded on a tropical island without straw, he would improvise a new one out of palm leaves or seaweed. He never needed a particular hat. Any hat will do, or he can go without. Character is not the same as its resources. Although it uses and discards materials, character is not the materials but the form given to them.

# The price of characters

The logic that associates these materials is dreamlike but not arbitrary. Why a straw hat? Why this song? Why Chevalier? Jerome Christensen might point out that the Marx Brothers made *Monkey Business* at the Paramount studio, and that Chevalier sings "You Brought a New Kind of Love to Me" in *The Big Pond*, also a Paramount production. The approximations of Chevalier in *Monkey Business* may be interpreted as signatures of the collaborative artistic process that Christensen describes as "studio authorship." One studio product learns from another how to pass through customs after crossing the Atlantic. How do Paramount screenwriters get their characters across the Atlantic without any trouble? By making them imitate Maurice Chevalier. "You've got to sing one of Chevalier's songs to get off this boat!"

The interesting possibility of studio authorship should be distinguished from the uninteresting possibility that a simple economic logic guides the decisions in this scene. Yes, it's true, at the time of the production of *Monkey Business*, the Paramount studio owned the rights to the song "You Brought a New Kind of Love to Me" and did not need to pay for the song to be reprised four, five, or six times, but this fact is not a compelling incentive for the studio to produce several new performances of the song by the Marx Brothers. If the studio's motive is to cut costs, then why hire four actors to do a job that one can do? In addition to owning the rights to the song, the studio also had a contract with Chevalier. So why doesn't he appear in *Monkey Business*? But why make another movie with Chevalier after the first one? If the answer is that a mass audience demands more of Chevalier, then why is that?

The desirability of more scenes in which Chevalier's character appears, or even the existence of one such scene, is ultimately an aesthetic problem, and requires an aesthetic solution.

What is the price of character? The scene from *Monkey Business* might be considered an exercise in economy. The performers are engaged in a price war in which they compete to see whose characterization of Chevalier is the cheapest. Produced in a period of economic depression, the film depicts serious social inequalities. For the stowaways on the boat, money is completely out of reach. Other characters might have money; the Marx Brothers never touch it.

In playing Chevalier, Harpo at first appears to use no resources at all, and Chico and Groucho do no more than sketch a vague outline. In Chico's rendition of "You Brought a New Kind of Love to Me" I discern no attempt to imitate Chevalier's French-accented English or to tone down Chico's absurdly Italian-accented English. "If-a da nightingale could-a sing like-a you," he sings. Groucho performs in his faint singing voice, skulking and slouching like Captain Spalding or Rufus T. Firefly but not remotely like Chevalier. Only Zeppo attempts a French accent; his own voice is so bland that it might as well be an unmarked surface capable of receiving any impression.

The vocal line of "You Brought a New Kind of Love to Me," as interpreted by Zeppo, Chico, and Groucho, is remarkably more tuneful than in Chevalier's interpretation. I have viewed *The Big Pond*, and I am here to tell you that Chevalier's delivery is talky, more patter than tune, even when he is using the song to seduce Claudette Colbert. (I would also note that he wears a casquette rather than a boater). Colbert trills ornaments in a fluty voice. Chevalier talks around the vocal line, reserving energy, as well as variation in tone and pitch, for the burbles and chirps that punctuate each phrase.

This is curious. The Marx Brothers add an unnecessary and unprecedented musicality to their interpretations of the song. Chico also adds some snaps and syncopates the rhythm; his brothers add their own stylistic traits. Perhaps I should reverse my initial assessment and say that the economy of their performances is one of excess rather than restraint. The resources of character are bountiful and fairly distributed. Each performer has access to an inexhaustible cornucopia of passports and straw hats. As in the miracle of the fishes and the loaves, the one passport that Chevalier has been issued by a government mysteriously becomes four, although it does not succeed in getting four men through customs. Harpo lacks money to pay for his passage, and he doesn't wear the straw boater, but he does have the means to mount a working gramophone on his back. He is also supplied with exactly the right recording in case he should need to synchronize the movements of his lips with Chevalier's voice.

It may be objected that the source of the wealth I attribute to character is really a corporation. Does the straw hat that Chico wears issue out of some vast reserve of the character of Chevalier? No, it comes from the wardrobe department—the same department that provides the spare hat that Maurice carries in his suitcase. The wealth of the Paramount studio is on display in the unending stream of hats and passports. But the studio can buy these items cheaply enough; Harpo shows that a straw boater can be replaced by a top hat or a cap. The real wealth of the studio is on display in the bodies of the movie stars, the Marx Brothers. They are the treasure the studio really pays for. Apart from Zeppo, they are talented and distinctive actors, and they command a high price. However, they can be replaced, just as they replace Chevalier.

The lyric of the song asks whether it would be desirable for nightingales to "sing like you," but the moral or scandal of the scene is that anyone can sing like you!

The real abundance of a character is the totality of examples that it collects. This scene offers four examples of the same character. To put it another way, the scene offers at least four examples. Why assume that the series ends when the four brothers have returned to the back of the line? The offended society woman and the little girl whose places in line Groucho commandeers may also claim to be Chevalier, and may support their claims with their own hats, passports, and songs. Maybe in an hour or two the brothers will reach the front of the line again and enjoy another opportunity to audition for the part. Maybe the cycle will end only when Chevalier himself, or a convincing facsimile, appears.

What is the value of this abundance? Why should performances be repeated? Why should anyone want more than one of Chevalier? The solution I propose belongs to the idea of character itself. A character, as I define it, collects examples of a kind. A character does not have to discover anything new. Chevalier never does. He discovers again and again what everyone already knows about French masculinity—all the clichés we know without visiting or researching France. The purpose of collecting examples is not to discover something new but to move materials from one location to another. That is the narrative of the scene in *Monkey Business*. Crossing the Atlantic, four bodies must pass through the narrowing conduit of Chevalier's character. In place of plot, which does not advance in this scene, the Marx Brothers depict the process of collection.

# The twofold truth of character in performance

I define character as a device that collects every example of a kind. Does that sound strange? If you have been reading novels, maybe it does. Most readers view characterization in novels as individuating rather than collecting. If you have been going to the theater or watching movies or television, then my definition should not be difficult to accept. Strange as it may sound, you already agree with me. Otherwise you would not know how to interpret a theatrical performance.

Here are two principles, which I will express initially as permissions. They might be called the rights of the actor, and they pertain to all actors, good ones and bad ones:

**1** Different actors may play the same character.

**2** An actor may play different characters.

The performance history of the character Othello illustrates the first principle. How many actors have played Othello? A few of the famous ones are Edmund Kean, Paul Robeson, and Orson Welles. Tommaso Salvini's interpretation of Othello delighted and instructed audiences around the world. One young member of his audience, Constantin Sergeyevich Alexiv, was so inspired by this touring production, which he saw at the Imperial Great Theater in Moscow in 1892, that in his later career as actor, director, and teacher of theatrical method, he assumed the surname Stanislavski, a Russian transliteration of Salvini. Stanislavski's career also illustrates the second permission. In addition to playing Othello he played Trigorin in Chekhov's *The Seagull*, Sotanville in Molière's *Georges Dandin*, and many other parts.

The two principles governing the serial accumulation of instances of a character across theatrical history should be easier to recognize in Shakespeare's memorable formulation. They are the argument of the "seven ages" speech. "One man," Jaques observes, "plays many parts" (2.7.142). The other side of the coin is that "all the men and women" play the same parts (140), which are the "seven ages" of life (143), and in the same order. The whole in which a part participates is both the career of the player who "plays many parts" and the character seen in all its aspects. By collecting instances of a character, repeating performances, objectifying dialogue as script, and by housing the stage in a building designed for this purpose, theater becomes artifactual (carrying materials across time) rather than merely occasional (holding a moment in time to itself). Does Salvini use up the resources of the character of Othello on the occasion of his appearance onstage? No, Stanislavski writes, "The Othello of Salvini is a monument, a law unto eternity which can never change" (Stanislavski 1933, 268).

This law unto eternity is not a special privilege granted to Salvini alone. Elsewhere Stanislavski explains that the ability to generalize an individual case is a mark of artistic genius. The context for his explanation is a comment on Molière, an artist for whom one would not expect Stanislavski to show much sympathy:

> Molière also embraces human passions and faults broadly. He describes what he has seen and what he knows. Being a genius, he knows all. His Tartuffe is not merely the individual Tartuffe, but all human Tartuffes taken together. . . . In this respect he is near to Pushkin and to all great writers generally, for in this respect all great writers are the same.
>
> **(STANISLAVSKI 1933, 151)**

Unlike Stanislavski, I am not concerned only with works of genius but with all characters. I am trying to show the sufficiency of the barest outline for the purposes of characterization. A "part," a "sketch." Even a prop such as a hat—that's all you need.

In the case of Tartuffe, as with Chevalier, I would argue that the character's participation is not limited to human instances. Tartuffe's defining quality of false piety might be more than adequately represented by a hair shirt. And it should be clear that the character includes the bad examples just as much as the good ones. As Auerbach points out, the comic element in Tartuffe, as with all of Molière's characters, is that he is a bad example (Auerbach 1953, 317). I am not just referring to Tartuffe's religious hypocrisy. He pretends to be pious but he is a poor pretender. He constantly betrays the worldliness of his ambitions to all observers with the exception of his willfully blind patron Orgon.

"Everywhere the ass looks out from under the lion's skin," Auerbach comments. Fernandez traces this tendency, where characters represent types without being good examples of the type, to Molière's early piece *Ballet des incompatibles*. Here dancers are paired with others who exemplify opposing or incongruous qualities. In the later theatrical masterpieces these "incompatibles" are fused in single characters. "A character in Molière is comic," Fernandez concludes, "for no reason but that he undertakes to merge attributes that are mutually contradictory" (Fernandez 1958, 34).

La Bruyère has his own joke about bad examples. In the grouping entitled "De la mode," the virtuoso Démocède has a mania that requires him to possess every print of Callot's, including "one print that is not, to be honest, his best work" (La Bruyère, 408). Earle's character of the Blunt Man includes the Blunt Man's "counterfeit," who, Earle warns, "is most dangerous" (Earle 1897, 36). Tartuffe is a bad example of piety, and, by the same token, he is as bad an example of hypocrisy. (A truly brilliant hypocrite would to all observers appear indistinguishable from a truly pious person.) And yet, as Stanislavski and many other readers and audiences attest, Tartuffe's image of hypocrisy has a remarkable power of generalization.

The eternal law of which Stanislavski speaks is the connection between a character type and a particular example. The tendency of character to universalize has all the force of a natural law and subtends the two principles of performance. These principles, stated as principles rather than permissions, are the abundance of character and the transformation of the actor. I initially stated these principles as permissions granted to actors, but really the first principle belongs to character, and only the second is a fact about actors. While a character uses any material, an actor performs as any character.

These two principles, abundance and transformation, are understood in all performances. For the most part they are merely understood; you don't usually see them represented. Watching Salvini as Othello you might be aware that other actors have played this part, and that Salvini will play other parts, but your knowledge remains in the background. The performance is supposed to collect every example of a character in one actor; Salvini's art is to sum up the entire history of producing the play, but without having Kean, Robeson, Welles, and the others join him on the stage. Productions that follow the parsimonious rule that assigns several characters to one actor, or the extravagant rule that uses several actors to play one character, take advantage of the two principles but still do not bring them into the foreground. In *Kind Hearts and Coronets*, where Alec Guinness plays all but two members of the D'Ascoyne family, no more than one of Guinness's roles is visible in any given scene; and in *I'm Not There*, where six actors play Bob Dylan, no scene directly represents more than one of Dylan's aspects.

The abundance of character and the transformation of the actor come directly into view only in a performance of a performance. The witches in *Macbeth* show that they are a single character by repeating their own and one another's lines; the incantation, "Double, double toil and trouble," invokes and enacts the process of doubling. They demonstrate the abundance of character by the simple expedient of appearing alongside one another onstage. In *King Lear*, Edgar disguises himself as Poor Tom; the actor in this role demonstrates the principle of transformation by acting simultaneously as Edgar and as Tom. (The double nature of Tartuffe has a similar effect, although Edgar, unlike Tartuffe, is supposed to be a decent actor.)

The Maurice Chevalier scene in *Monkey Business* is an extraordinary performance of performance in that it puts both principles on display simultaneously. The four Marx Brothers play a single character, Maurice Chevalier. Each one plays himself while playing Chevalier. Abundance and transformation.

# What characters can't do

The joke in *Tartuffe* is roughly the same as the joke in *Monkey Business*. The difference is that Tartuffe's poor performance succeeds in getting him what he wants. Orgon is convinced of Tartuffe's piety despite the overwhelming evidence of his hypocrisy. The audience witness an underlying worldliness constantly breaking out as the mask of piety slips from Tartuffe's face. Closer to the action, Orgon does not see the slips, so determined is he to spite the members of his family who point them out. And that's the joke: the tension between the clearly visible failure of the performance and its improbable success in the community of the play.

The performances in *Monkey Business* do not succeed in getting the Marx Brothers off the boat. We in the audience are supposed to recognize that the brothers are playing the part of Chevalier, and maybe the customs official does too, but still he is not willing to accept their passports as genuine. He makes a distinction that the brothers either do not see or do not care about. Character is not enough. And that's the joke: the brothers ask the character of Chevalier to do something for them that it can't naturally do. For me, then, the scene provides an opportunity for separating the meaning of character from other meanings for which it is commonly mistaken.

(1) *Character is not individuality.* The official who inspects the passport is looking to identify exactly one person as "the movie actor" Maurice Chevalier. But he is faced with four actors who present Chevalier's passport for inspection. When asked to "identify themselves" ("Are you going to identify yourself?"), they offer to confirm that they are who they say they are ("Wait, I prove it!") by performing one of Chevalier's songs. The customs official asks the four Marx brothers to individuate. They, in turn, ask character to individuate. The official rightly refuses to accept this attempt at individuality, since the abundance of the character contradicts the passport's work of individuation.

(1a) *Does character entail identity?* I do not think so. If it did, then the four actors playing Chevalier would be identical but discernible. The risk of treating character as identity is to violate Leibniz's law, which says that only indiscernible things are identical. Carole Bouquet and Angela Molina, the two performers playing Conchita in *That Obscure Object of Desire*, would be thereby identical but discernible. Tartuffe would be indiscernible from but not identical to himself.

(But this is the case for Viola and Sebastian in *Twelfth Night*. They are not identical but they are indiscernible. The only way to tell them apart is by pointing. Their problem is family resemblance, not character.)

The Marx Brothers themselves set the lowest possible standard for identity.

—Do you know who's on this boat?
—No.
—Maurice Chevalier, the movie actor. I just ran into him.
—Did you hurt him?
—How do you know it was Chevalier?
—I got his passport. Right there.

"How do you know it was Chevalier?" An excellent question. Zeppo's answer, "I got his passport," is inadequate, as the following scene will show four men who are not Chevalier presenting Chevalier's passport. He accepts with unwarranted innocence a policy of lax security that identifies any passport with any bearer.

(2) *Character is not iconic resemblance.*

—Hey, he looks like Chevalier!
—Yes, there's a striking—
—And I can look like Chevalier.
—Well, I certainly look like Chevalier.
—But that's not enough. You've got to sing one of Chevalier's songs to get off this boat.

As they speak these lines, the brothers make a slight effort to caricature Chevalier's face. They don't try to mimic his face with any exactitude. They put their chins up and their lower lips forward (and Harpo points to his chin to make sure that everyone knows where to look); Groucho's eyes widen. Zeppo tells them that facial resemblance is "not enough" and must be supported by a performance of "You Brought a New Kind of Love to Me." He seems to understand that there is a distinction between character and resemblance, but he tells it backward. Performing in the character of Chevalier is not enough to pass through customs. Resemblance would be much better. Looking like Chevalier and carrying Chevalier's passport would be just enough to pass through customs. The customs official would like nothing more than to match the face in the passport photo to the face of the man who carries it.

By the time the brothers reach the front of the line they seem to have forgotten how to compose their faces. Maybe they have simply given up on achieving a "striking" or "certain" resemblance. The official complains:

—This picture doesn't look like you.
—Say! This picture doesn't look like you.
—Say! This picture doesn't look like you.
—Well, look at that face!

The customs official is surely correct. The Marx Brothers do not look like the picture. The best that can be said for their physical resemblance, I would say, is that they look somewhat more like Chevalier than does Pépé le Pew. That is, they look as much like Chevalier as any humanoid masculine figure. The brothers put little energy into disputing this observation. Chico admits that his face is all wrong, but suggests that the back of Chevalier's head "looks just like" him. Groucho points out that the picture "doesn't look like" the customs official either, as though repeating a personal insult.

It is not clear whether the customs official even recognizes that the four brothers are performing as Chevalier, whether he associates the hat and song with Chevalier (or, to put it another way, whether he recognizes that the hat and song are part of an association), or whether he has seen any of Chevalier's films. His outrage is provoked not by their travesty of Chevalier's character but by the fact that there are four of them, standing together in line, all claiming to be the same individual, and failing miserably to look like the picture. Again the Marx Brothers substitute character for personal style.

(3) *Character is not style.* I said that the genre of this scene is travesty, a debasing of form, as opposed to parody. The distinction may sound rather fine but it isn't. It depends on the difference between form and style. Parody isolates and exaggerates elements of style. For Chevalier, these could include the accent, the cooing and burbling, the wild gestures, the wide-eyed expression, the strutting, and the talky way of putting across a song. (The trick of parodying Chevalier would not be discovering these mannerisms, which are written in letters that one who runs may read, or copying them, which anyone can do, but figuring out how to exaggerate them more than he does.) Travesty of the pure sort practiced by the Marx Brothers is a blunt instrument that ignores style and merely reproduces character. If the Marx Brothers wished to parody Chevalier, they would need to hew closer to the model. Their performances are funny because they aren't trying very hard. They either don't bother to try or they are not sensitive enough.

I know that they are sensitive enough. They are capable of subtle parody. (Groucho's parody of *Strange Interlude* in *Animal Crackers* is more sensitive to O'Neill's style than the parody of the same play by Spencer Tracy and Joan Bennett in *Me and My Gal*.) Instead their project is to sever Chevalier's character from his personal style and attach it to their own styles. In doing so, they treat character as a formal device rather than a personal stylistic preference. Their performances are exercises in character, which forms a collective, but not portraiture, which individuates. They are interested only in what Arendt, in her discussion of the ancient meaning of character, calls "whatness," the characteristics that associate persons and things, rather than "whoness," the positing of a unique human image (Arendt 1958, 181).

Critics who expect character to do the work of individuation are as mad as the Marx Brothers, who think that carrying Chevalier's passport obligates them to sing one of his songs, and that the song and the papers together are enough to get them smoothly through customs. They are as mad as Chevalier himself, who when Jeanette Macdonald raises the objection that it would be unseemly for her to accept help from a stranger, gives his name: "I am Maurice." (He also thinks that any woman he loves may be addressed as "Mimi.") Ferguson gave this madness a name. It's the confusion of form for style.

# Characters lounge

What happens when characters get together? If each character is an individual, the outlook is bleak for relations between characters. The best example I have found is *Steven*, a weekly comic strip by Doug Allen. *Steven*, like *The Merchant of Venice*, is a work of theory in that nothing happens. Such events as there are tend to be overwhelmingly mundane. Steven, a little boy wearing a lumpy hat, orders drinks in a bar or sits in a chair watching television. In response to every question or suggestion, he says, "No." Sometimes he adds some obscene words.

The lack of other events, even the lack of comic business, is one of the main themes.

   —C'mon, can't I come with you on this comic adventure?
   —I'm just going to the Goodwill to get a new table.
   **(Allen 1983 [Because the comic book Steven is unpaginated,
   I am citing the year of serial publication.])**

   —Now I have enough for a bottle of Vat 12.
   —Oh boy, this is going to be a good comic.

**(1988)**

These exchanges remind me of *Merchant*. The characters define themselves not by performing but by anticipating and evaluating their performances. They know that some of their adventures will have better jokes than others. The characters are known to one another as characters. The background they inhabit is known to them as a comic strip. For example: "I hate all the characters in this comic strip" (1984).

If this comic strip is mainly theoretical, what is the theory? Woodrow, the rodentlike character who enthusiastically anticipates a trip to the Goodwill or the liquor store as a "comic adventure," seems designed to advance the argument and connect it to the mundane actions and squalid background. Woodrow doesn't drink but it still makes sense for him to contribute money for Steven to buy a bottle of Vat 12, just because it gives him an opportunity to appear as an image in one or several panels.

The loss of the money is not significant because he cares more about his status in the society of cartoon characters. It doesn't make sense for him to care about anything else. His refrain is, "Can I be in this one?" The phrase has a magical effect. It inserts him into "this one," contradicting Steven's habitual answer, "No." The only thing better than appearing in the *Steven* comic would be having his own "Woodrow Comic" which he gets, briefly, in exchange for bailing Steven out of a holding cell (1983).

This social theory looks quite different from that of *Merchant*, where each character makes a collective. In *Steven* each character is pitted against all the rest in a winner-takes-all competition to be the protagonist, the title character, the center of attention. Steven complains, "Everybody's always trying to take over my comic strip. . . . Now it's some stupid cactus plant" (1989). He isn't exaggerating. In some episodes the cactus plant does effectively take over, appearing in most or all of the panels. Then Steven occupies only the title, in which he desperately asserts, "This is *my* comic strip, *I'm* the star, I'm *Steven*" (1990). Or he is squeezed into a small final panel, where he has the last word: "The plant's not funny" (1990). Or, in a different mood, he surrenders: "Go back to the plant. Nothing's happening here" (1990).

The cactus plant is only one of the minor characters who are plotting to take over the comic strip. Fifidoodle, a dog drawn to resemble a deformed Snoopy, talks candidly about his ambition: "I want it to be my comic strip" (1984). Fifidoodle even tries to convince the other characters to join him: "We must plot to overthrow the evil Steven" (1984). I think Fifidoodle is right. Steven is evil, both passively, in that he only says no and gets drunk, and actively, in that he has a pattern of assassinating any minor character whom he views as a threat to his status as protagonist. This is a social theory that can have violent consequences, such as Steven firing at Fifidoodle with a shotgun, or Mr. Owl Ph.D. firing at Woodrow with a cannon.

But it's hard to argue that Fifidoodle is more virtuous than Steven. He also tries to murder Steven. Later he tries to murder the cactus plant. In one episode he and two other dog characters kidnap Steven's friend Brock and threaten to keep him locked away until they are featured more prominently. Steven is not intimidated: "You have Brock hostage, so what. Kill him" (1986). His friendship with Brock is already strained from an earlier conflict: "Brock used to be my friend, but now he's taken over my comic and ruined it" (1981).

Even the collective action represented by the dogs' attempted mutiny would normally be impossible since each dog is working on a separate plan to be top dog. The dogs are competing with each other as well as with Steven. Mr. Owl Ph.D., the academic in the group, explains that these competitions are based on desires shared by everyone: "A lot of people would give anything to have their own comic strip" (1988). Because there are not enough comic strips to go around, the characters compete brutally for the one thing that everyone wants: to occupy more space in the panel. "One of the things we do in the comic business is to fill space. . . . And around here at Steven's, we do it pretty well" (1986).

I am not the first literary critic to use *Steven* for its theory of character. For Lynch the conflicts in Steven's "comic strip business" can be generalized to include the "character business" of the literary novel (Lynch, 3). Woloch, in his account of the formation of hierarchical, centralized communities of characters *The One vs. the Many*, does not discuss the comic strip, but he has the same social theory. As his title suggests, Woloch thinks the characters gathered in his study are competing with one another. Each one wants to be the protagonist. What Woloch calls the "character space" of the novel is finite, and the protagonist has a disproportionately large share, while the many minor characters occupy unfairly small, confined spaces.

Behind the various plots of the realist novel is a metaplot that pits characters against one another in a contest for maximum attention within a limited space. The particular shape of the metaplot is determined by the patterns of attention of a given novel's readers, which are determined by the novelist's artistry. Woloch calls this relationship behind the metaplot the "actual social basis" for the character-system, one of the "larger social processes" in which readers and novelists are embedded" (Woloch 2003, 157, 237). However, he is not saying that the fictional metaplot reproduces the inequalities of historical societies. The protagonist in a novel does not even have to be the center of attention for other characters in order to capture the attention of readers. In these respects the character-systems Woloch describes are truly dynamic: the contest is always open to all characters.

What Woloch identifies as the metaplot of the realist novel is simply the plot of *Steven*. In the comic strip, because the social theory is laid bare, it becomes possible to calculate precisely how space is distributed among the characters. At any moment the character who acts as protagonist is easy to identify. The protagonist is the character whose name appears as a banner in the title.

The Famous Steven of Providence (1983)

Steven: The Boy, The Legend (1985)

The title changes, sometimes radically, to reflect changes in the hierarchy.

Steven and Brock, Comedians (1984)

Brock (1981)

Woodrow Comic (1983)

Steven and His Plant (1990)

The population of characters, the "many" against whom the "one" protagonist shines, has a precise number: "Steven gives up counting morons on 14th Street in New York City. Three million twelve, oh, I give up" (1987). The amount of space allotted to a character can also be measured and even quantified: one can count the panels in which a character appears, and one can measure the space a character occupies in relation to the others. Because this is a cartoon that calls itself a cartoon, and because Steven is never shown in profile, there is no discrepancy between the actual space of the panel and the illusion of space that it creates.

(Even in a community of flat characters there can be spatial anomalies. Brock's refrigerator box is larger inside than outside, like a spooky house in a gothic novel, and somehow the box is more elegantly appointed than Steven's apartment. "It's because of the way I decorate it" [1981]).

Allen gives the character-system itself a precise volume and spatial location. All characters who are not part of Steven's current weekly comic adventure are gathered in a small room called the "Characters Lounge." Every time a mutiny fails, the rebel character is returned to the lounge. The same thing happens when characters die. "I don't kill them, I just retire them to the Characters Lounge" (1986). The lounge is a stark image of the system Woloch describes, in which the centrality of the protagonist is achieved against a background of foreshortened minor characters. Fifidoodle complains, "This place isn't a lounge, it's a prison" (1984).

The Characters Lounge shows that the idea of the character-system, despite a seeming dynamism that would potentially allow for a moment-by-moment reordering of the hierarchy, actually is a principle of severe closure. Erving Goffman has a good name for this kind of space: the comic strip or novel becomes a "total institution" for the characters. Goffman coined this term to designate institutions such as mental hospitals, prisons, monasteries, military camps, and boarding schools, because they tend to include the entire lives of the inmates, both before and after they enter the institution. The determining fact in the "moral career of a mental patient" is not the mental illness and its attendant symptoms but rather a relationship to the hospital shared by other patients: "Persons who become mental-hospital patients vary widely in the kind and degree of illness. . . . But once started on the way, they are confronted by some importantly similar circumstances, and they respond to these in some importantly similar ways" (Goffman 1961, 129).

For Goffman the totalization of institutional experience can be symmetrical or reversible insofar as the institution sometimes also includes the entire lives of those who administer it, such as doctors, guards, and teachers. A novel could not ordinarily be considered a total institution for readers and writers, although, if you think about it, there are some interesting exceptions in literary modernism. I'm thinking of Joyce's incredible suggestion that it should take at least as long to read *Finnegans Wake* as it took to write the thing. The cult audiences for certain novels such as *The Lord of the Rings* might also be committed to a total institution.

For Woloch the most important fact about a character is not the possession of intrinsic qualities. Not the characteristics, in other words. Instead the determining fact in the existence of a character is the relationship to a character-system elaborated sentence by sentence: "Narrative progress always entails a series of choices: each moment magnifies some characters while turning away from—and thus diminishing or even stinting—others" (Woloch 2003, 12). A novel's character-system is a zero-sum economy in which attention given to one character has to be taken from another.

—Does this mean that I can take over your comic?
—No . . . But I've decided to add you to my cast of extras.

**(1984)**

# The spider community

In the model I am proposing, the ability of a character to generalize is not limited by the boundaries of a work of art such as a novel or comic strip. In other words, there is no character-system, no cast of characters. I try, when I can, to take examples from critics who disagree with me. One of Woloch's examples will illustrate the indifference of character to the frames that separate works of art from one another.

When Woloch describes the character-system of Balzac's novel *Père Goriot*, he argues that the system must include characters who recur throughout the *Human Comedy*. In this way he begins to imagine the society that a character automatically establishes, if it is truly a character. However, Woloch's concept of the character-system is limited historically to Balzac's lifetime and generically to the novel. It does not acknowledge and cannot sustain the inclusion in *Goriot* of characters from other novels, plays, and books of characteristic writings by other authors.

Jeanie Deans from Scott's *Heart of Mid-lothian*, Alceste from Molière's *Misanthrope*, Jaffer from Otway's *Venice Preserved*, Ménalque, the distracted man from La Bruyère's *Caractères*: these characters and others appear in

*Goriot* (Balzac 1995, 165, 165, 196, 190). Some of their names also appear in the "Avant-propos" to the *Human Comedy*, where they are integrated into a society that also includes Balzac and his readers. They also have some affiliation with the state of nature through Balzac's comparison of his project to that of naturalists such as Buffon. If Buffon described all of nature, Balzac asks, couldn't he do the same for human society? (8).

Even considered apart from its influence on Balzac's ambitions, Buffon's natural history makes an important contribution to literary character. Peter Demetz incorrectly describes Buffon as a strong nominalist for whom "the individual horse or lion was the 'real' thing and all 'genres, ordres, et classes' merely a necessary evil" (Demetz 1968, 399). Although Buffon opposes the systematic taxonomies of Linneaus and his followers, and although he makes fun of the notion of kingdoms and families of creatures, he is strongly committed to the reality of the species. His pragmatic definition of species as a group of creatures that can reproduce themselves within the group remains useful in modern biology (Roger 1997, 309–35).

The bulk of Buffon's *Natural History* is devoted to character sketches of the traits of animals. Here is his character of "The Cat":

> The cat seems to have feelings only for itself, to love only conditionally, to lend itself to relations only in order to abuse them; and because of this natural disposition it resembles men more than does the dog, which is entirely sincere.
>
> (Quoted in **ROGER 1997, 283**)

Character is given at the level of the species and also crosses species. Balzac understands this very well. "When Buffon paints the portrait of the male lion, he dispatches the female lion in a few phrases; but in society a woman is not always the female of the male" ("Avant-propos," xlii). Balzac's point is not to assert the radical particularity of social as opposed to natural families. Rather he wants to emphasize that in human society the gender of a character makes a difference.

Balzac's response to Buffon suggests that character is not limited to human examples even in a series of novels with the general title *Human Comedy*. Character does not respect divisions between biological species, or between life and death, for that matter. Ordinary household objects, places, machines, and abstractions—obviously these can be examples of a character. In *Steven* a cactus plant becomes the most interesting character. In novels such as *The Adventures of a Bank-note* and films such as *The Counterfeit Coin* the protagonist is a piece of money. John Earle's *Microcosmography* gives the characters of generic places such as "A Prison" and particular places such as "Paul's Walk." Earle sometimes describes persons as places. ("A Gallant," he says, is "a walking mercers shop" [Earle 1897, 18, 61, 30].)

The same thing happens in Woloch's other examples. Here is a passage from *Great Expectations*:

> An épergne or centerpiece of some kind was in the middle of this cloth . . . and, as I looked along the yellow expanse out of which I remember its seeming to grow, like a black fungus, I saw speckled-legged spiders with blotchy bodies running home to it, as if some circumstance of the greatest importance had just transpired in the spider community.
>
> I heard the mice too, rattling behind the panels, as if the same occurrence were important to their interests. But the blackbeetles took no notice of the agitation, and groped about the hearth in a ponderous elderly way, as if they were short-sighted and hard of hearing, and not on terms with one another.
>
> **(DICKENS 1950, 98)**

"These crawling things," Pip continues, "had fascinated my attention," and for a few paragraphs he describes the social lives of spiders, mice, and blackbeetles. This scene is organized like the character-systems that Woloch studies, except that the human examples, Pip and Miss Havisham, are not at the center. They look on from the outermost periphery, along with the blackbeetles, who are less observant. Most characters in this scene give their attention to the "great cake," which Pip helpfully describes as the "centerpiece" and which therefore might be called the protagonist. Pip attributes "public importance" to mice and spiders, whose "interests" converge in the centralized cake on and around which they live.

An accurate account of communities of characters in the novel should include not only those who walk on two legs but also those who crawl on several legs—the "spider community," in other words. Spiders are connected to other spiders and to the community of mice through shared interests. They are connected to the human community through Pip's fascination, as well as through the cake, a talismanic object for people and for spiders. Membership in this society is not limited to examples of characters who are represented directly in the pages of the novel. "Spider community" means what it says: all spiders and everything that spiders are interested in and everyone who is interested in spiders and (peripherally) everyone whose interests coincide with those of the spiders.

Even the minor characters in *Steven*, stuck in the cramped Characters Lounge, easily form associations with other figures outside the frame.

The example of *Steven* might seem to show that Woloch's model of the character-system is actually the right one, or right in at least one instance. But characters in the comic strip repeatedly discover openings in the panel. In a late episode, Steven fires the minor characters. "I don't regret firing all my characters one bit! . . . I can have big empty panels like this where nothing happens" (1990). Then he jumps out of the panel altogether and lands in the real world. "Goodbye cartoon world. I'm jumping" (1990). The plot of the comic strip remains the metaplot that Woloch studies in the realist novel. But the metaplot of the comic strip is something else. The fired minor characters continue to be represented in the story. "Didn't you notice that you've been in it more since you were fired?" (1990). Conversations cross the border separating the panel and the margin. Mr. Owl Ph.D. finally explains, "There's no difference between the comic world and the real one" (1990). The owl's general statement seems wrong to me, but, as far as character is concerned, he's probably right.

Communities of characters bridge individual fictions and genres, as well as orders of reality such as history and fiction, given and made, and life and death. The best example of these crossings is not a comic book or a novel or a group of novels but a work of criticism such as *The One vs. the Many*. In one passage Woloch performs a thought experiment in which he invents a new Characters Lounge for the entire history of literature: "Imagine a Hall of Fame for minor characters—ranging from Pylades to Lucky and Pozzo, with a handful of Mercutios and Fridays in between—where fictional characters were suddenly plucked from their relative obscurity within the dramas and narratives that they enchant" (Woloch 2003, 214). His book is that Hall of Fame. It collects characters from various novels, plays, poems, and works of criticism and gives them a new significance.

The problem is that Woloch has no way to account for the act of collecting. The concept of the character-system only describes communities within novels. It does not describe the community established by his own study, in which the entire cast of *King Lear* is attached to *Père Goriot* and then to the names of professors of literature who study Balzac and Shakespeare. If Woloch is right about the functioning of the character-system, then criticism should be impossible.

Woloch's position is closest to mine when he describes the "fifty adjuncts" to "a single cup of tea" in *Great Expectations* (Woloch 2003, 191–94). Those fifty adjuncts are only the beginning, far from a complete list of the ingredients that go into a cup of tea. Woloch quotes the epigraph to Auerbach's *Mimesis* as an expression of scarcity: "If Dickens had 'but world enough and time' perhaps he could avoid condensing the crush of humanity into its 'most peculiar' element" (190). My point, which I believe to be

Marvell's point and Auerbach's point, is that there is just enough: the whole world and all of time.

# Why the sky is blue

There will never be justice in the novel as long as there are characters. One character inevitably focuses attention, and the many others are reduced to minor status. Criticism cannot rectify this problem, which Woloch calls "the problem of narrative fairness" or "the labor theory of character" (Woloch 2003, 41, 27). At best critics can address the problem by making good on an ethical imperative to recognize the deformation of minor characters.

Marx's labor theory of value fits this argument uneasily. The social universe of the novel is unjust to minor characters, "the proletariat of the novel," in that it does not exploit them *enough*. This is also the demand of the minor characters in *Steven*: to be made to do more work. "All I get is complaints from my employees about not working enough." "Can I be in this one?" "No" (Allen 1990). To call minor characters "the proletariat of the novel" may provoke a knee-jerk materialist response. Why are you worrying about characters in novels when the owners continue to exploit the workers of the world?

Still, this call for justice for characters is interesting. Woloch's concept of character space allows him to discriminate between just and unjust uses of characters within the total institution of the novel but not to rectify injustices. The advantage of a sociological approach such as Fowler's or Brewer's, which tracks the uses of characters by readers, is the ability to discriminate between good and bad uses in a community of actors that can be reorganized (Fowler 2006, 60–63). How does the formalist model of character, which makes a seam between fiction and history, address this problem? Can it make similar discriminations?

Here is one more example of something that translates:

—Oh, Ingrid Bergman, now she's low maintenance.
—Low maintenance?
—There are two kinds of women: high maintenance and low maintenance.
—And Ingrid Bergman is low maintenance?
—An L.M., definitely.
—Which one am I?
—You're the worst kind. You're high maintenance but you think you're low maintenance.

—I don't see that.

—You don't see that? Waiter, I'll have the house salad. But I don't want the regular dressing. I'll have the balsamic vinegar and oil, but on the side. And then the salmon with the mustard sauce. But I want the mustard sauce on the side. On the side is a very big thing for you.

—Well, I just want it the way I want it.

—I know. High maintenance.

The career of the offensive notion of interpersonal maintenance begins, as far as I am able to determine, in the foregoing Socratic dialogue from the film *When Harry Met Sally*. From there it migrates to other novels and fiction films (*Bridget Jones's Diary, High Maintenance*), to articles in newspapers and magazines (some of which are reviews of the novels and films, others of which are straightforward applications of high and low maintenance as demographic categories), and even to pet stores, and finally gets absorbed into folk psychology in a chain of influences that it would be instructive to trace in detail. (This is the kind of microhistorical research in which Brewer excels.)

Details are not necessary for following the process of translation that occurs in the dialogue itself. The speaker, Harry, is not claiming that "there are two kinds of women in the community of this film" or that "women in this film and women who see this film and are influenced by it can be divided into two categories" or even that "in the experience of the screenwriter Nora Ephron, there are two kinds of women." The claim is for a complete taxonomy: "There are two kinds." Maintenance does not have to migrate successfully from the film into other fictional and non-fictional environments (although, coincidentally, it does) because it's supposed to be everywhere already. The only obvious limit on the universality of the translation appears to be gender. Society is organized so that men do the work of maintaining cross-sexual relations, and women, who are maintained, require maintenance at varying levels of intensity. Although this organization must include men to do the work as well as women to be worked on, it is expressed as a fact about women rather than men.

As though to illustrate the process of translation, the categories of high and low maintenance emerge in a place where this film is in direct contact with another film: Harry and Sally in *When Harry Met Sally* are watching Rick and Ilsa in *Casablanca*, and they make no distinction between the actors and the characters they play. "Ingrid Bergman, now she's low maintenance." The actor becomes the character. Or, as in Jean-Luc Godard's iconic view of film performance, *Casablanca* becomes a documentary about Ingrid Bergman, whose talent as a movie star is to embody an ideal form of womanhood not only in the community of the film in which she appears but also in other films, and in New York, and elsewhere (Godard 1986, 120–22). Harry and Sally demonstrate this function of her performance not only by giving a name and an abbreviation, "L.M.," to the kind of woman she represents, but also through their willingness to replace her with their bodies. Earlier in the scene they ask whether, in Bergman's situation, they would choose to spend their lives with Paul Henreid or Humphrey Bogart. They agree on Bogart. Not only could they act as Ilsa, maybe they could do it better than Bergman.

The social organization proposed in this scene does not respect boundaries between one film and another, or between cities such as New York and Casablanca, or between the aesthetic and the historical. It does not really have to travel across these boundaries but instantly occupies every point on the map. Even the primary, unspoken difference between women and men turns out to be collapsible, as Harry shows when he imagines himself portraying the character of the low maintenance woman, or when he speaks as Sally ("Waiter, I'll have the house salad").

There are only two remaining obstacles to the universal translatability of this crude taxonomy. One of them is Sally's declared blindness: "I don't see that." This is a rather weak obstacle. She sees and does not question the validity of the categories, but doesn't see that she belongs to one of them. Her refusal to see becomes evidence that she has been assigned to the right category, the third "worst kind" of woman who doesn't know what kind she is, confirming that she has somehow internalized the taxonomy before Harry introduces it. (Here, as in Plato's dialogues, education is a process of recollecting what one already knows.) Her declaration might be said to interrupt but in fact instantiates the recursive movement of the dialogue, the way the two speakers bombard each other with affirmations and echoes of what has just been spoken.

The second obstacle is that the transportation of elements from one film to another occurs in a limited, asymmetrical economy of vision. Rick and Ilsa do not look back from their film (as Rick does in *Play It Again, Sam*) at Harry and Sally in theirs. However, exchanges between the films can go in more directions than one. When Harry talks about kinds of women, he includes the female lead in *Casablanca*. When Rick, who shares the screen, says, "The problems of three little people don't amount to a hill of beans in this crazy world," he also universalizes. His statement includes triangular relations on both sides of the screen.

Rick's cosmology sets the scale differently. For him the maintenance of a relation between two men and one woman is comparable to and diminished by geopolitical relations. The Vichy France colonial apparatus? Now that's high maintenance. The boundary between films is effectively porous in both directions. Each film universalizes its characters in a way that includes the entire cast and audience for the other film.

Now let's test the limits of the translatability of high and low maintenance. Compare this scene with one from a film that might seem to fall outside its sphere of influence, *Yeopgi Girl*.

(The Korean word transliterated as *yeopgi* literally means "bizarre" or "curious." I am leaving it untranslated because it has more importantly come to mean the aggressive, unpredictable quality exemplified by the character in the film—who is given no other name—and because the translation for English-language release and for the Hollywood remake, *My Sassy Girl*, is even more condescending. Another plausible translation, although not exactly an improvement on the existing one, would of course be *High Maintenance Girl*.)

Here is the dialogue:

—You know why the sky is blue?
—The reflection of the sunshine—
—Nope. It's for me. I want it to be blue, so it's blue. You know why the fire is hot? It's all for me. I want it to be hot, so it is. You know why we have four seasons here in Korea?
—Because of you.
—That's correct. And why were you born here? It's for me as well.

This short dialogue, which takes the form of a catechism, localizes its generalizations: "We have four seasons here in Korea." The film is, in a sense, very Korean: the characters tend to speak on behalf of the moviegoing public ("Koreans love melodramas," "Koreans love sad movies, all because of *Sonagi* [Shower]"), and to colonize popular Korean films in the mode of parody—for example, the *yeopgi* girl changes the ending of *Sonagi* so that the dying heroine, now played by her, asks to be buried not with the clothes worn by her lover, but with his living body.

It may be objected that calling this dialogue a catechism imposes a Christian interpretation on an obviously secular and non-Western piece of popular culture. The Christian typology becomes explicit in the next line of the dialogue. Gyeon-woo objects that he could not have been born "for" the *yeopgi* girl since he is slightly older. She explains that he is a figure like John the Baptist, sent before her to announce her imminent arrival. In another scene, Gyeon-woo writes a new decalogue, the ten rules of dating, for the *yeopgi* girl's new boyfriend. For example: "Drink coffee instead of Coke or juice." "If she says she'll kill you, don't take it lightly."

The acknowledged regionalism of *Yeopgi Girl* could confirm a pattern that Moretti has identified in international film distribution. Comedies (which, Moretti speculates, depend significantly on effects that will be intelligible only to audiences fluent in the language spoken in the film) do not export as well as some other genres, such as action films (Moretti 2001). However, the marked tendency of *Yeopgi Girl* to play toward and speak on behalf of a Korean audience did not prevent the film from achieving extraordinary success throughout East Asia, including Hong Kong, a market notoriously resistant to imports. Nor did it prevent the optioning of the story and the subsequent production of a Hollywood remake.

It would be possible and might even be interesting to retrace each step in the process of exporting *Yeopgi Girl*. Instead, as always, I am interested in the immediate translation that occurs in the dialogue itself. The *yeopgi* girl's catechism is self-consciously local, Korean; on the other hand, she is not reluctant to universalize. She lives in a world centered on herself, in which all objects intelligibly swear their fealty to her: "It's all for me." Like a god, she makes the climate, the color of the sky, physical law, birth, and death, subject to her will. As Sally says of her dinner, "I just want it the way I want it." The *yeopgi* girl also wants it the way she wants it, but the scale has changed.

Sally lives in a universe in which there is nothing bigger than a salad. Everything can be lined up and placed "on the side" of everything else. Only gender roles, which contribute to the social universe its definitively asymmetrical shape, are exempt from this horizontal organization. In *Casablanca*, meanwhile, salads are so small as to become invisible. No one orders dinner at Rick's Café Américain. Even interpersonal relations are dwarfed to the status of "a hill of beans" when compared with governments and armies and resistance movements. The *yeopgi* girl lives in a universe in which (like Sally's) nothing is bigger than a cup of coffee. "Wanna die? Order coffee!" Even the solar system and the fact of mortality can fit into a cup of coffee. Unlike Sally's, the *yeopgi* girl's universe includes stars and mortality, and, along with everything else in the universe, they are organized around her. Everything contributes to the maintenance of the universe, and everything matters, which is why she has to be vigilant about things like coffee and clothes, even going so far as to approach a stranger in the park to demand that he change his sweater because "you can't wear the same color as mine." The same thing happens in the sky: "I want it to be blue, so it's blue."

I don't mean to overstate the value of *Yeopgi Girl*. I suppose I am glossing over the fact that the title character sometimes treats people, especially Gyeon-woo, unfairly. Why should he be responsible for her? In a perfect society maybe no one would be responsible for anyone else. In a better society we might be better at it, and the *yeopgi* girl is a little better than Harry and Rick at justly distributing responsibility.

Her catechism exposes what is so offensive about the expression "high maintenance," even apart from sexist usage. "I just want it the way I want it" is not "high maintenance," it's a tautology, no more intense for its specificity or emphatic repetition than anyone else's wants. The problem with Harry's account of maintenance is that it is unevenly applied. It ignores the work that goes into maintaining any relationship, the tools that anyone has to use in order for relations between persons and things to have any continuity. The work of maintaining relations is always multidirectional. Both parties in the dyad contribute to it, and so do salads, salad dressings, hills of beans, armies, microclimates, the heat of fire, heaven and earth, and life and death. No item on this list is automatically bigger or smaller than any other. All things carry the same weight more or less well, more or less quickly, more or less comfortably, and without spilling a drop. It's the weight of the universe.

# 2 BANISH THE WORLD

## Negative anthropology

Sometimes I call myself a professor of negative anthropology. As far as I know, there isn't any such thing. The reality that negative anthropology has is that it's a joke. It isn't even my joke; it's from Raul Ruiz's film *Three Lives and Only One Death*. Here is a short voice-over from this movie:

> It is 10:45. Professor Vickers ascends the main Sorbonne stairs ten minutes before giving the opening lecture at a major conference on negative anthropology. Suddenly, he pauses. Something strange is happening.

A bit of dialogue from a later scene suggests other possible meanings for negative anthropology:

> —I'm sorry, but this book [by Carlos Castaneda] is awful.
> —What?
> —This is awful stuff. This guy's a fraud.
> —Are you interested in this?
> —I should say so.
> —[Voice-over] The professor spent the rest of that night explaining negative anthropology to Maria Garbi-Colosso, better known as "Tania la Corse."

It isn't clear what negative anthropology means to the characters in the film, but it must have something to do with the running joke about Carlos Castaneda. Applied to me, the nonsense phrase "negative anthropology" is funny because it sounds just a little too pretentious to be real, and because it casts a skeptical light on my actual academic career in literary studies. At the same time, despite its silliness, the phrase is evocative. Negative anthropology could mean something useful.

It could be something that isn't humanism. It could be a different way of doing humanism. Or it could mean postcolonialism, something like Africans studying Europeans—that could be negative anthropology—like in *The Mad Masters*, a film by Jean Rouch documenting the Hauka cult in Ghana performing a ritual where they are possessed by figures from the French colonial government. It could be a social science, like Bruno Latour's "symmetrical anthropology," which I'll talk about a little bit later. Or, as Julia Lupton suggested, negative anthropology could be an account of culture where you subtract the human beings. Think of all the artifacts that aren't produced by human civilization, like beehives and seashells and things like that. Those could be the objects of a negative anthropology.

It could also be a way of thinking about theatrical performance, or specifically about performance in the movie *Three Lives and Only One Death*. The conceit of the movie is that Marcello Mastroianni plays three parts, each of which is a double role. (Ruiz originally intended to have the title say *Three Double Lives and Only One Death*.) In the sequence I was just talking about, he is both a professor and a panhandler, and he is pleased to discover that his salary is exactly the same in his two roles.

So much for "double lives." What about "only one death"? The significance of the second part of the title is that being an actor usually means having more than one death.

An elegy for Shakespeare published in 1632 in the second edition of the folio collection of Shakespeare's *Works* says that "the actor's art" is "to die, and live, and play another part." A simple example of that art would be the career of the actor James Cagney, who dies in *The Public Enemy*, and then he dies again in *The Roaring Twenties*, and he dies in *White Heat*, and in every one of these movies he has a drawn out, stagy death scene. "Oh! You got me, etc." His art is to die, and then live, and then play another part.

The speaker's point in the elegy is that Shakespeare died, but we should be careful when we mourn for him, because he was an actor, and his death is not singular as it would be for an ordinary human being. We have seen him die before. How do we know this is his final death? The surprise in Ruiz's movie is that Marcello Mastroianni plays essentially six parts (or three parts, each of which is two parts) and dies only once.

These attitudes toward the singularity of death—uncertainty in the elegy for Shakespeare, and surprise in Ruiz's film—suggest a comic account of tragedy. There's a freedom that you weren't looking for, a move that you didn't know you could make, a choice where you didn't think you had a choice. I would compare these attitudes to a terrible movie by Jules Dassin called *Never on Sunday*, which has one really interesting idea, which is a comic reading of Greek tragedy. A woman in the film named Ilya has a wonderful, personal appreciation of Greek tragedy where she adds a happy ending to the denouement. The play ends, "and then they go to the beach." All the great tragedies end the same way, with an extra beach scene.

Finally negative anthropology could be an unrecognizable name for misanthropy. I'm interested in activating all of the possible meanings of negative anthropology, but this last one is that one that I really care about. As a critic I have a professional interest in misanthropy. This is a book about the idea of character. For me, the character of the misanthrope is paradigmatic of what all characters do.

People often write books about personal enthusiasms, and I want to be clear that that isn't what misanthropy is for me at all. I don't view myself as a misanthrope. But I thought it might be appropriate in this book to say some things that I don't usually say about the topic of misanthropy when I present this material at conferences and schools, when talking with students in classrooms and colleagues in literature departments. I want to reflect a bit on why this topic interests me and why I've chosen to dedicate part of my life to it.

I was saying earlier that you always end up inhabiting whatever you write. Maybe other people understand this better than I do. Maggie Nelson seems to understand this very well. Sometimes she writes about things she loves, like her partner Harry or the color blue, and sometimes she writes about things that repel her or that might be dangerous for her, such as the murder of her aunt Jane, but she always deliberately chooses what she wants to inhabit. Maybe if I understood this principle better I would write about different subjects. Things I like. Maybe, at least, I would be more deliberate in my choices. Why am I writing about misanthropy, with the guarantee of associating myself with misanthropy, which is potentially a toxic concept?

Here's what I think about the character of the misanthrope. I think the misanthrope is essentially unworldly. The misanthrope wants to get out of the world, to "flee all humankind," as Alceste says in Molière's play. The paradox at the heart of misanthropy is to be in the world and not in the world.

This paradox should not be confused with what Hans Robert Jauss calls "the paradox of the misanthrope." Jauss isn't talking about unworldliness but about self-hatred. The misanthrope hates all humanity but is a member of the human species; therefore the misanthrope is self-hating. Empson observes the same "logical puzzle" in the invective of Timon and Apemantus: "They cannot escape being men, so that there is some logical puzzle for them in railing against mankind" (Empson 1951, 179). For Jauss and Empson self-hatred does not compute because to hate oneself would be to "act against one's own nature" (Jauss 1983, 307).

Jauss and Empson are both great readers but they are making a mistake. Unlike unworldliness, self-hatred is not a paradox. At least, I would say, self-hatred is no more a paradox than any other reflexive emotion or action. I can hate myself just as I can pity myself, comb my own hair, or brush my teeth, without asserting that I am anything other than myself. All that I need are separate parts in my organization: my hand holds the comb and my hair receives its part.

Self-hatred becomes a paradox if you are a monist. The first principle of the creature in Spinoza's *Ethics* is "conatus," self-preservation, "with which each thing endeavors to persist in its own being" (Spinoza 1991, 108). That is why the biggest problem for Spinoza's ethics is suicide, which he calls "absurd," and that is why he responds almost superstitiously to Descartes's thought experiment that begins by doubting his own existence and ends by separating mind from body. According to Spinoza, this experiment is a kind of "madness" outside the field of creaturely possibility whose only exemplary value is to demonstrate that Descartes is clever enough to make the position of self-hatred seem credible. "In my opinion," Spinoza says, "he," Descartes, "has shown nothing else but the brilliance of his own genius" (102). Descartes's first meditation looks to him like a suicide note, an absurd contradiction of the truths that "nobody will desire to suffer hurt" (130) and "no one thinks too meanly of himself by reason of self-hatred" (146).

Spinoza has a point. I mean, why would anyone want to be a dualist? It comes with so much unpleasant baggage. It means being separated from your body. It means being separated from the world and from other people. It's a very uncomfortable intellectual position. But, you know, we live in a world of discomfort, awkwardness, pain, and conflict, and dualism may be the bitter truth of this world.

There is a line in William James's psychology that says, "Every creature likes its own ways." Which is obviously false. Not every creature likes its own ways. Some creatures hate themselves and want to injure themselves. James knows it is false, which is why he opposes the "sick soul" to the cheerful one. Maybe Jauss and Empson do not know this because, like Spinoza, they are what James calls "healthy-minded." It is not in their nature to doubt themselves.

The first task for negative anthropology will be to put misanthropy on a more objective footing.

# Softer signs

Here is a beautiful passage from the last act of Molière's play. Alceste, the misanthrope, says that he will forgive Célimène, the coquette, on one condition:

> Yes, you betrayed me, yet I am prepared to forget what you did and shall find it in my heart to excuse your behavior by attributing it to the waywardness into which the wickedness of the age has led you because you're young—provided you will agree to join me in my plan to flee all humankind and undertake to accompany me forthwith into the rustic solitude in which I have sworn to live.

**(MOLIÈRE 2000, 5.4)**

One idea this translation misses is the sense of will. Célimène has to be not just agreeable but really, really willing to follow him into solitude, to turn her back on human society. Not just to please him but because she wants to very much.

What happens to the world when the misanthrope withdraws from it? Two things. First, all human society is constituted through the exclusion of one individual who withdraws from it. Second, that individual represents a society of misanthropes who also flee human society. So you can see that Alceste collects two kinds of persons in his speech.

He underlines this point by inviting Célimène to "flee all humankind" with him (5.4). Alceste is solitary. He retreats to a place that he calls "rustic solitude." But his peculiar kind of solitude can accommodate the company of Célimène. The presence of Célimène will not disturb Alceste's solitude because if she were to turn her back on human society she would no longer be a coquette but rather a misanthrope, hence no more disturbing than any other member of the community of misanthropes. The misanthropes do not disturb one another in their solitude because they are collected without relating to, acting on, or knowing one another, or wanting to.

In this gesture of withdrawal from the world, Rousseau saw the possibility of a new, just society. He thought that Molière did not fully understand this vision and mixed it with other gratuitous notions. "The character of the misanthrope is not at the poet's disposal," he complained (Rousseau 1909, 203). Despite Molière's bungling, and despite the distortion of the spectacular medium of public theater, a better way of life was still tantalizingly evident.

This is the same vision of society that the classical misanthrope Timon proposes to Apemantus when they participate in the Festival of the Pitchers, an unusual memorial holiday in which the celebrants are expected to drink silently rather than perform songs and toasts. Plutarch tells the story in the *Life of Antony*:

> And once, at the Festival of the Pitchers, the two were feasting by themselves, and Apemantus said: "Timon, what a fine symposium ours is!" "It would be," said Timon, "if thou wert not here."

**(PLUTARCH 1920, 299)**

That is a vision of society: two misanthropes sitting together and drinking silently. Or two misanthropes drinking together but not sitting together. You might not agree with Rousseau that such a society would be perfect. You might not even agree with Timon that it would be a "fine symposium." But it would be a kind of society.

I want to caution against a cynical reading of misanthropy. Many readers of this passage and of Molière's play see Alceste as a kind of narcissist. (And obviously self-hatred is different from self-love, but they do share an underlying self-fascination.) The compelling evidence for this supposed narcissism is a line that occurs in an earlier scene. Alceste says that he wants to be "distinguished." That is, he wants Célimène to distinguish him, to love him more than her other suitors. He wants everyone to recognize him for the righteous man that he is. His misanthropy potentially takes on a cynical cast. He wants to get out of the world because the world does not reflect him, does not show him as he wants to be seen, does not reinforce his self-fascination.

I read that line differently. The way in which Alceste wishes to be distinguished is consistent with his withdrawal from society. The distinction he wants is really a variety of discretion. Instead of shaping the way others talk about him, his distinction would render all such talk superfluous; he wants others to take him for granted, just as he takes himself for granted. If everyone did that, he would not have to participate in social relations. He would not have to defend his reputation. He could win his lawsuit without having to appear in court or arrange to have witnesses establish his character, as he proposes in the play's first act. Or he could be in the right without winning the lawsuit, which is the situation in the last act.

Célimène, the coquette, shares the same principle of discretion. Here is a translation of her great speech at the end of the play. She is refusing to accommodate the demand that she state a clear preference for one of her suitors:

> Heavens! Your insistence is quite inappropriate! How unreasonable you both are! I'm quite capable of making up my mind. It's not my

heart that hesitates; I'm in no doubt—there's nothing simpler than making a choice. But what I do find very awkward, I must admit, is having to state my preference to you personally. I feel that one should not have to say such disagreeable things in the presence of the people concerned. One can give sufficient indication of one's preference without being forced to throw it in a person's face. Some gentler form of intimation should be enough to convey to a lover the failure of his attentions.

(5.2)

Célimène is a coquette not because she loves or wants to be loved by many people, but rather because she wants her love to be taken for granted. Alceste insults her when he demands that she make an unambiguous declaration of her love or aversion. She knows that she prefers Alceste but she does not want to reject her other suitors because she believes that it would be impolite to state "disagreeable things" directly. It's rude to make a display of her love. Maybe it's even rude to deny love to someone who asks for it. Her heart, anyway, knows softer signs to indicate its preference.

In other words, she is a coquette by dint of her expertise in maintaining a web of relations that are invisible to Alceste. He can't interpret a code that he doesn't even see! Nonetheless he suspects the existence of this code and wants to escape it. Discretion may be the one quality that Alceste and Célimène have in common.

Most people don't read the play like that. For some reason I want to give the most sympathetic possible interpretation of these two characters.

In fact I do know why I want to give the most sympathetic possible interpretation. This is one of the things that I don't often say, but I'll say it here. How did I start working on this project? A few years ago I went on a date that went badly, I guess you could say, and it ended with the woman saying that I was a misanthrope. At the time I reacted defensively. "What?! Where did that come from? I think that I am a very loving person, etc." Because most of the things that I associated with misanthropy (cynicism, hatred, cursing) felt foreign to me.

But the woman who said this is one of the smartest people I know, and it seemed possible that she knew something I didn't know. I kept turning it over in my head until I remembered Molière's interpretation where the misanthrope operates on a principle of universal discretion that sometimes looks like stubbornness and sometimes looks like total withdrawal from and indifference to the environment. That was an interpretation of misanthropy that I thought I would be able to claim without embarrassment. And that is how my attempt at self-justification became a research project! Which, now that I think about it, doesn't bode well for making a clean separation between misanthropy and narcissism.

# Poets are always gay

Most people don't read Molière the way I do. But I'm not completely alone. One person who I think really understands Molière is the filmmaker Hal Hartley. In an interview Hartley acknowledges that the determining influence on the verbal style of his films was an intensive reading of the complete works of Molière, undertaken just before the composition of the screenplay for his first film, *The Unbelievable Truth* (Hartley 2008, 17). What interests Hartley in Molière's theater is the dominance of poetry over dramaturgy. "The words themselves were the action," he says. "The rhythm and melody of what is said almost by itself creates action, generates momentum, creates space, even" (19).

The influence of Molière may account for the peculiar solidity of Hartley's screenplays. As an artist Hartley resembles Meredith in his tendency to project an imaginary document out of which his individual works are chiseled. Hartley makes the script present onscreen by staging scenes of reading and recitation that situate human actors alongside books and other documents. *Henry Fool* shows an especially dense accumulation of text onscreen. A partial catalogue of the library of *Henry Fool* would include Simon's poem in blank verse (in handwritten, electronic, and printed incarnations), Henry's suitcase packed with the volumes of his *Confession*, two editions of Wordsworth's *Prelude* (one rescued from a dumpster and the other checked out from a Long Island public library), Simon's contract with a literary publisher, and the extensive file of rejection letters he receives from other publishers. In *Flirt*, Dwight carries a German-English dictionary that he uses to translate the words of the script. For example, *schlampe* translates as "loose," which Simone has already offered as a mean-spirited translation of "lucky." "You're not lucky. You're loose" (Hartley 1996, 44). In the third and final sequence of *Flirt*, the screenplay itself appears in the hands of the character Hal, played by the director, who cites lines from the first two sequences as though reading them into the record of a court case.

The script becomes still more palpable by means of the framing and performance of the dialogue. The actors speak their lines clearly and never overlap. In many scenes each line has its own shot; this is especially striking in the "three counselors" scenes from *Flirt*. The actors speak as though taking dictation, or learning their lines rather than putting on a show. They insert pauses within lines and observe short but definite pauses between lines; their clear, slow diction reinforces the separation of each line by an edit. Only Stuart Klawans has noticed this trait, which is Hartley's most consistent and distinctive practice as a director. The line readings of the actors "live inside little cushions of air," Klawans remarks, with the result that "conversations . . . last almost twice as long as you'd expect" (Klawans 1998, 35). Even when no documents are visible in the frame, the techniques of ventilating the dialogue and limiting single lines to single shots objectify the script, making the lines feel not merely written but epigraphic. The characters talk like books. Every word they pronounce recalls its origin in the script waiting at the edges of the frame or behind the screen.

The extent of Molière's influence that Hartley acknowledges is mainly stylistic. His films are also notable for their explicit, continuing engagement with the themes of Molière's plays. I am interested in Hartley's treatment of these themes, because his characters read them as I do. Here is a scene from *The Unbelievable Truth* that efficiently summarizes *The Misanthrope*:

—Are you the misanthrope?
—No, I wanted to be, but they wouldn't let me play a man, so instead I play a flirt.
—Is that an interesting role?
—Being a flirt? Sometimes, but the thing about flirting is that it can lead to harder things.

—Is that bad?

—It turns out badly for the woman I play.

—What happens?

—She can't stop flirting.

—Ever?

—That's just how some people are. She flirts herself to death.

—It's a sad play?

—She doesn't die, actually, but the only man who really loves her has impossible standards.

—That's too bad.

—Yeah, it is.

—Does it have a happy ending?

—No one gets what they want, and they all go away frustrated and sad.

—It's a tragedy.

This is a good exposition of the common value of discretion shared by the misanthrope and the coquette. (Hartley translates coquette as "flirt.") In this scene the subject of Célimène's deep flirtation becomes a pretext for the superficial flirtation of two other speakers—one of whom plays Célimène, but not in this movie, not directly. The pretext of Molière's play stands between the two speakers almost as a chaperone. It allows them to keep talking and guarantees the discretion of their conversation insofar as it resists defining their relationship.

The fatal consequence of flirtation is the implication of a tragic reading of comedy, which, like the comic reading of tragedy, takes as its premise the repetition of performances. According to the speaker of Yeats's "Lapis Lazuli," Hamlet and Ophelia "are gay" because the closure imposed by the curtain at the end of the fifth act is not terminal but will be repeated in tomorrow's performance and in every production of the play, because, as Ilya puts it in *Never on Sunday*, the unspoken last line of every classical tragedy is: "And then they went to the beach." Audrey's intuition of the unfreedom of Célimène's flirtation is also based on this fact of dramaturgy. "She can't stop flirting." Célimène's frivolous actions might be motivated by a desire to cheat death, but her actions suffer a kind of death through repeated performances that make them seem increasingly mechanical. Nothing new or spontaneous can happen here. Her performance can only serve to objectify the script that dictates every word and gesture.

This scene may be open to the cynical reading that it presents an image of seduction. Hartley calls it flirtation. There is a big difference. Hartley insists on it, and I think he's right. Seduction, one of the "harder things" that flirtation can lead to, almost never happens in his films. Instead Hartley depicts flirtation, which he defines as a wish to remain in a state of frivolity and ambiguity forever.

# Yes, Dwight, like Bill in New York City, is a flirt

This is such a good idea that Hartley made it the premise of another film.

—The point is, Dwight's been given an ultimatum. He should know how he feels. He's acting in bad faith. He wants the situation to remain ambiguous indefinitely.

—He's a flirt.

—Exactly.

—To flirt is to exist in ambiguity. Flirtation denotes nothing more and nothing less than chaste amorous relations generally devoid of deep feelings. Yes, Dwight, like Bill in New York City, is a flirt. For people like this to define what the situation really is between themselves and . . . well, the other . . . this is to destroy the very possibility of flirtation.

**(HARTLEY 1996, 46–48)**

In an essay from a few years ago on Aphra Behn's novels, I misidentified the source of this idea as the introduction to Adam Phillips's collection of essays *On Flirtation*. I now believe that the common source for both Phillips and Hartley is Toril Moi's study of Simone de Beauvoir. The above lines from *Flirt* are spoken by the three construction workers who counsel Dwight in the middle sequence of the film, set in Berlin. The third construction worker, Boris, is reciting a doctored passage from Moi:

According to *Le Petit Robert*, a flirtation designates "more or less chaste amorous relations [*relations amoureuses*], generally devoid of deep feelings." . . . Flirtation, then, is based on ambiguity: it is a game in which one does not declare one's hand. To have to "come clean," to confess what is "really" the case, is to destroy the very possibility of flirtation. In this sense, flirtation is not a goal-oriented activity. . . . The point of the game is to make all participants feel good: you make me feel attractive, I make you feel desirable, I brighten your day, you brighten mine.

**(MOI 2008, 149)**

The character of the flirt is the central figure in the film's three movements. What Boris calls the film's "situation" is as follows: a "loose," "aimless" "flirt" has been involved with a "beautiful," "extremely intelligent" person for six months, an unusually long time for a flirt. This beautiful person is at the same time involved with someone else, "talented, successful," and "really nice," in a foreign city. Meanwhile the flirt is intrigued by a fourth "very attractive" person who has recently separated from a fifth "successful and well-thought-of" person. Each sequence traces a complex network of interpersonal relations: a long-distance relationship, an affair, a troubled marriage, an ultimatum, a rivalry, always ending with an accidental gunshot to the face. The distinctiveness of *Flirt* is that it traces precisely the same network of relations three times, preempting some of the work of structural analysis and rather insistently formalizing the scenario. The space between characters in three different cities mysteriously acquires the same shape.

Such networks are an effect of any narrative and can be objects of contemplation and appreciation in their own right. Hitchcock admired the "fascinating design" of Highsmith's *Strangers on a Train* so much that he was moved to reproduce it imprecisely in a film. "You could study it forever," he later said of that pleasing shape (Hitchcock 1985, 195). If Warner Brothers had let him get away with it, perhaps he would have done as Hartley did and made it into two more films set in other cities, like a gambler feeding coins into a slot machine until its display finally returned the crude image of a cherry stem three times. Hitchcock may have tried to do the same thing with the spiral motif in *Vertigo*, which spreads from Madeline's hair onto every surface in San Francisco.

*Flirt* objectifies its plot, but plot is not the object of aesthetic value that it really wants to display. I am trying to make rather complicated point with this movie and I am not completely sure that the movie is strong enough to bear the weight that I want to put on it. I mean, this film was admittedly a critical and commercial failure. And in my own experience, I've shown the film to a number of people, and they tend to hate it.

I've also read most of the reviews that were published around the time of the film's release, and critics really hated it. The critics agree that *Flirt* has a narrative but perversely refuses to develop it and replaces it with absolutely nothing. "Vacuous," declares Stanley Kauffman. The same scenario three times isn't a bad screenplay, it's simply "not a screenplay." Kent Jones, in an insightful survey of Hartley's work through *Henry Fool*, is mystified by *Flirt*. The film, he writes, is a "puzzle" and "a dead end": "The same story told three times" is, of course, redundant, producing only the impression of "the same story told three times" (Jones 1996, 72). Jones also quotes an anonymous viewer who personalizes the problem: "This is the work of a pretentious wanker."

Hartley, unrepentant, continues to speak in interviews of *Flirt*, a critical and commercial failure, as his best film, just as one would expect from a really pretentious wanker. Far from being obsessed with his stunted scenario, Hartley describes its writing as "going through the motions" (Hartley 1996, xiii). Like the text of a book of characteristic writings, his scenario is carved out of clichés: "Why is she doing this to me? . . . She loved me once. Why can't she love me now?" (20). "We are at a party. She and Walter had a fight. She was upset. I got her a drink. She cried on my shoulder. I told her a joke. We kissed" (12). What makes the film valuable, then, if the thrice-recycled and already conventional plot and lines of dialogue are of no interest in themselves, and do not emerge from particular situations but instead are "like reciting a particularly apt passage of a traditional text" (Hartley, xiii)? What can this film deliver other than the generic plot and dialogue that it repeats and never develops?

Kauffman thinks he knows: "The manifesto for such an enterprise is, predictably, that the trio will dramatize cultural differences." The first requirement for such a project would be to locate some differences in each city. Then, in order to dramatize the differences, the film would need to connect them, and, if they are real differences, show how they conflict. Kauffman probably thinks he is watching a film about circulation. A common element circulates within a broad network, cementing relations and bringing distant elements of the network into relief. This manifesto would be familiar to Kauffman because he has seen it in many of the successful films of the period. *Pulp Fiction*, for example. Or *Mystery Train*, or the *Three Colors* trilogy. Like *Flirt*, these films have a three-part structure. Unlike *Flirt*, they follow three extremely different scenarios that unfold simultaneously, brushing against one another. The points of contact between the narrative strands are minimal and momentary, but consequential, frequently violent. For example, the various characters of the *Three Colors* films are serendipitously assembled as the French non-national survivors of a ferry disaster at the finale of *Red*. The result in each case is a satisfying dramatic irony inviting viewers to trace between characters the connections to which the characters themselves are blind. The films might dramatize globalization by showing the relations between persons that the market obscures. Or they might dramatize the fate of the nation following European unification (which is the background for *Three Colors*). Or they might, as Kauffman suggests, frame a clash between cultures.

*Flirt* resembles these films but is ill-equipped to realize their projects. Instead of framing the momentous intersection of three narratives, Hartley both isolates each iteration of the scenario and impresses the same shape on it. Meanwhile, in the negative space around the network, a second shape gradually comes into relief. The second shape looks more or less like a person. This shape, this fascinating design worthy of a lifetime of study, is the declared subject of the film: the flirt. The film is character-driven rather than plot-driven, and, as Hartley puts it, "The character of the film was accumulated" (Hartley 2008, 82). Although skeptical, Jones sees something similar: Hartley "builds emotions structurally rather than underlining or expressing them virtuosically" (Jones 1996, 71). The plot stops developing after thirty minutes. The collection of additional examples of a character becomes a different kind of plot.

Kauffman may be misreading a line from the film: "If we are to believe what he tells us," the construction worker Boris says, "the film-maker's project here has been to compare the changing dynamics of one situation in different milieus" (Hartley 1996, 49). However, instead of depicting changes in dynamics, instead of finding and highlighting differences, Hartley collects examples of the same thing from every city. In other words, the real manifesto for the film is that "people are the same no matter what the milieu is," as Boris goes on to say.

The very fact of a scene in which one of the characters summarizes "the film-maker's project" means that the film cannot be limited to the realization of this project. The work of this scene, which suspends the progressive development of the plot, is theoretical. As he reflects on the project of the film, Boris collects examples of a character: "Yes, Dwight, like Bill in New York City, is a flirt" (46).

In linking Dwight (the flirt in the Berlin sequence) to Bill (the New York flirt), Boris takes himself out of the plot. He gives a character to Dwight and to Bill; he gives them the same character, that of the flirt. Then when he comments on the director's project and expresses skepticism, finally judging the film a "failure," he gives Hartley a character. The endpoint of this trajectory is for Hartley to appear onscreen in the third sequence playing the role of the "disgusting" two-timing boyfriend, involved with both the flirt in Tokyo and a "very nice person" in Los Angeles. For his part, Boris seems to step out of the film and regard it, and Hartley's decisions, aesthetically, from the position of a spectator.

This episode, too, is repeated in each sequence. The flirt asks, "Am I wrong to want more time? More proof? Is it wrong of me to be scared?" and three counselors provide, not practical advice exactly, but thoughtful, literate reflection in lines that, contrary to the established practice of the film, change every time. Maybe the question is an invitation to speculate, to step out of the film for a minute or two and view the flirt as a piece of art.

The episode has a choral relationship to each sequence and to the film as a whole. The changing dialogue is only one of the devices by which Hartley severs the chorus from the stubbornly repeating narrative. In New York Bill is never shown reacting to the three men in the "gentlemen's" toilet whose advice he solicits. Each gentleman is shown in a separate shot; because there is no establishing shot, the actors appear not to occupy contiguous spaces. The three construction workers in Berlin do share a space—they are grouped around a pillar in a scaffolding—but after asking if he is "wrong to want more time," Dwight pointedly turns and races out of the shot, with the tails of his coat flapping behind him, and disappears from the scene entirely. He does not allow himself to receive their advice, let alone respond to it. In the Tokyo sequence Miho solicits advice from three women in a cramped holding cell. Here Hartley shows the detachment of the chorus not by isolating the actors and ventilating the dialogue, but rather by an uncanny compression of the soundtrack: all the lines are spoken simultaneously, with the three voices layered directly on top of one another with minimal articulation.

The structure of the film is circular. The shape of the network of relations becomes increasingly clear with each turn of the wheel. By the time the film ends, it has traced three such shapes and stacked them. At the center of each shape is a hole. If you line up the holes correctly, they turn into a conduit. "Yes, Dwight, like Bill in New York City, is a flirt." The association of Dwight and Bill is purely formal; they exemplify a type.

I am not saying that the flirt is somehow not relational. Flirting is a mode of relation, albeit a noncommittal one. The flirt is the most heavily trafficked crossing in the network: Bill is seeing Emily, intrigued by Margaret, attacked by Walter, and also becomes an object of fascination for a doctor, a nurse, and a woman in a phone booth who asks to borrow a quarter. The only character to whom Bill does not relate directly is the ghost character in Paris who is Emily's other boyfriend.

I am saying that the characterological aspect of the flirt is not relational. There is no relationship at all between Dwight and Bill. Bill is in New York trying to decide whether he wants Emily or Margaret, and Dwight is in Berlin trying to decide between Werner and Johan. With reference to each other, they are associated but not related.

# Every anvil

I say that the character of the flirt collects examples, that it associates but does not relate its members. To see an image of collection, look at the poster used to publicize *Flirt*. Three people are gathered in a small room. In the center Miho is dancing with both arms raised and her feet a few inches from the ground. Dwight, shirtless and in tight leather pants, leans into the corner window, smoking thoughtfully. Bill reclines on an unmade bed in the foreground, hugging himself loosely, staring vaguely at the viewer, toward whom he also extends a bare foot, perhaps as an invitation.

It is tempting to read this poster by itself as an image of association without relation. Tempting, but a mistake. There may be a weak sort of unrelation in the failure of the three figures to acknowledge one another, and by the same token a weak sort of relation. True, there are no eyeline matches between them: Dwight looks past Miho, who smiles and looks down, absorbed in the gaiety of her dance, and Bill looks toward the viewer without particularity or intensity. The same sort of inattention is familiar from groupings in public transit, where passengers forced into close proximity learn to stare directly at one another without seeming to pay attention. Their "civil inattention" is obviously a mode of relation, a protective response to what could easily be an intrusive and unbearable closeness (Goffman 1971, 5). Three people couldn't get this close without some give and take.

The poster becomes interesting as a comment on the film, because no such scene occurs in the film. Images in advertisements are often made specifically for publicity or taken from deleted shots or production stills that do not exactly reproduce shots from the film they advertise. This scene is set in an impossible, or, better, unthinkable space. Where is this space? It might be an apartment in any of the three cities (New York, Berlin, Tokyo) in which the action takes place, or it might be in one of the other cities (Paris, Los Angeles) implicated in the action as destinations rather than locations. In some versions of the poster, the words "NEW YORK BERLIN TOKYO" are superimposed on the image. The bed looks a little like the one from which Bill has risen at the start of the film, but it looks just as much like the bed on which Miho exposes and appreciates the naked back of one of her lovers at the end.

This is an international film, and its locations are announced by intertitles and marked by local colors (although not by establishing shots, which Hartley consistently avoids). The characters, the flirts, are cosmopolitan, sociable, promiscuous: "You are with a different man every time I see you" (Hartley 1996, 44). They know lots of people, and they get around; their lovers are always taking off for cities on other continents, and they sometimes spontaneously run after them. The setting of the poster, however, is unmarked, indeterminate, and, as I have said, unthinkable, because these three, Miho, Dwight, and Bill, have absolutely nothing to do with one another. Nothing, that is, except that they are the same character.

In the film, the chorus maintains this unthinkable space. The chorus is the motor driving Dwight and Bill through the conduit, and the motor is powered by meaning alone. The job of the chorus is to define the meaning of the flirt and illuminate the collection of examples. "Flirtation denotes nothing more and nothing less than chaste amorous relations generally devoid of deep feelings. Yes, Dwight, like Bill in New York City, is a flirt." The Berlin chorus consists of builders after all, and they are building a kind of person. But while the chorus theorize the collection of examples of flirtation, and while each episode of the film dramatizes it, the same process occurs less obtrusively for the other characters in the film, including the chorus. In the network of relations, each character is both a point that relates to others and an empty space in which examples of a kind collect. Like the flirt, Walter, Greta, and Yuki are the same character played by three different actors. Their type has a repeated description in the screenplay—"pretty successful and well-thought of . . . most of the time." Margaret, Werner, and Ozu are also the same character, although only Ozu is represented directly onscreen, realized in the body of an actor.

The chorus represents a rather special case. The speeches in the choral episodes are exceptional in their failure to repeat, but the three speakers in each episode duplicate the three-part structure of the film. The construction workers in Berlin do not only correspond to the gentlemen in the New York toilet and the women in the holding cell. Each construction worker also corresponds to the other two. They are all playing the same character, the chorus. Whereas three actors play the flirt, and only one actor plays the alienated spouse of the "successful and well-thought of" character, it takes nine actors to play the chorus. The special interest of the chorus is not the greater number of instances that it collects, which is striking but not important. The choral episode makes it possible to show multiple instances of a single character in a scene (New York), in a single shot (Berlin), and even speaking simultaneously (Tokyo).

The chorus in *Flirt* shows a moving image of the unthinkable space depicted in the poster, where several examples of a character gather. This image helps to clarify what Boris means when he says that "people are the same no matter what the milieu is." Obviously the individual members of the chorus are not the same. They are the same character, not the same people. These three construction workers, played by three different actors, have different names (Boris, Mike, Peter), and they speak different lines. They don't even agree on the question of the success of the film in which they appear. The three women in the Tokyo chorus represent three distinct types: a punk, an office worker, and a housewife.

The three flirts are not the same either. They display numerous significant and minor differences. They have different races, genders, sexualities, occupations, nationalities, languages. One is a professional dancer. Another wears a beautiful coat. The third is nearsighted. The lesson seems to be that people are not the same within a milieu, let alone between milieus. Nonetheless, despite being different persons, the flirts are the same character, as are the members of the chorus.

A single space that collects various examples of a character is rarely shown on film outside of musical scenes. Why, in *Swing Time*, is Fred Astaire sometimes flanked by a group of male dancers whose movements duplicate his movements? Why, in the ballet scene in *Singin' in the Rain*, is Debbie Reynolds abruptly replaced by the more skilled dancer Cyd Charisse? Why, in a single shot from *Sayat Nova*, does Sayat the boy vibrate alongside Sayat the man? This extravagant rule of performance is authorized by the collective meaning of character.

A character forms a community by associating without relating examples. This is the real space of character. "The most terrible isolation," as the construction worker Mike puts it. That is why, for me, the misanthrope is a paradigmatic character. Association without relation is the society of misanthropes. A character forms a society by collecting every example of something. For the misanthrope, collection is paradoxical. The misanthrope establishes a collective by denying membership in any collective.

# A hereafter in the here

Misanthropes conventionally are expected to express hatred for humanity in general, and impatience with individual members of the species. It seems to me these feelings are fleeting and incidental. The misanthrope is better characterized by objective actions: in the interpretations of Lucian and Shakespeare, long speeches of invective; in Molière's, withdrawal from the world.

The performance of the double action of withdrawing from the world is a paradox. Molière emphasizes the paradox by having Alceste ask Célimène to "flee all humankind" with him (5.4). In addition to despising the world and being impatient with others, Alceste is loving, and he saves his best love for the world's most worldly representative. As he offers to detach himself from the world, he also offers to attach himself.

Milton draws attention to the same paradox by having the pensive one in "Il Penseroso" wish for solitude by asking to join the "company" of a personified abstraction named Melancholy. This company is not just a couple like Alceste-Célimène, but includes Silence and other personified abstractions. Like the misanthrope, Silence has a company. The figures who idealize solitary living are social by virtue of their characterology, because they collect every example of their kind.

I am ultimately going to propose an easy way to resolve this paradox. First, I want to distinguish my way of doing it (which I take from Shakespeare) from two other ways.

The first possible resolution is based on a cynical reading of misanthropy that comes from later adaptations of *The Misanthrope*. In his essay "Of the Comic Spirit" Meredith observes that generations of English writers had been trying to rewrite and resolve the scene in which Alceste invites Célimène to join him in solitude (Meredith 1906, 26–27). Meredith participated in this tradition. The running joke in *The Egoist* is that Willoughby Patterne's way of courting his fiancée Clara Middleton is to demand that she renounce the world: "He explained to his darling that lovers of necessity do loathe the world" (Meredith 1979, 40). One of the two narrators in *The Amazing Marriage* offers this truism: "The condition [of love] . . . prepares true lovers, through their mutual tenderness, to be bitterly misanthropical" (Meredith 1923, 309).

Meredith sees something in the scene from *The Misanthrope* that he thinks other English writers missed. For example, in *The Plain Dealer*, an interesting adaptation of Molière's masterpiece, Wycherly resolves the paradox by turning it into a geographical movement. Manly, who is not exactly a misanthrope but, to use Wycherly's term, a "plain dealer," invites Fidelia, who, as her name suggests, is a loyal person (pretty much the opposite of a coquette), to join him in retiring from the world. This time the act of escaping the world does not imply cosmological dualism. Manly turns out to mean another place on a map of this world, India, which he lamely calls "the *Indian* World," as though recalling the higher stakes for which his model Alceste plays this game.

> Now, Madam, I beg your pardon . . . for lessening the Present I made you; but my heart can never be lessen'd; this, I confess, was too small for you before, for you deserve the *Indian* World; and I would now go thither out of covetousness for your sake only.
>
> **(WYCHERLY 1966, 5.3)**

When Manly rewards Fidelia's loyalty with the promise that she "deserves the *Indian* World," he is not offering to withdraw from the world of relations. He has no thought of retiring with Fidelia into a paradoxical solitude. His plan is to replace the relations of English society with those of a different, Indian society.

A few lines later, Manly defaults even on this compromise and offers to "reconcile," to become "friends with the world," which now seems to mean the English world.

> Nay, now, Madam, you have taken from me all power of making you any Complement on my part; for I was going to tell you, that for your sake onely, I wou'd quit the unknown pleasure of a retirement; and rather stay in this ill World of ours still, though odious to me, than give you more frights again at Sea, and make too great a venture there, in you alone. But if I shou'd tell you now all this, and that your virtue (since greater than I thought any was in the World) had now reconcil'd me to't, my Friend here wou'd say, 'tis your Estate has made me Friends with the World.

The geographical reading reduces to the cynical reading that Manly's "quarrels with the world," his incessant "railing," were all along a kind of seduction, a way of dancing attendance on something that "[he] cou'd not enjoy, as [he] wou'd do." To commemorate his reconciliation with the world, Manly proposes the following odd moral:

> There are now in the World
> Good-natur'd Friends who are not Prostitutes.

The normative implications of this moral are worth drawing out. Either friendship is ordinarily practiced as a kind of prostitution, or else only prostitutes are truly good-natured. The rule in this community is that people "dissemble love" out of a "real passion" for money. The question is whether friendly prostitution might be not just an incidental accommodation to material commitments but an ideal, an expression of "good nature." The rule of universal prostitution reinforces the cynical account that only a "real passion" for the world's gifts could motivate Manly's railing against them. Misanthropy becomes an elaborate game of playing hard to get.

Wycherly develops this account by assigning it to the character Olivia, a coquette whose "aversion" to the world acts by negation. For instance: "I must disobey your commands, to comply with your desires" (2.1). Olivia performs the misanthropic gesture of withdrawal as seduction, "a constant keeping gallant" that explicitly rejects what it most wants in order to enframe it. Her refrain, which is to say that a thing (a gown, a visit, a person, or "the world" in its entirety) "is of all things my aversion," has the effect of picking out parts of the world as possible objects of attraction. The cynical reading is destructive to the quality of discretion that misanthrope and coquette originally share. Different gestures of flirting and railing turn out to have the same seductive effect.

This cynical reading may diminish the scene from Molière, Meredith complains, but it is instructive. Olivia understands Manly but he doesn't understand her. He takes her at her word: "She is all truth, and hates the lying, daubing, masking world" (1.1). To the misanthrope, the coquette looks like a member of the society of misanthropes.

Why doesn't Manly see the irony in Olivia's railing against the world? If the characteristics of the plain dealer are that he is "honest, surly, nice"—if, in other words, he is untrusting and impatient to an extreme degree—why does he trust his mistress's declaration of aversion? Olivia diagnoses the problem: "He that distrusts most the world, trusts most to himself" (4.1). Like Alceste, Manly is unlikely to interpret a code correctly if he doesn't know there is a code. He is blind to the attachments of the world because he has not done the preliminary work of accepting their existence.

His potential rejection of the world is prefigured by the world's aggression toward him. Merely loitering in front of Chancery court, he "draws" on himself three challenges "and two lawsuits," because he is, as his non-friend Freeman observes, "too curst to be let loose in the World" (3.1), or, as one of Lermontov's narrators says of the character Pechorin, he neither belongs in this world nor in any other.

# Trenton makes/the world takes

What other worlds are there? To describe the cosmos of the misanthrope I want a social theory that will not reduce to one world. Another promising place to look might be Bruno Latour's "sociology of associations" or "symmetrical anthropology." Symmetry means that fieldwork is supposed to include the outraged responses of people who have been studied by social scientists. The method of symmetry solicits responses from all actors— not only humanoid ones, but also plants, diseases, stars, and concepts. Everything that makes a difference makes a world, and has to do the work of making it all the time.

Not even this universe of conflicting worlds will satisfy the demands of the misanthrope. Latour is patient, and recommends patience to his actors, warning them not to "travel without paying," to make a world without doing the work of maintaining it. The misanthrope, on the other hand, is impatient. The misanthrope wants to get out of the world not soon but immediately; Alceste demands that Célimène cut her ties with the world and follow him "forthwith." Latour recognizes and celebrates the reality of many worlds, but he will not admit a second world whose content is not totally unfolded and maintained through a network of relations. To do the misanthrope's work, you need some of the tools of art that Latour rejects.

In what is simultaneously one of his best jokes and most instructive examples, Latour observes the hand gesture that people use when they want to indicate worldliness. When they talk about the Big Picture, or the Social Context, or Neoliberalism, or Globalization, they make as if to embrace the world, but "their hand gesture is never bigger than if they were stroking a pumpkin" (Latour 2005, 186). Latour uses this image to exemplify the forbidden method of "travel without paying," in which you reduce one thing (the world) to something else ("a reasonably sized pumpkin"). From reading poetry, however, we know that if a pumpkin can be part of a society, it can also stand for society; that is a figure of speech. Let's do a quick iconography of this gesture using some other poetic tools that Latour has cast down.

The first stage on our journey might be the motto and emblem of Shakespeare's theater, the Globe. The emblem shows Hercules spelling Atlas in supporting the world. The motto, according to E. R. Curtius, is a slightly altered tag from John of Salisbury's treatise *Policraticus*: "Totus mundus agit histrionem" (The whole world plays the actor). The theater of the world would not be complete without an audience, so Salisbury adds another level of reality, Heaven, where the "divine and wise" view the endlessly repeating actions of this world's inhabitants from a safe distance (Curtius 1991, 139–40). The position of the divine and wise gives a name to cheapest seats in the nineteenth-century music hall, which are called "The Gods" or "Paradise."

The second stop might be the "seven ages" speech from *As You Like It*, in which Jaques loosely translates the theatrical motto into the proposition that "all the world's a stage." Commentators like to point out that the speech may once have referred to the recent construction of the Globe, and could even have inaugurated performances in it (Curtius 1991, 140–41). Jaques's speech is provoked by a homily spoken by the deposed duke:

This wide and universal theatre
Presents more woeful pageants than the scene
Wherein we play in.

**(2.7.137–139)**

The emphatic preposition "in" at the end of the half-line serves to insert the duke into a scene after the previous lines have removed him to a place in the audience. The duke excels at putting people in a frame so that he can appreciate them.

Other characters in the play seem to want to do the same thing. Corin uses the same word, "pageant," to frame an exchange between Phoebe and Silvius when he invites Rosalind to "see a pageant truly play'd / Between the pale complexion of true love / And the red glow of scorn"

(3.4.49–51). Unlike Rosalind, the duke will not "prove a busy actor in their play" (3.4.56). The duke is an Aristotelian, aesthetic humanist, and will not violate the frame that both shows him "woeful pageants" and protects him from their woe. The duke is a spectator, or, to borrow the word he uses to describe his relationship to Orlando, a "witness," within the community of the play.

This is especially how he relates to Jaques: "But what said Jaques? / Did he not moralize this spectacle?" (2.1.43–44). These lines suggest the possibility of second-order spectating, where the duke could assign to subordinates the work of framing pageants, witnessing them, and summoning the appropriate moral. He would like to look at Jaques looking. "The Duke . . . hath been all this day to look you" (2.5.29–30). If the duke seems to pursue the choice spectacle of Jaques's melancholy with unwonted vigor and duration, his preferred mode seems to be extreme passivity. He receives even the winter wind with pleasure as plural "counsellors / That feelingly persuade me what I am" (2.1.10–11). The counsellorship of the wind does not advise the duke to follow a course of action; nor does it communicate any knowledge of air or seasonal change. It mirrors the duke, providing him with a knowledge that he might already have of "what he is." Even in the absence of his favorite performer, Jaques, the duke receives the elements of the given world as pageantry. He lives in a world in which all things, including "trees," "brooks," and "stones," perform in his personal pageant of self-inspection (2.1.16–17).

The duke has studied Salisbury and clearly wants to occupy the position of the divine and wise. The background for his spectatorial attitude is an unfair two-world cosmology in which the theater of the world empties itself and the other world, a deeper, divine and wise level of reality, receives its bounty. Many critics have found a similar dualism at work in the two settings of the play. For Wolfgang Iser, the pastoral world is secondary, presenting a "counter-image" of politics but not a "counter-reality" (Iser 1983, 312). The function of the forest is to "make manifest" the "latent" energies in the primary reality (308). Cynthia Marshall, building on Iser's asymmetrically realized doubles, argues that the play's chief devices are "substitutions," "negations," "conversions of troubling material," as when the fratricides that would be necessary at court become brotherly love in the forest (Marshall 1986, 379). The forest represents a sort of time-out, a "holiday" in C. L. Barber's formulation, from the "everyday" violence of court life (Barber 1972, 239).

This unfair two-world cosmology becomes a model for the relationship between stage and audience in scenes that acknowledge theatricality. Louis Montrose makes strong claims for the "theater of the world" trope as a sociology of theater for the Renaissance. Unlike the old duke, Montrose identifies with actors rather than spectators, and organizes the universe so that relations between worlds favor the stage. If everyone plays a part, then spectators are also players, which gives the professional players a power to establish conditions of possibility for the social universe. The players become, in Montrose's phrase, "experts" from whom the spectators learn their roles in society. "People might go to playhouses," Montrose suggests, "to learn, from experts, how to play" (Montrose 1996, 211).

These accounts of the play's dualism have some value insofar as figures such as the duke and Jaques can be made to speak for them. They are not going to help me establish the misanthrope's second world. Thus far the stages in the iconography of the world-gesture might be, for Latourian sociology, object lessons in the folly of formalism. This is what you get, Latour might say, if you "try to imitate Titan and carry the world on [your] shoulders" (Latour 1993, 189). You get an inferior second world, one that is going to fall apart immediately after you put it together, to paraphrase Philip K. Dick. This is what you get if you travel without paying: someone else always has to foot the bill.

If the first world pays for the second world, then it gets everything it pays for, which is everything. The second world is sustained by imports from the first world, which it pays for in the end by exporting everything it produces. On this interpretation, the motto "All the world's a stage" tells a story of uneven development similar to the one narrated in the motto on the Delaware River Bridge. "Trenton Makes/The World Takes." Which seems simultaneously to complain about the exploitation of labor and to celebrate it.

# I hold the world

There is another critical tradition concerned with the two settings of *As You Like It*. In *Second World and Green World* Harry Berger discovers in the double movement toward and away from the world a central preoccupation of Renaissance thought. Berger acknowledges that many cultures have techniques for producing second worlds, or, in Doderer's phrase, "a hereafter in the here," through art, the study of ancient languages, sexual fetishism, patriotism, or narcotics. In Berger's view, Renaissance thinkers distinguish themselves by a persistent "doubling of the pattern," so that the "second world" of art presents itself as a "green world," a given, out of which the world of ordinary experience is produced. Berger classifies the two stages of this double movement by attributing them to two generative books for the humanist movement in northern Europe: Erasmus's *Praise of Folly* enacts a "pastoral misanthropy," a withdrawal from the world, whereas More's *Utopia* enacts a "utopian misanthropy" or "false return" to the world that would avenge the misanthrope's wrongs on the lives of citizens while pretending to reform them.

Rosalie Colie likewise insists on a cosmological rather than geographical interpretation of the pastoral escape from the world. The forest is not a place on the map; Colie calls it a "cartographical fiction" (Colie 1974, 249). Nor is it a period in history, a golden age, but rather "Golden Agelessness" (250). The forest is an independent world, essentially parallel to the world of the court. The two worlds are separated not by distance or chronology but by the institution of time. The inhabitants of the forest "fleet the time carelessly as they did in the golden world" (1.1.114–15); they "lose and neglect the creeping hours of time" (2.7.112).

How might this other tradition organize a universe in which "all the men and women [are] merely players"? If, following Montrose, we take "merely" to mean "that they are wholly, entirely players—'without admixture or qualification,'" where does that leave the spectators? (Montrose 1980, 51). What Montrose calls the "privileged visibility" given to players and political figures seems less privileged when everyone performs and no one occupies a space offstage from which to observe. Instead of amplifying the duke's homily, Jaques offers a correction. Instead of an aesthetic humanism that solicits identification while ensuring a conventional distance, Jaques proposes a radical humanism that makes a seam between stage and world. His is a phenomenology of theater where there is no audience, a world of "merely players" in which, as Allen Grossman puts it, if there's tragedy, then "no one goes home" (*Summa Lyrica*, 3.2.2).

What kind of theater would be so indifferent to its impact that it would leave no space for an audience to stand? Jaques is concerned with two other, neglected features of theatrical practice. "One man in his time plays many parts" and "All the men and women" play each part (2.7.142, 140). This is simply true. A character is played by an actor; the same character can be played by different actors in different performances and revivals. Performances are repeated in rehearsals, in productions, and, in the case of traveling companies of players, in different spaces and towns. A play can also be revived in later seasons and generations, and sometimes other languages and cultures.

Jaques distributes these repetitions across the "seven ages" in the life of "one man." To each age he assigns a stock character from comedy—lover, soldier, pantaloon, and a few others. Barber associates these repetitions with the recursive paradigm of holiday. Montrose identifies them as "the Elizabethan life-cycle," with the qualification that Shakespeare's great characters do not correspond to the seven ages, but fall "precisely between the social acts" (Montrose 1996, 33).

A better gloss on this speech might be Schopenhauer's observation that commedia dell'arte, because it only presents stock characters in stock situations, is the most realistic kind of theater, because people in history make the same mistakes every day of their lives and with every new generation, without ever learning anything or recalling their past mistakes. Schopenhauer even revives the "lean and slipper'd pantaloon" (2.7.158) from Jaques's speech: "After all experience of former pieces, Pantaloon has become no more agile or generous" (Schopenhauer 1907, 1.237).

On the other hand, Montrose is right to point out that most of the stock characters in Jaques's great speech, with the possible exceptions of "the lover, / Sighing like furnace" (which could refer to Orlando, Rosalind, Phoebe, Silvius, and other characters [147–48]) and "second childishness and mere oblivion" (which may refer, tactlessly, to Adam [165]), do not appear anywhere else in this play. They are ghost characters, part of the language of the play but not part of its spectacle. (This does not compromise their ability to carry meaning, and would not be a disadvantage in the theater of the world that Jaques proposes, which does not value visibility.)

An actor plays different characters, and different actors play the same character. "One man in his time plays many parts," and "all the men and women" play each part. Note that Jaques does not wait through the seven ages of a long and varied lifetime to collect every example of the seven stock characters. He does not even have to perform as the seven characters in order to activate their meaning. This is the real point of his speech. He can collect all the examples pertaining to seven different characters in a speech of barely thirty lines. In short, Jaques travels without paying.

In addition to translating the motto of the Globe, Jaques also restates an exchange from the earlier comedy *The Merchant of Venice* (which, by the same logic, would also seem to be a candidate for the play that celebrates the company's move to a new performance space). Antonio "holds the world but as the world," by which he turns out to mean "a stage" (1.1.77–78). Like the duke, Antonio has been reading *Policraticus*. He seems to assume a Christianized reading of the trope, where the theatricality of this world indicates its transitoriness, its secondariness—the fact that it is derived from, reflective of, and therefore distant from another, better world—and ultimately its lack of value. Gratiano offers an alternative to this interpretation by pretending that Antonio has not been assigned his "sad" part, but has chosen it out of a personal preference for sadness. Gratiano likewise chooses, or asks for the power to choose, his part: "Let me play the fool" (1.1.79).

The conditional is the guarantee of artifice, like Touchstone's "if," whose "virtue" is that it sustains form (*As You Like It*, 5.4.101). As Stanislavski, the celebrated teacher of theatrical method, puts it: "If acts as a lever that lifts us out of the world of actuality into the realm of imagination" (Stanislavski 1989, 49). Through the lens of Gratiano's conditional, Antonio's declaration that he "holds the world" looks less like a Herculean effort and more like an Archimedean one. Antonio "holds the world" and thus holds himself apart from it. He does not give the world structure and is not oppressed by its weight. Instead he projects himself out of the world, and in the space between his part in the world and the otherworldly place from which he speaks, that part has the potential to take a different shape, to participate in new wholes.

# Excursus: Why Latour's actor-network theory, although great for studying things in the public world, is a dangerous method for literary studies

I am not a scientist, social scientist, or philosopher; I am a literary critic. Latour's sociology challenges us to describe social organizations in which nonhuman actors make a difference, to imagine a history of symmetrical and multidirectional movements in time, and to set the scale for social groups so that microactors summon macroactors as well as the reverse. I have learned a lot from Latour's projects. Nonetheless I think his methods are wrong for literary studies. Here's why.

(1) *Latour is not a formalist.* Graham Harman points obliquely to Latour's antiformalism in the main title of his monograph *Prince of Networks*. A form of government such as a prince is precisely what reality lacks once Latour has networked it.

One dramatic expression of Latour's thoroughgoing rejection of formal principles will suffice. In an astonishing passage from *Irreductions*, his most systematic statement, Latour denies that all of Euclidean geometry is contained in Euclid's *Elements*:

> No one has ever deduced all of geometry from the axioms and postulates of Euclid. But "in theory," they say, "anyone can anywhere" derive "the whole of" geometry "at any time" from the axioms of Euclid "alone." In practice, this has *never happened to anyone.*
>
> (*Irreductions*, **2.1.7.1**) (Italics in original)

In other words, there is no such thing as potential. Only actualities are real. Discoveries in geometry do not unearth what is implicit in Euclid's *Elements*. Later geometers translate the axioms and postulates into something completely different. Each postulate is a translation, and translations are incommensurable. (On the reality of the dormant, see Harman.)

(2) *Latour does not care about poetry.* Although in *Irreductions* Latour is not actively hostile to poetry, he gratuitously declares its irrelevance:

> I speak only of those weaknesses that want to increase their strength. The irreducible others have need of poets rather than philosophers.
>
> **(1.3.1)**

Here is an unlikely but fair comparison. Latour is no better than Bourdieu at valuing art. One can say, for Bourdieu, "At least he admits that the rules for art differ from the rules for the rest of society. He allows art a kind of autonomy, albeit a worthless kind, impossible to desire, that no one would accept as a gift." For Latour, one can say, "At least he describes a world to which something can be added. He allows artists to create something." The deficiencies of their accounts are complementary. Bourdieu thinks that art is special but adds nothing to the world; Latour, that art adds something to the world but is not special.

(3) When Latour prohibits travel without paying, he does not intend to prohibit travel, only to regulate it. He expects his actors to pay for their transport by becoming different actors in new locations. An actor exists "only once, and at one place" (*Irreductions*, 1.2.1); a different set of coordinates requires a different actor. In effect, Latour puts his actors on the "basic-cash subfloor" where Joe Chip, the hapless protagonist of Dick's *Ubik*, must pay a small sum of money when he wants to perform an action—open a door, put cream in his coffee, use the sidewalk (*Ubik*, 23).

That is too high a price for art. We do not make art for one time and one place alone. The vital purpose of art is to move in time. *Poetry is the forbidden method of travel without paying.*

# With his hated hand

In his dramatization of one of the key texts in the literature of classical misanthropy, *Timon of Athens*, Shakespeare seems to be concerned with the style of misanthropy more than with its form. Most critics agree that the invocation of misanthropy in *Timon* is cynical, "a dilettante festival of cynicism," as G. Wilson Knight puts it (Knight 1949, 225). Empson reads this cynicism as literal dogginess. He identifies two kinds of canine behavior in the community of the play, the flattery of the Athenians and the disdain of Apemantus, both accommodations to things one wants and can't have. Dawson affirms that the coordination of "aggressive self-assertion and ironic self-contempt" is rooted in envy (Dawson 2009, 205). Timon gratifies a desire for an object he can't possess by imagining its destruction.

I agree that Timon, at least in Shakespeare's play, emphasizes the subjective characteristics of misanthropy and their cynical interpretation. What does misanthropy mean to Timon? Hatred: "I am *Misanthropos*, and hate mankind" (4.3.54). In the voice of Misanthropos, Timon speaks for absolute reality. As he establishes the society of misanthropes he also involves himself in personal relationships with every member of the human race. He hates them all. This moment of self-definition fulfills Timon's ambition when he asks the gods to "grant" that "as Timon grows, his hate may grow, / To the whole race of mankind, high and low" (4.1.39–40).

(The characterization of Timon as a misanthrope is arguably closer to misandry insofar as the play is populated by men almost without exception. Women appear as dancing ladies in 1.2, and in speaking parts as prostitutes in 4.3. Only in the latter scene does Timon remember to include women in his general hatred of "the whole race." When misogyny emerges it does so as a reflection of the original misandry. For example, Timon hates women by association, because they are "nearest" to men [4.3.322]).

The difference between Timon and Apemantus rides on the false question of whether "the race of mankind" includes the misanthrope. This is Timon's question to Apemantus: "What wouldst thou do with the world, Apemantus, if it lay in thy power? . . . Wouldst thou have thyself fall in the confusion of men, and remain a beast with the beasts?" (4.3.323–27). Apemantus's pastoralizing hatred points to a state of nature in which he could live as "a beast with the beasts," whereas Timon insists that the animal kingdom is inseparable from the world of social relations called "the world": "Wert thou a leopard, thou wert germane to the lion. . . . What beast couldst thou be that were not subject to a beast?" (4.3.342–46).

Apemantus's hatred is part of a complex feedback system that generates love as a tertiary response to hatred. As the character called the Poet puts it, he "few things loves better / Than to abhor himself" (1.1.60–61), which is to say that he experiences hatred in a mode of nostalgia. Apemantus reflects on himself, hates himself, reflects on his self-hatred, congratulates himself, and feels much better. Timon's hatred is not more direct, but it is more intense: "His semblable yea himself, Timon disdains" (4.3.22). This hatred never turns into a positive feeling; instead, as it reflects on itself, it "grows" (4.1.39).

The crucial point on which Timon agrees with Apemantus is the reflexivity of hatred. The misanthrope is not just any kind of creature (a beast, for example) that hates mankind but a man who hates every kind of man, including himself. Timon does not save his abhorrence only for the "feasts, societies, and throngs of men" that he has deserted (4.3.21). He divides himself only enough to reflect on himself in the third person: "himself Timon disdains." The third person expresses some of the discomfort of dualism. Third-person disdain, which touches everyone without being anyone's possession, is like the weather. To say that "Timon disdains" is like saying, "It's raining."

Timon does not always express these sentiments in the third person. "I'd throw away myself" (4.3.222). "Take away thyself" (4.3.286). In these instructions the misanthrope potentially takes on a more objective character, defined by reflexive actions rather than reflexive feelings. How could they not be paradoxes? How can I throw or take away myself? Maybe like this:

> Build from men;
> Hate all, curse all, show charity to none . . .
> Give to dogs
> What thou deniest to men . . .
> Ne'er see thou man, and let me ne'er see thee.

**(4.3.529–40)**

These instructions sound easier to perform, although the final command, not to see or be seen, discounts the symmetry of vision. Whether we see each other depends on you as well as me. In Shelley's *Frankenstein*, Victor tells the Creature, "Begone! relieve me from the sight of your detested form." The Creature responds, logically but inappropriately, by placing his "hated hand" over Victor's eyes: "Thus I relieve thee, my creator" (Shelley 1992, 104). He replaces a vision framed by hatred with a relationship that is probably more intense, and a sensation that is probably more intimate.

In the command to "build from men" Timon articulates the defining misanthropic gesture of withdrawal from the world. Timon "of Athens," at the center of his own play, throws himself away, takes himself away, builds from men, by leaving Athens. If the feeling of self-hatred is externalized as invective (which admittedly is the most striking of the play's discursive modes), unworldliness becomes an object of contemplation in the political program of self-banishment. This is one of Shakespeare's favorite insights: that banishment is reciprocal. To banish oneself is to banish the world.

# The breath of kings

"Banishment!" Alcibiades exclaims in *Timon of Athens*. "It comes not ill. I hate *not* to be banish'd" (3.5.114–15). The italics, which are mine, indicate a possible interpretation. "I hate not to be banished" could mean that Alcibiades does not especially mind being banished, or it could mean that he prefers banishment. He hates it when he *isn't* banished.

Like many characters in Shakespeare, Alcibiades not only accepts but relishes his banishment, and turns it back on the senators who hand down the sentence: "Banish your dotage, banish usury / That makes the senate ugly" (3.5.101–102). Banishment is reciprocal not only because Alcibiades gives the senators the power to judge and banish him, while he retains and exercises a symmetrical power over them, but also because he carries out his own sentence. Unlike deportation, where a representative of the state physically removes the deportee to a place outside of the state, banishment is a reflexive action. The execution of the sentence will even give him a tactical advantage: "It is a cause worthy my spleen and fury, / That I may strike at Athens" (3.5.116–17). If you want to raise an army against Athens, the first step is to occupy a place on the map outside of Athens; before you take that step, it helps to have a reason, a "worthy cause" for doing so.

This trope is obviously an attractive one. It is the basis of Gaunt's advice to Bolingbroke in *Richard II*: "Think not the king did banish thee, / But thou the king" (1.3.279–80). Bolingbroke is notable for his failure to maintain his side of the reciprocal banishment. If we take him at his word, he fails because he is not a poet. He is not able, he says, to "hold a fire in his hand / By thinking" (1.3.294–95). In this he resembles Orlando, who is unable to "live by thinking" (*As You Like It*, 5.2.50), and Latour, who denies that all of Euclidean geometry is contained in Euclid's *Elements* (Latour 1993, 2.1.7.1). He can't add to the materials of the given world, and expresses awe and envy at the creative power of majesty, "the breath of kings," to cut and shape time (*Richard II*, 1.3.215). Bolingbroke wishes he could be like Richard and "be his own carver, and cut out his way" (2.3.143).

His son is more ambitious. "Banish plump Jack," Falstaff warns, "and banish all the world" (*1 Henry IV*, 2.5.473–74), and Hal receives the admonition as a contract awaiting his signature. "I do; I will" (2.5.475). The two parts of his answer maintain both sides of the bargain. Not only does he already intend to banish Falstaff, the collector of worlds, but he is also going to constitute an entire world through his exclusion.

The example of Coriolanus, who banishes Rome, starts to explain how it's possible to do that. Where in the world can I go that isn't in the world? Wrong way of asking the question. You can get out of the world only by occupying another world. "There is a world elsewhere" (*Coriolanus*, 3.3.135). In order to banish the world, first you need more than one world. You have to be, at least, a dualist.

One might expect this trope to achieve its full bloom in *Lear*. From the perspective of a connoisseur of misanthropy, Kent begins promisingly: "Freedom is hence, and banishment is here" (1.1.182). It sounds like Kent is preparing to banish the world. Unfortunately, Kent's career does not take him "hence"; a few scenes later he returns in disguise to the old king and offers his services. The reason he originally gives for preferring banishment is political. Banishment is reflexive, therefore reciprocal, and therefore a gift of "freedom." His reason for returning to "serve where thou dost stand condemned" (1.4.5) is not political but social. He discovers that the bond between master and servant remains intact even when political alliances have been dissolved and political institutions have been reconfigured. Kent is no longer Lear's subject since Lear has banished him, abdicated his powers and divided his territory, but Kent continues to love him and wants to serve him.

Shakespeare undertakes his most sustained investigation of the trope of world-banishment in the comedy *As You Like It*, which will be the subject of my next section.

# How to banish the world

*As You Like It* constitutes the given world from outside. The production of the given world through the strategic exclusion of elements of the made world is a political project, planned and executed by Duke Frederick. In his first appearance, Frederick expresses dissatisfaction with the materials he has been given. Unlike "the world," which calls Rowland de Bois "honourable," Frederick knows him to be "still mine enemy." The only solution he can think of is to assign Orlando, Rowland's son, "another father," "some man else" (1.2.213–19). This startling revision of family relationships is consistent with his earlier political career. Before the play begins, the "old news" is that Frederick has banished the "old duke," his own brother, and absorbed his dukedom as well as the "lands and revenues" of his retainers (1.1.96–100).

This impulse, ultimately fratricidal, is normal in the community of the play, but not natural. The separation of the normal from the natural is so thorough that Oliver becomes a "villain" for insulting his brother Orlando (and therefore, implicitly, their father), and ultimately "no brother" at all (2.3.19). Oliver plots to kill his brother, a normal impulse that occurs to all brothers, but acting on this impulse goes against the laws of nature. Similarly, Rosalind and Celia share a love unusually surpassing that of "natural sisters" (1.2.266), since biologically related sisters would probably just want to kill each other.

The engine that normalizes society is a particular kind of dyadic relationship. Oliver and Orlando, Celia and Rosalind, the old duke and the new duke, Touchstone and Jaques—these are pairs of doubles. (Iser for some reason denies that either Touchstone or Jaques has a double, [313].) Note that there is no confusion between the doubles. They never get mixed up with each other. That is because the doubles are not equals. By contrast, in *Twelfth Night*, the doubles are precisely equal, symmetrical, and indiscernible, like the halves of "an apple cleft in two" where there is no bigger share and no remainder (5.1.219). The doubles in *As You Like It* are almost equals—commensurable, but not equal. Children of the same parents, but occupying different positions in birth order. Or a duke and a deposed duke. Or a duke's fool and a former duke's would-be fool. Each one of the two possesses the necessary qualifications for occupying the other's place. Thus each could envy the other's place, but the two could never be mistaken for each other. (On near equality as an occasion for envy, see Ferguson 2002).

When one member of a pair takes the place of another, the former is "made," and the latter is "marred," "misprised," "misconstered" (1.1.27, 29, 163; 1.2.255). Misconstering is not at all like the mistaken identities of *Twelfth Night*. Making and marring are a single process, as Jaques also suggests when he counsels Orlando to "mar no more trees" by decorating them with rhymes (3.2.256). The reciprocal action of making and marring explains the fratricidal impulse. Oliver does not "teach" Orlando to "make anything," because what Orlando makes will mar Oliver. Both share the same set of materials, the "blood" and "spirit" of their father (1.1.44, 21); what each brother makes is cut out of his brother's resources. The same goes for the other pairs of doubles. Frederick correctly observes that Rosalind robs Celia of "her name," because they share one substance between them (1.3.77).

Banishment, Frederick's political play, rewrites the rules of the world so that younger sons inherit wealth and position while their older brothers become vagabonds, and children are reassigned to different sets of parents. As his daughter Celia puts it, Frederick makes it possible to "change fathers" (1.3.88). He facilitates the exchange by progressively banishing all the characters in the play. The exact opposite of Falstaff, who collects worlds gradually, making two where there was one, seven where there were two, and eleven where there were seven, Frederick reduces the population of the court serially, starting with his brother, then Orlando, then his niece and daughter, then the "villains of my court" (2.2.2), then Oliver, at each step absorbing the property of the courtiers within the dukedom. When Frederick is finished, "all things that thou dost call thine" belong to him (3.1.9).

This process ends with a strange conversion:

> And to the skirts of this wild wood he [i.e., Frederick] came
> Where, meeting with an old religious man,
> After some question with him, was converted
> Both from his enterprise and from the world,
> His crown bequeathing to his banish'd brother,
> And all their lands restor'd to them again
> That were with him exil'd.

**(5.4.157–62)**

What happened?
Frederick just banished the world.

Here's how. He sends everyone away, until he has actually depopulated the court. (One of the play's running jokes is that the Forest of Arden is called "a desert" [3.2.122], "a desert place" [2.4.71], even a "desert city" [2.1.23]! But the desert is the center of population, and civilization is empty. The court has become Death Valley.) Now Frederick has no alternative, no one left to banish, but himself, which he does as though pulling up the ladder after him. When he crosses the mirror, he changes, becomes a "convertite," a religious hermit, in what is now the most densely populated area.

The play ends with the establishment of new families, presided over by the god of marriage, as well as the restoration of ancient kinship bonds. But let's pause to consider how this two-world universe is organized at the moment when Frederick completes his project. The court is empty, and its neglected resorts and mansions will become havens for deer and endangered species of birds. The desert, meanwhile, has become "the golden world." The inhabitants of the golden world have a society. What they lack is relation, just like Hesiod's golden world, where fathers do not recognize their alienated daughters. (At 3.4.33, the old duke, Rosalind's father, asks her "parentage." I think he really does not know her.) The inhabitants of the golden world "fleet the time carelessly," because, like animals, they have no memory to experience the passage of time as pain, or because, like gods, they know that time is an illusion. As Celia says, Frederick turns penalty into pleasure, offers "liberty . . . not banishment" (1.3.134–35).

One might call Frederick's political maneuvering the underplot of the play. However, since, as Marshall observes, this is "not a heavily plotted play" (Marshall 1986, 381), Frederick's world-banishment is actually the plot, or as close as the play comes to having one. The play has no other mechanism for its transformations than the serially prosecuted program of universal banishment. The "magician uncle," who, according to Ganymede's promise, will resolve all of the characters' desires into nonconflicting object-choices, is Rosalind's natural uncle (working for normativity and against nature), Frederick. Montrose remarks that Frederick is "the effective agent of a dramatic resolution which he himself does not intend" (Montrose 1981, 41). Doesn't Frederick do exactly what he sets out to do? He offers to banish the world. Unique among characters in Shakespeare who imagine this as a desirable outcome, he achieves it.

# Timon's epitaph

In *Timon* Shakespeare does not seem to be terribly interested in the problem of the misanthrope's unworldliness. Instead he uses the exchanges between

Timon and Apemantus as an occasion for self-hatred and invective. The one episode from Plutarch that Shakespeare retains and embellishes is the composition of Timon's epitaph.

In his last scenes Timon becomes a poetic figure: first a writer, and finally a poem. As a writer he is quite different from the Poet who appears in the play's first scene. The Poet is a Shakespearean figure who composes without effort, and his book is, in his own words, "a thing slipp'd idly from me," "a gum which oozes / From whence 'tis nourish'd," in other words, a material that does not resist (1.2.20–22). Timon, by contrast, writes slowly and without concealing the effort. He starts working in 4.3, instructing himself, "Make thine epitaph" (4.3.382), and is still at work several scenes later: "Why, I was writing of my epitaph" (5.1.185).

Along with the difficulty of writing, Shakespeare highlights the difficulty of reading the epitaph. A soldier from Alcibiades's army first has trouble finding Timon's grave, then announces his illiteracy ("I cannot read") by contrast with Alcibiades who "hath in every figure skill." Finally the soldier has to transport a wax impression from the grave so that Alcibiades can speak the poem in a later scene (5.3.6–7).

Why, at the end of the play, does poetry become difficult? There may be a kind of realism at work in this story. Timon's writing takes time because he carves in stone, a material that resists, and not all soldiers are skilled in elocution. I believe the difficulty of Timon's epitaph stands in for other difficulties that become mysteriously easy.

The first difficulty is the grave. How does Timon get into the grave? Maybe he has servants to do his work. His withdrawal from the world would not necessarily be compromised by the presence of servants if the entire household is conceived as intermediary for the master; moreover, the servants remain loyal enough after Timon leaves Athens to consider themselves still his servants. "Our hearts wear Timon's livery" (4.2.17).

I don't think so. Two scenes are reserved for Timon to dismiss the servants and to instruct his faithful steward Flavius to "build from men" and avoid seeing or being seen by Timon. The servants probably don't bury him. No, the grave is a do-it-yourself project: Timon, addressing himself, commands, "Timon presently prepare thy grave" (4.3.380). Timon digs his own grave, just as he slowly carves his own epitaph, perhaps using the same spade with which he digs for roots and finds gold; he also transports his corpse into the grave, fills it in, and places the stone over it. These are reflexive actions that should really be impossible.

The second difficulty, closely related to the first, is death. How does Timon die, exactly? "I am sick of this false world," he says (4.3.378). And: "My long sickness / Of health and living now begins to mend, / And nothing brings me all things" (5.1.186–88). There's a name for this sickness whose symptom is a wish not to persist in one's own being, and that is suicide. Timon desires, intends, and executes his own death, and miraculously arranges his own burial after death.

The first difficulty may help to explain the second if he commits suicide by burying himself alive. Both difficulties may help to explain the problem of assigning a genre to this play. Unlike most comedies, *Timon of Athens* takes place in a community in which death is possible. Unlike the way death happens in most tragedies, the unlikely, unnecessary death of Timon, the hero, occurs offstage, so the audience are both not required to participate in death and simultaneously protected from such participation. The sharing of Timon's death occurs not through tragic catharsis but through a different form of participation. Here is the suicide note:

> Here lies a wretched corse,
> Of wretched soul bereft:
> Seek not my name. A plague consume
> You, wicked caitiffs left!
> Here lie I, Timon, who, alive
> All living men did hate.
> Pass by and curse thy fill, but pass
> And stay not here thy gait.

**(5.5.71–78)**

The epitaph fuses two distinct poems (attributed to Callimachus and to Timon himself) in Plutarch. (These poems represent a small selection of the many funeral epigrams for Timon, a popular subgenre in classical literature; others are collected in Fantuzzi and Hunter [2005, 202–06].) Crossing the two poems produces the familiar paradox of the misanthrope's unworldliness. The speaker in the epitaph refuses to name himself, and then gives his name; commands the addressee to join him in death (even nominating a mechanism, plague, to carry out the instruction), and insists that the addressee avoid his grave, repeating the word "pass" twice, and emphasizing the act of withdrawal from the world rather than the invective.

The only community in this play that satisfies the unworldly demands of this misanthrope is that of the dead. No relation obtains for the dead, not even Timon's powerful hate, which extends to "all living men" only while he is himself "alive."

# A heart in winter

Let me take a moment to explain again why this idea appeals to me. I moved to California a few years ago and it wasn't an easy adjustment. In many ways I still have not adjusted. Basic features of the place like the weather and the light and the landscape seem alien to me. Of course I have developed habits of living and working. And the way I have adapted to this alien environment is by cultivating an almost pathological indifference to it.

I will give two examples. I didn't unpack my stuff for a whole year after I moved here. I had all of my boxes, still completely packed, piled up in the living room. Then, for my second year in California, I moved the boxes into the bedroom. I still didn't unpack them, I just moved them into the bedroom.

And also, my first year here—I think the bursar's office at the school where I work will never forgive me for this—I didn't cash any of my paychecks. And then, after a year, I finally, in response to these baffled phone messages from the bursar's office, finally started a bank account to deposit the money that I was earning. But I didn't use any of that money for another year. I made an effort, not really a conscious effort, not to take anything from this place. I couldn't do it.

Eventually I ran out of the money I had saved from my previous life before moving to California. I finally had to accommodate my circumstances and try to live with what I had in the place where I was actually living. No doubt that was a healthy decision. The fantasy of remaining indifferent to the place where I live is also, no doubt, part of what makes the misanthrope my favorite example of a character and the one toward which every stream of my argument funnels.

I'll conclude with an example that I don't understand too well. This is a painful dialogue from a film by Claude Sautet, *A Heart in Winter*:

—I want you. I'm not usually so forward, but I had to tell you.
—Camille, I don't think I can give you what you're looking for.
—You're looking for the same thing. I know you and accept you as you are. This world that you built for yourself long ago, closed off from everyone else—that doesn't matter to me. I'm here for you. Look at me. You can't go on like this. You have to accept that you're changing.
—Camille, you're beautiful, rare; you're going to be a great musician. You have almost a surfeit of gifts—
—Well, then, since I'm perfect—
—But you're making a mistake. You see me as you want to see me. But that's not what I am.

—Stop lying to yourself. This is really so simple.

—I must tell you the truth. I had decided to seduce you, without loving you. As a game. Probably because I wanted to take something from Maxime. That's what I decided.

—You can't "decide" something like that!

—You don't understand, Camille. You're talking about feelings to which I have no access. I don't love you.

—Don't talk to me. Don't look at me.

Camille offers herself with total confidence; Stéphane rejects her with absolute certainty. Sautet had the actors, Emmanuelle Béart and Daniel Auteuil, play the same roles in other films from this period. At the end of his life, Sautet got interested, almost as a formal problem, in making films in which a character played by Béart would not be desired. So, in *Nelly et Monsieur Annaud*, Béart's character is distant enough from the elegant older gentleman Monsieur Annaud for flirtation, but too distant for seduction.

Sautet was also interested in using Auteuil as a figure of extraordinary passivity. In *A Few Days with Me*, the film that inaugurates Sautet's late period, he has Auteuil's character Martial emerge from a paralyzing depression in a state of universal acceptance. Martial is a guy who says yes to everything—job offers, friendship, love, crime, violence, prison. *A Heart* is almost the opposite. (Well, the true opposite would be Kieslowski's *Blue*, in which the character played by Juliette Binoche does really say no to everything.) Stéphane is a guy who sends nothing and therefore receives everything. In any situation, he quickly acquires all knowledge and remains himself unknown.

This scene might be read as a variation on the scene from *The Misanthrope* where Alceste invites Célimène to join him in solitude, but the film is only distantly related to Molière. It consciously adapts Lermontov's novel *A Hero of Our Own Times*, which interprets misanthropy cynically, as narcissism and seduction. (Seduction is an element in Molière too. "The issue," as Stanley Cavell points out, writing directly to Alceste, "is why the others care that you are not convinced" [Cavell 1998, 98]. Cavell is right; Alceste has some kind of "hold" on the others. The last thing that happens in the play, after Alceste exits, is that Philinte and Éliante follow him, because they don't want the world to continue without him.)

One could say that Stéphane is being honest with Camille and in a sense respectful in rejecting her. But he does so at a moment when truthful, complete disclosure would be the most hurtful thing he could do to her.

What makes him this way? Why does he do this to her? Characters in the film suggest a number of possible explanations: he feels inadequate, unworthy, or jealous of Maxime, or jealous of Camille. Hartley might say that this movie is never about seduction, and only about flirtation. Maybe. Maybe Stéphane's passivity is a code of discretion. These explanations all mean that he cares about something, about someone, more than he realizes. As Slavoj Zizek points out, the best explanation is the one Stéphane gives, which is that none of these feelings touches him. He has a heart in winter, right? "The trap one has to avoid," Zizek writes, "is the search for any kind of 'psychological' background or foundation that would account for Stéphane's incapacity to love" (Zizek 1996, 243).

This does not mean that Stéphane has no feelings. That isn't quite what he says. He just has "no access" to them. He has feelings but he doesn't feel them. He adopts an attitude of detached curiosity and appreciation toward musical instruments, other people, and toward his own feelings. He is impossibly objective, as Zizek puts it: "He 'wants nothing' because he lacks nothing . . . because he himself occupies the place of the object" (Zizek 1996, 244).

What would that be like? You would behave like anyone else, approaching and attempting to engage the things that you care about, and care wouldn't happen. Sort of like the Grimm Brothers' tale about the boy who did not know what fear was. Because that's what you would do if you didn't feel fear. You would go on a quest for it. You wouldn't think that there was anything wrong with you. You wouldn't think to ask, why am I not responding to things that I obviously care about? If anything, you would ask, why are these things not doing their work?

In other words, for the misanthropic gesture to be truly objective, the world itself has to withdraw.

# 3 WHAT FICTION MEANS

## Decorum or discretion?

The subtitle of *The Importance of Being Earnest* is: "A trivial comedy for serious people." If I understood the meaning of this generic description, I would know everything there is to know about Wilde.

Don't I already understand? The meaning seems straightforward enough. Comedy is trivial in the sense of frivolous. It offers a bit of momentary fun. If it fails to improve the people who are its audience, at least it does not put them in actual danger. People are serious because they take themselves seriously. They exist for themselves, not for something else. In that case, the two modifiers are redundant for the strangely unsettling phrase: "A comedy for people." This abbreviation only emphasizes the redundancy. "For people" as opposed to what? Bears? Ghosts? Why not simply say: "A comedy"? What could be more human than that?

The unsettling implication of these descriptions is that they are not redundant. Some people are not serious, just as "some aunts are not tall" (*The Importance of Being Earnest*, 1.145–46). Some comedies are not for people, and some are not trivial. In declaring a genre and a species, the subtitle seems to refer to unexplored modes of the comic and to unachieved visions of humanity. The parallel construction implies that these categories are opposite ends of a spectrum, but I am not ready to say that a nontrivial comedy would be a serious one. (Is triviality opposed to seriousness? In a line spoken just before the final curtain, Jack, now called Ernest, implies that the opposite of triviality is importance, which may not be the same thing.)

The parallel construction may have another meaning if its form is identical to the play's distinctively shiny, funny talk. Although there are several kinds of people in *Earnest*, there is only one kind of talk. Wilde formalizes talk to the extent that every character talks in the same voice, which is Wilde's own voice. A figure of speech such as parallelism, which in most circumstances would be a stylistic choice, in this community is a formal principle with the same status as the alexandrine couplet in Racine. Algy treats his share of the play's talk as an element of personal style in an appreciative comment on the phrasing of one of his own lines, but neglects to observe that every line spoken in the play, clever or not, trivial or not, is equally "perfectly phrased" (1.608). The capacity of Wilde's voice to assimilate details of plot and psychology as well as rhetorical figures is shown by the tendency in the third act for Gwendolen to speak in unison with Cecily, and Jack with Algy. The characters of Jack and Algy are highly distinct, but their talk does not differentiate them—not a bad trick in such a talky play. A better tool for differentiating them might be the idea of seriousness, but, as I have started to indicate, this idea has its own difficulties.

In his wonderful essay "What Does Jamesian Style Want?" David Kurnick makes a similar observation: everyone in James's novels, including the narrator, speaks with the same voice. My account differs from Kurnick's in that I view talk in both James's novels and Wilde's plays as form (a principle that organizes what the characters say, thus interestingly separable from the form of character itself) rather than style (a personal choice that each character makes, thus expressing character).

If the subtitle talks the same talk as the characters, then readers may suspect that it performs a rhetorical operation that displaces the terms of a commonplace. (I am trying very hard not to call this figure of speech paradox, antithesis, or inversion.) The adjectives serious and trivial vibrate with a barely suppressed inclination to switch positions. Or maybe some exchange between the two has already taken place. In fact, early drafts have a slightly different subtitle: "A serious comedy for trivial people." The same perfectly phrased parallel construction. Is the meaning the same as in the final draft, or different? The earlier version confirms the existence of an interpretive problem, but does not offer a key.

Here is another indication of the problem from Wilde's earlier comedy *An Ideal Husband*. Is Lord Goring serious or not?

—Humph! Never know when you are serious or not.
—Neither do I, father.

(4.34–36)

He doesn't know. What's more, he doesn't want to know.

—Do you always really understand what you say, sir?
—Yes, father, if I listen attentively.

(3.146–49)

In order to understand what he says, Lord Goring only has to listen to himself; this procedure "always really" works. The fact that he "never" knows whether he is speaking seriously or not suggests that he is not even curious. He might know if he paid attention to what he was saying. He does not do this. His deep uncertainty on the subject of himself embraces not just his sayings but also his feelings, and maybe even the question of whether he feels anything.

—You are heartless, sir, very heartless.
—I hope not, father.

**(1.298–99)**

Which means that he doesn't know. He could try consulting his own feelings for an answer! This time his uncertainty seems ineffectual rather than feckless, because he at least expresses a wish to have a heart. Some part of him has a hopeful feeling as to whether he has feelings. (By contrast, note that when Jack accuses Algy of being "perfectly heartless" for eating muffins, Algy pointedly repels the accusation and explains his eating habits as both practical and expressive of disappointed love [2.810–20].)

Critics make an interpretive error when they assume that Wilde is obviously and without complication on the side of the trivial. They make a strategic error when they try decorously to replicate Wilde's elegant voice in their own critical discourse, whether because they want to assume his powers or because they are capitulating to them. Sontag's impressive essay "Notes on Camp" takes its structure from this mistaken decorum. Since it would be "embarrassing to be solemn and treatise-like about Camp" (Sontag, preface), she presents a paratactic list of "notes" in lieu of argument or analysis. Basing her essay on the premature conclusion that "Camp is playful, anti-serious," she makes it impossible to test her best insights— for example, that "Camp involves a new, complex relation to 'the serious'" (Sontag 1966, paragraph 41).

At the risk of begging the question, I propose to take Wilde's language very seriously. This is partly to correct an imbalance, and indicate a neglected path through Wilde's thought and writing. For the decorum that guides the symptomatic readings, I would substitute a method of discretion. Objectifying figurative language for the purposes of study destroys neither its beauty nor its humor. In fact a "solemn and treatise-like" delivery can make for an effective comic routine. The difficult modifier "serious" also appears in the stage directions for *Earnest*, where Wilde repeatedly directs the actors to read their lines "very seriously."

# For he who lives more lives than one/more deaths than one must die

Did you ever notice how many times the word "tragedy" occurs in Wilde's society comedies?

> —All women become like their mothers. That is their tragedy. No man does. That's his.
> —Is that clever?
> —It is perfectly phrased! And quite as true as any observation in civilized life should be.

(*Earnest*, **1.605–09**)

This taxonomy of literary genres is glaringly incomplete insofar as it excludes the very play, a self-described "trivial comedy," in which it is pronounced. Algy confines his observations to tragedy, leaving comedy untheorized; as with Aristotle, either he neglects comedy or the continuation of his remarks on poetics is not extant. The social taxonomy of "all women" and men seems to include the complete set of ontogenetic possibilities for the characters, but like the subtitle it vaguely gestures at other combinations of literary forms and interpersonal relations not directly represented in the play. Within its horizon may appear family romances with happy endings, and previously unexampled, happier human creatures such as male mothers. Is there a genre that depicts men in a process of becoming and women in a position of equality? If there is one, it might be called comedy.

With considerably less authority, Dumby (not as remarkable a figure in philosophy as Algy), reads a lecture on the same literary taxonomy in *Lady Windermere's Fan*:

> In this world there are only two tragedies. One is not getting what one wants, and the other is getting it. The last is much the worst, the last is a real tragedy!

(Lady Windermere's Fan, 3.332–35)

Unlike Algy, Dumby strangely prefers unfulfilled desire to satisfaction. He agrees with Algy in universalizing tragedy: the two kinds of tragedy in his taxonomy cover every human possibility if not every literary object. (Do they include this play? I don't think they do, although the subtitle, which identifies it only as "a play"—to be specific, "A Play about a Good Woman"—is inconclusive.) The fineness of the distinction between the two kinds could give new meaning to the word trivial. Whether a tragedy is best or worst, or fake or real, seems unimportant if there is nothing "in this world" that isn't tragedy.

Between "not getting what one wants" and "getting it," the unexplored possibility is not wanting. D. A. Miller sees this possibility realized in the impersonal narrator who speaks in Austen's novels, who is "not in want of anything." Is there a genre where characters enjoy such ease? It might be called comedy; at least, Wilde's society comedies approach this condition by making the same elegant talk available to all characters, even the slowest, even the "demmed fool" Tuppy.

I could go on building a concordance of tragedy—in the same play, Lady Windermere distinguishes between tragedies of action and words, implying that the tragic arena includes all actions and all words. (Unlike Dumby, she has trouble deciding which of the two is the "worst," authentically tragic class [4.35–36]); her mother, meanwhile, makes the unpleasant discovery that "life repeat[s] its tragedies" (2.478). You get the picture. Tragedy is far from off-limits in these comedies. On the contrary it defines the limits of representation, spreading from the center and nearly reaching the outermost edge, and leaving a tiny corner offstage where, in theory, comedy might flourish.

Recall one of Sontag's propositions. According to Sontag, "Camp proposes a comic vision of the world" (Sontag 1966, 44). And again: "Camp and tragedy are antitheses. . . . There is never, never tragedy" in camp (39). Since Sontag takes the pattern of camp from Wilde's society comedies, she not only ignores but denies the existence of one of the main topics of these comedies. What if I said: "There is always, only tragedy"? I would not be going farther than Lady Windermere.

Lest I overstate my case, however, Lord Goring appears to inject what I am starting to see as his characteristic note of confusion:

> —And as for trusting us, it is tragic how much they trust us.
> —Perfectly tragic.
> —Or comic, Lady Basildon?
> —Certainly not comic, Lord Goring. How unkind of you to suggest such a thing!
>
> (*An Ideal Husband,* **1.334–39**)

Which means, as usual, that he doesn't know. He might investigate the question by paying attention to his responses. For example, does the open, trusting nature of Mrs. Marchmont's perfect husband amuse Lord Goring or terrify him? He does not ask himself this question.

Whether Lord Goring is speaking seriously or not makes little difference to me. I just want to know what it would mean for him to speak seriously. In this instance, he is surprisingly helpful. His question proves that comedy is a possible topic and a worldview; Lady Basildon's response suggests that its expression is somehow unmannerly. Their exchange discloses a scale of literary values that the other discussions of tragedy allow but (apparently for reasons of politeness) prefer to obscure. Sontag discloses the same possibility when she qualifies her assertion that "Camp is playful" by saying that "Camp involves a new, more complex relation to 'the serious.' One can be serious about the frivolous, frivolous about the serious" (Sontag 1966, 41). This admission violates the decorum requiring Sontag to perform exclusively in the mode of play, but it is not a misstep; it is one of her finest insights. In short, what she calls "a comic vision of the world" (44), because it is a vision of the whole world, has an account of tragedy. This combination, a comic view of tragedy, is central to Wilde's comedies.

In a classical tragedy, such a wise saying as Algy's might be spoken by the chorus, whose job is to remain onstage to witness and comment on the action as it unfolds. The chorus is detached enough to frame the action but embedded enough to be implicated in the meaning of its own moral commentary. The chorus is a membrane connecting the actors to the spectators while keeping them from running together, ensuring exactly the right aesthetic distance.

By comparing Algy to Aristotle I mean to suggest that his position is essentially critical rather than choral. The choral position is not just compatible with tragedy; it's a classical convention of the genre. The critical position, while not a requirement for comedy, is definitive of the comic account of tragedy. Corneille's *L'illusion comique* clarifies this account by turning it into plot. The revelation in the denouement, which installs a happy ending after the death of the protagonist, is that Clindor is not a tragic hero but an actor in a tragedy, that is to say, a "comedian." The narrator Alcandre helpfully defines the "theatrical illusion" as the actor's practice of dying not once but repeatedly:

> These are the members of an actors' troop
> Who share their takings based upon their parts.
> One kills, one dies, one causes tears to flow,
> But it's the stage that shapes their enmity.
> They fight in verse. Death follows on their words.
> Dropping the borrowed passions of their roles,
> The traitor, the betrayed, the live, the dead,
> Are, when the curtain falls, friends as before.

(5.5)

What is an actor? Someone who has multiple deaths. Ordinarily death is a singular, atomic fact. My death is my own, inalienable destiny; I can't give it away entirely or divide it to be given to others in pieces or experienced by myself in stages. In its extreme privacy, death resembles sleep, but I transport materials into and out of sleep, and I can't do that with death. So great is the privacy of death—in a sense, death is my only real possession since it's the one thing I can't give up—that its experience is kept secret even from myself. Mortality makes me an individual in the weak sense of singular and the strong sense of indivisible. I can't die twice. As Phèdre puts it, no one can return from the settlements of the dead (*Phèdre*, 2.5).

But *Phèdre*, the play, tells a different story. Thésée does return from the land of the dead; this event sets the plot in motion. This mythical fact is also a formal one. Considered as a play, *Phèdre* divides and shares the death of Hippolyte, which is repeated in every performance of every production so that different audiences may experience someone else's death in controlled circumstances. Actors are defined by this strange relationship to death. As the elegy for Shakespeare says, the "actor's art" is "to die, and live, and play another part."

The trade secret of actors is how to share death. Their eyes, as Yeats says of the eyes of actors playing Hamlet and Ophelia, "are gay" because they take the comic view of the tragedy they perform. Actors rarely get the opportunity to communicate this practical knowledge directly. The choral speeches in a classical tragedy emphasize the singularity of the death that they are meanwhile quietly working to undermine. The responsibility of communicating this knowledge belongs not to actors but to critics, who see the form of the play.

The two positions may overlap somewhat. In my terms, the position of the narrator Alcandre shifts from choral to critical within a single speech. In *Earnest*, Algy's perspective is critical rather than choral in that he is concerned exclusively with the "perfect phrasing" of his speech, which is the form of the play. I might have saved time substantiating the similarity between Algy and Aristotle by quoting *The Critic as Artist*, where Gilbert observes that the *Poetics* is the "one perfect little work of aesthetic criticism" because it is about tragedy without being tragic (Wilde 1989, 352).

# An example of the dominance of form

The area of talk in Wilde's society comedies is nearly wall to wall. If you view the comedies only as texts, apart from the dimension of performance, then talk covers the entire area, since the speeches, titles, and stage directions are univocal. All characters, costumes, props, and settings have equal access to the one voice from which they take the pattern for everything they say and do.

What are the limits on what this voice can represent? In theory, at least, there are no limits. As Basil Hallward, the painter in *The Picture of Dorian Gray*, observes, "There is nothing that Art cannot express" (Wilde 1989, 56). (See also "Preface," 48.) Dorian's personal beauty may be unusual but it is not inexpressible, and Basil is enough of an artist to capture it in a painting. Because an artistic medium is finite, it can't say everything at one go; but because it is a medium, it can be made to say anything. If the medium seems inadequate to the task of representation, that is only because the artist has not acted artfully enough.

I agree with Basil. Accordingly I argue that the emphasis on tragedy in the vocabulary of the society comedies expresses a preference rather than an absolute limit. The characters could talk about comedy but they usually do not. They are comic characters, but they are as discreet as possible in their performances. They speak "very seriously," giving no indication as to whether they are joking or not, whether they themselves know, or whether they could recognize a joke if they saw one. They share talk but not laughter.

This is surprising. In fact the evocation of laughter often has an ugly or painful implication. Think of the "thin and shrill" laughs of the skeletons in "The Harlot's House." Or, better, think of Mrs. Erlynne's wish to protect her daughter from "the horrible laughter of the world, a thing more tragic than all the tears the world has ever shed," suggesting a tragic account of comedy to complement the comic account of tragedy (*Lady Windermere's Fan*, 3.145–47).

(The tragic reading of comedy is likewise premised on an ability to distinguish form, only it perceives a kind of fatality rather than freedom in the repetition of performances. All theater becomes a house of death insofar as the words are dictated by a script and the actions have been rehearsed. Comedy in particular becomes deathly because, Bergson argues, it discovers a mechanical element in living human actors. The characters make the same foolish errors every time. There are never surprises. Tragic!)

It may be unfair to bring one of Wilde's poems into the discussion but I am not cherry-picking. What does laughter sound like? The pages of *Dorian Gray* include a "nervous" laugh (Wilde 1989, 81), a repetition of "the same nervous staccato laugh" (82), "a bitter laugh of mockery" (161), "a hideous laugh" (188), "a bitter laugh" (191), and a "mocking laugh" (213). These laughs might imply the feeling of superiority that Hobbes discerns in all laughter, or the fantasy of assaulting and devouring the vulnerable object of laughter that Canetti discerns in Hobbes's interpretation. (This feeling is surely the implication of Wilde's most famous comic revision of tragedy, which is his joke about the unintended comedy of little Nell's death, at which, he says, any minimally sensitive reader would be compelled to laugh.)

The main force of these descriptions is aesthetic. The experience of laughter—the sound, the contortion of the face, the feeling—is ugly and somewhere between unpleasant and painful for those who express it and those who witness it. This may not be the most original interpretation of laughter, but it is kind of surprising coming from Wilde. This great conversationalist who drew people to him by making them laugh, who knew, as well as anyone has ever known, the value of a sense of humor, never represents it in his writing as an attractive quality.

(I do not agree with the cynical view that would discount the value of a sense of humor in romantic relationships. "What qualities are you looking for in a lover?" "Sense of humor." The cynical view is that this answer is hypocritical or delusional. "A sense of humor" is the conventional answer because it's an innocuous cover for other truly attractive qualities such as beauty or power that the respondent won't or can't admit. I would not deny that people are often attracted to physical types, to confident displays of mastery and majesty, or to those whose exquisite vulnerability makes others feel strong. Nonetheless, I do not think we are fooling ourselves when we say we are attracted to funny people. There is more than one sense of humor; like the human body, humor has its own morphology that includes masterful and vulnerable modes. I can laugh because I feel superior to something—Hobbes is right about that—and I can also laugh when some brilliant joker picks me up and plays me like an instrument, dragging me up the scale of laughs from titter to belly laugh and back. How these and other modes contribute to the eroticism of an erotic object is debatable and, by the same token, a promising area for further research. These investigations will have to wait for another occasion, since Wilde's corpus is perhaps the worst conceivable archive for carrying them out.)

Who can blame Wilde's aesthetically sensitive, culturally refined characters for protecting themselves against this ugly human expression? They do so by muting the beginnings of laughter whenever they occur. They say: "Don't laugh like that" (Wilde 1989, 199). And again they say: "You laugh. Don't laugh" (209). "You laugh, but . . ." (88). Explosions of laughter are far less frequent in the society comedies, and they are stifled by the same methods. Again the characters try to protect themselves by discouraging the perception that they have a sense of humor: "You may laugh, my boy, but . . ." (*Lady Windermere*, 3.222–23). "No," they say, "I am talking very seriously," just as the stage directions call for a "very serious" delivery, and so "you mustn't laugh" (1.40). "You must not laugh at me, darling" (*Earnest*, 2.496). Laughter is a human possibility that no one wants to feel, no one wants to provoke, and no one wants to see. Lady Basildon bristles when Lord Goring asks if her husband could be a comic figure, as though his seemingly innocent question violated a rule of good taste.

I feel a certain satisfaction in compiling concordances of usage like the one in the last paragraph. There is a rich tradition of them in studies of Wilde. One stunning example is Eve Kosofsky Sedgwick's catalogue of the ubiquitous terms of affectionate address exchanged between Jack and Algy within a single act of *Earnest*: "My dear fellow," "dear boy," and so on (Sedgwick 1993, 69). Jeff Nunokawa catalogues complaints of boredom and shrugs of indifference in *Dorian Gray* (Nunokawa 2003, 72–74). These catalogues are possible because Wilde, justifiably proud of the new way of talking that he created, constantly repeats himself without embarrassment. He meets new and unforeseen situations by proudly playing his tape.

My sampling of statements of the tragic theme in the society comedies has the same structure. When Sedgwick, Nunokawa, and I present these catalogues, we are pointing out the existence of open secrets. These repeated usages—terms of homosocial endearment, complaints of boredom, propositions about tragedy—are taken for granted and thus not noticed in the plays and novels, and previous critics, taking their cues from the characters' speeches, have not commented on them either. "Here is something that you already know if you have read Wilde's work, but you might not know that you know this."

My claim about the resistance to comedy is not like the others. It isn't an open secret. The attempt to stifle laughter before it begins is a conscious effort at repression. Lady Basildon contributes to it when she calls Lord Goring "unkind" for bringing comedy into the conversation. Lord Goring, meanwhile, collaborates with her on the maintenance of an atmosphere of discretion.

Another word for this atmosphere might be antitheatrical. Unlike a laugh track or a reaction shot, techniques that endeavor to anticipate and train an audience's response, Lord Goring's question about comedy puts any response in doubt. What does he mean by that? Is he serious? Does he even know? Is Lady Basildon in on the joke, assuming it's a joke? These lines can be played archly, and in performance they frequently are, but I suspect that Wilde is trying to avoid that interpretation when he instructs the actors to deliver "very serious" line readings.

In another scene, Lord Goring labors to maintain an atmosphere of discretion, but this time he seems to take Lady Basildon's part, and the transaction occurs without being put into words:

—Extraordinary thing about the lower classes in England—they are always losing their relations.
—Yes, my lord! They are extremely fortunate in that respect.
—[Turns round and looks at him. Phipps remains impassive.] Hum! Any letters, Phipps?

(*An Ideal Husband*, **3.34–38**)

The look that Lord Goring directs at Phipps implies the question that everyone else has for Lord Goring. Is he speaking seriously? Does he know? This is the effect, neither arch nor deadpan but deeply uncertain, that Wilde consistently goes for and consistently achieves. He can't possibly mean that! But it's unthinkable for him to mean the other thing!? The characters strive to achieve this effect. That is to say, they take a position of critical detachment that makes possible a comic account of tragedy, and they work to avoid hearing the comic implications of their speech. This is the "new relation to the serious" that Sontag proposed. In the above stage direction, Wilde calls it impassivity. In another stage direction, he calls it "the dominance of form":

He [Phipps] is a mask with a manner. He represents the dominance of form.

(*An Ideal Husband*, **3.1, S.D.**)

What is the dominance of form? Lord Goring recites epigrams, and Phipps contributes a line that also sounds like an epigram. Phipps could be basically empty, so dominated by form that he recites lines without intending anything by them. Or he could be indulging Goring's fondness for this kind of talk as a butler's professional obligation, while remaining privately, philosophically superior to this witty talk. Or he could seriously intend a bitter statement about family relationships—this could be an autobiographical speech. Or he could intend to suggest that Goring is wrong, to remind him why people in the lower classes keep dying—this could even be a passage where Wilde imagines a person reading his books in a condition of poverty. Or, finally, Phipps could be the source for Goring's ideas and sense of humor.

I do not know. But I don't think Wilde wants the tone to be completely inscrutable. It's more that he wants to keep the sense of humor private. Everyone in the audience is supposed to think, "This line was meant just for me, and I'm the only one who knows how funny it is."

# Wilde in the age of ideals

How do you periodize an ideal?

> We live, as I hope you know, Mr. Worthing, in an age of ideals. The fact is constantly mentioned in the more expensive monthly magazines, and has reached the provincial pulpits I am told: and my ideal has always been to love someone of the name of Ernest.
>
> (*Earnest*, **2.47–53**)

Gwendolen does it month by month. An article in a magazine communicates to her the spirit of the time, and she lives according to that spirit for the duration of an age—that is, one month, until the new age begins with the appearance of the magazine's next issue. Like styles in fashion, ideals change with the seasons, coming and going in cycles.

Between Gwendolen's age and mine there is a gap in literary history. One way of measuring the gap would be to say that I do not live in an idealistic age. To judge by the evidence of recent magazines, the last age of ideals was the 1960s. A second, more telling way of measuring the gap would be to say that literary historians do not use Gwendolen's term to periodize her age. Wilde's critics talk about movements and styles such as realism, naturalism, aestheticism, decadence, preraphaelitism, impressionism, romanticism, utilitarianism, and positivism. They do not talk about idealism. They do not live in an age of ideals, and they do not think that Gwendolen does either.

Idealism is Wilde's term as well as Gwendolen's. Wilde and the characters to whom he lends his voice are constantly talking about a literary style that they call idealism or arguing with an intellectual position that they call idealism. They are constantly denouncing and defending objects that they call ideals. "The harmony of soul and body," Basil expostulates in *Dorian Gray*. "How much is that! We in our madness have separated the two, and have invented a realism that is vulgar, an ideality that is void" (56). "The true tragedy that dogs the steps of most artists," Gilbert observes in *The Critic as Artist* (incidentally generalizing tragedy as a side effect of the creation of art), "is that they realize their ideal too absolutely" (Wilde 1989, 370). Gertrude in *An Ideal Husband* declares her love for her husband in these terms: "To the world, as to myself, you have been an ideal always. Oh! be that ideal still" (1.806–08). "There was your mistake," her husband replies at the end of the next act. "There was your error. The error all women commit. . . . Women think they are making ideals of men. What they are making of us are false idols merely" (2.815–28).

What are they talking about? A few literary historians have supplied an answer. In *George Sand and Idealism*, Naomi Schor argues that Sand's novels have fallen out of the canon of realism because they belong to a different but closely related tradition, idealism, that makes claims on reality not by accumulating private, mundane details of personal hygiene and local color, but rather by engaging in a negative process of paring away details to reveal the essential nature of things, and concurrently in a positive process of enhancing the best qualities of things, offering them as exemplars of beauty and goodness.

Two other critics have started to explore the territory opened up by Schor's pioneering research. In her article "Comparative Sapphism," the modest scope of which belies its breathtaking revision of the history of art in nineteenth-century Europe, Sharon Marcus shows how small, insignificant, and at the same time disturbing realist gestures appear to critics working within an idealist paradigm. English idealist critics of the late nineteenth century deploy realism as a phobic response to images of carnal (as opposed to Platonic) love between women, and to discipline writing that deals in such images. The international canon of realism appears to these critics to be nearly identical with what they call Sapphism. They see both realism and Sapphism as a kind of fetishism, an idealization of the abject, a library of novels, poems, and stories (by Balzac, Baudelaire, Zola, and Swinburne) that perversely idealize fingernails, hair, and female sexuality.

Toril Moi's monograph *Ibsen and the Birth of Modernism* tells a fascinating story about Ibsen's long struggle to break out of "the idealist straitjacket," and uses this story to advance a compelling new definition of modernism. According to Moi, modernism rejects the conventions of idealism and unworks the braid of truth, goodness, and beauty. For example, Baudelaire depicts beauty without goodness; Zola writes in the name of a truth that it would be wrong to beautify. (What happens to goodness? Maybe Dostoevsky depicts a goodness that fails to get itself taken seriously as true or beautiful. Maybe Conrad depicts a goodness whose noble appearance always turns out to be an ugly lie.) Moi says that critics are wrong to oppose modernism to realism. On the contrary, she defines modernism as the programmatic separation of idealism from realism, and the single-minded pursuit of the latter. Modernist art claims to represent reality without idealizing it.

It's no accident that the task of excavating the literary history of idealism has fallen to three prominent feminist critics. To a feminist, idealism presents an unfamiliar configuration of the familiar problem of essentialism. Maybe any feminist research program needs to figure out some meaningful way—not necessarily recognizable, but meaningful—to conserve the general category of women. For some feminists, the trick is to do so without essentializing; for others, to distinguish womanhood as a category while allowing individual women to represent humanity universally.

However, although the same concerns may lead both Schor and Moi to study idealism, the two critics reach almost opposite conclusions. Schor comes close to being converted by the object she studies. According to Schor, Sand is drawn to idealism in part because of its power to reorganize society: "The quest for an ideal, animated by an unshakable faith in the perfectibility of humankind, was throughout the nineteenth century a powerfully mobilizing force for change" (Schor 1993, 14); and idealism retains some of the same "transformative, revolutionary potential" for Schor. For Moi, on the other hand, idealism is a reactionary aesthetic, "hugely oppressive to women" in that it "offers women only a restricted range of roles compatible with its lofty ideal of beauty" (Moi 2006, 184, 186).

Marcus has an ingenious way of getting around this impasse. In just a few pages, she manages to convey the emancipatory potential of idealism in its romantic origins, the stifling effects of idealism when established in institutions of popular and academic art, and the subversive impact of realism when it confronts this establishment. There is no contradiction in Marcus's account, because idealism's capacity to liberate or oppress depends entirely on what it idealizes. (Sand, de Stael, and Swinburne have totally different visions of human perfection.) This is just to say that idealism is a language of evaluation. In fact art has no way of communicating values that isn't idealizing. Apart from the idealist paradigm, realism conducts no energy because by itself it lacks a discourse of value. Realist art achieves its maximum impact only as long as we assume, along with the idealists, that whatever is represented in art is an idealized image. The job of realism's kitchen sink is to set an example. Thus the kitchen sink is a figure of absolute rather than contingent reality. (Now I am paraphrasing Rosemond Tuve's discussion of the character of Mirth in "L'Allegro" but contradicting Tuve's historical thesis.) If the kitchen sink is radically particular, then it's just a plumbing problem, not an aesthetic one.

Moi's account of modernism is pretty compelling. She is clearly right to say that modernist art rejects the conventions of idealism (such as the nobility that characters achieve by sacrificing themselves for one another). She is inarguably right that idealism as a name for a constellation of values has been eclipsed by realism and largely forgotten by literary history, and she makes a convincing case that Ibsen's influence bears some responsibility for this. However, Moi does a disservice to modern artists, including Ibsen, insofar as she cuts them off not just from a conventional set of values but from a capacity to generalize that is a crucial source of aesthetic value. (The Bourdieuvian analysis that occasionally surfaces in Moi's monograph takes for granted the complete unreality of ideals, and describes an art without truth, goodness, or beauty.) In doing so, Moi even undercuts the feminist argument "that a woman can represent the universal (the human) just as much or just as well as a man" (Moi 2006, 243–44), since, without some technique for generalizing, no one, man or woman, can represent universal humanity. (Moi is referring to an exchange between Nora and Helmer in A Doll's House: "You are first and foremost a wife and a mother." "I no longer believe that. I believe that I am first and foremost a human being.")

I propose to rethink Moi's account of modernism from the vantage of idealism. The most effective rhetorical move would be to go back to the plays by Ibsen that make up Moi's archive, and reread them for what they idealize. Here I find myself at a disadvantage, because I do not know anything worth mentioning about Ibsen that does not come directly from the pages of Ibsen and the Birth of Modernism. Fortunately for my purposes, Moi also has a few suggestive pages on Wilde's role in the modernist rejection of idealism.

# The necessary idealizing of you reality

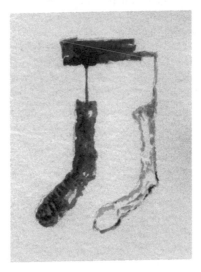

What is fiction?

—Do not speak slightingly of the three-volume novel, Cecily. I wrote one myself in earlier days.

—Did you really, Miss Prism? How wonderfully clever you are! I hope it did not end happily? I don't like novels that end happily. They depress me so much.

—The good ended happily, and the bad unhappily. That is what Fiction means.

(*Earnest*, **2.47–53**)

In other words, fiction means idealism. Letitia Prism's lost three-volume novel rewards virtue with happiness and punishes vice with unhappiness. Thus the novel arranges the parts of the world into more perfect shapes than those of nature. Its modality is not just as-if but should-be. Sidney, who says that poetry turns the brass of nature's world into gold, would approve.

Other characters in *Earnest* have similar intuitions, although they might not be able to express them as precisely as Letitia, who is an educator by trade. The very premise of the play is an idealism that has broken into the plot if not quite into the conscious lives of the characters. The "ideal" shared by Gwendolen and Cecily is "to love someone of the name of Ernest" because "there is something in that name that inspires absolute confidence"

(1.381–83, 2.498–99). Supporting their confidence in the name Ernest is a more basic confidence in the act of naming, as Joel Fineman once argued. The characters have somehow intuited that their names confer ontological status. The name identifies the type of which the bearer is an example. (Fineman 1991, 142.)

Jack may be a bad example, since he thinks he is lying when he says that his name is Ernest. Still, the name he gives, which turns out to be the name his parents gave him, accurately describes what Gwendolen calls "the simplicity of his character" (1.691). There is little choice between Jack and Algy in terms of their behavior. Jack calls himself by an assumed name, tells stories about an imaginary brother, and is as "advanced" a "Bunburyist" as Algy (1.217). They are as alike in their actions as in their speech.

Yet their characters are remarkably different. Algy is the "reckless" one, "very bad in my own small way" (2.127), and Jack is the "serious" one who "has to adopt a very high moral tone on all subjects" (1.202–03). This does not mean that Algy is entirely lacking in values. He is "serious about meals" (1.279) and a "serious Bunburyist" (2.778), whereas Jack is "so serious that he cannot be quite well," "serious about everything" (2.13–14, 2.783). The one difference between Algy and Jack is what they are serious about. To put it another way, they differ in the ideals they project.

What does Toril Moi mean when she describes Wilde as anti-idealist? She does not mean that idealism is not a topic in his writing. She is aware of the vocabulary of idealism that saturates every page, but she interprets it differently. Moi sees Wilde as "a virulent opponent of idealism" on a par with Ibsen himself: "Wilde's brilliant paradoxes, his searing indictment of moralism, are as anti-idealist as Ibsen's turn to the ordinary" (*Ibsen* 2006, 101). Wilde's treatment of idealism resembles Ibsen's in that both writers make the conflict between idealism and realism a subject for debate within their writings. They do not reject idealism by simply doing something else, as later writers might have the luxury of doing. They confront it head-on and defeat it, exposing the mutual incompatibility of truth, goodness, and beauty, and showing the inadequacy of any projected ideal to the variety of things in the real world.

If, on Moi's account, modernism reveals a world without ideals, then artists such as Ibsen and Wilde are tasked with the heavy lifting. They take the ideals out of reality so that later generations of modernists are left to play with a "void ideality" (a phrase that Moi borrows from *Dorian Gray*). Ibsen and Wilde show the work of derealizing ideals on paper. They even put it on the stage so that the defeat of idealism can occur publicly, ritually, over repeated viewings.

The passages from Wilde's writing that I have quoted to demonstrate an ongoing concern with idealism might therefore be taken as signs of struggle. Let's look at one of the passages.

> It is sometimes said that the tragedy of an artist's life is that he cannot realize his ideal. But the true tragedy that dogs the steps of most artists is that they realize their ideal too completely.

**(WILDE 1989, 370)**

These two sentences from Gilbert's first discourse on criticism as art seem to confirm everything that Moi says about Wilde's project. In a "brilliant paradox," Gilbert restates a commonplace from the annals of past idealisms and ironically reverses it. Simultaneously, he restates Dumby's remarks on tragedy from *Lady Windermere*. There are two kinds of tragedies, not getting what you want and getting it, and the latter is, for Gilbert as for Dumby, "the true tragedy." The lesson seems clear. The objective for art is to get ideals out of reality.

However, Gilbert, a loquacious character even for Wilde, is not finished yet.

> For, when the ideal is realized, it is robbed of its wonder and its mystery, and becomes simply a new starting-point for an ideal that is other than itself.

The continuation of the passage shows that Gilbert naturalizes idealism along with tragedy. For Gilbert, as for any idealist critic, art cannot avoid the process that Barbara Guest describes in a beautiful apostrophe as "the necessary idealizing of you reality."

Art communicates in ideals and has no other language. An unraveling of the fabric of goodness, truth, and beauty will consequently incorporate the threads into a different weave, "a new starting-point for an ideal that is other than itself." A different pattern, but a figure in the carpet nonetheless.

Is this what Moi means—that Wilde replaces one idealism with another? Instead of reproducing a checklist of cultural commonplaces (the symmetrical classical body, the nobility of sacrifice), he affirms a different, modern, progressive set of values? If that is Moi's argument, I would not disagree, or not very strenuously. But I think she is saying something else. She implies that Wilde's method destroys idealism so thoroughly that no ideals will remain for future generations of artists. Maybe the destructive feature in Wilde's writing is comedy. According to Moi, "the very genre of comedy pulls in the direction of the low and everyday," and thus is anathema to idealism (Moi 2006, 184). So far I have sketched Wilde's comic view of tragedy and the complex relation to seriousness that it makes possible. Now I want to ask the question in general terms. Does comedy idealize?

Let's ask someone from a period when artists and critics saw idealism as a force at least as powerful as realism. Schor's study of Sand includes a remarkable engraving by Honoré Daumier, "Battle Between the Schools—Idealism and Realism." This image might serve to illustrate Moi's definition of modernism. A more effective illustration, however, would need to show the aftermath: Realism triumphant over the vanquished corpse of Idealism. In the battle as seen by Honoré Daumier, no actual fighting takes place. At most the figures representing the two schools exchange menacing looks and brandish the tools of their art, the paintbrush, maulstick, and palette, which, presumably, both of them would use to make a painting. Maybe a violent struggle will occur in the moment after this tense scene. But what are they really going to do? Paint each other? If that is their plan, then they are too late, because someone beat them to it. Daumier has already converted both schools of art into an image.

And what side is Daumier on, anyway? The picture includes an idealist and a realist, but no obvious figure for the comic art that Daumier practices. Who is going to win this fight? Which one is Daumier betting on? Realism has exaggerated facial features and a short, stocky body, and appears in modern but not sophisticated dress, with, as Schor points out, peasant shoes (Schor 1993, 28). Idealism's body is unclothed, which, along with the Roman military headgear, gives him a classical appearance, but also implies weakness, as though he had been caught unprepared by Realism's sneak attack. The spectacles on his face suggest some impairment of his vision along with the teacherly and scholarly associations of academic art.

Daumier reproduces conventions of realism and idealism in order to caricature them, and in this sense does not prefer one to the other. Although caricature does not limit itself to one set of conventions, it idealizes in two other senses.

1   It epitomizes many artists, thinkers, and artifacts in the compact form of a personified abstraction. The figure of Realism collects all realist artists and works of art in one man's body. The conflict depicted in this image occurs on the level of absolute reality.

2   Daumier exaggerates the mundane characteristics in realist art and the pretensions of idealist art in order to find value in them. This value is not nobility, virtue, sympathy, justice, or beauty, but everyone knows its name and most people affirm that it is a value, so it should not be difficult to recognize. It's called humor. Daumier confers value on the two schools by making them look funny. In his

perceptive essay "Daumier Caricaturist," Henry James remarks on the compatibility of Daumier's comedy with idealism in terms that Wilde would recognize when he says that the themes of Daumier's engravings are "peculiarly serious . . . so serious that they are *almost* tragic." (James 1954, 28)

I don't think that Moi sees the humor of comedy as destructive to idealism for the simple reason that she is totally insensitive to it. Comedy, for Moi, consists of an orientation toward "the low and everyday," which explains why Ibsen's puzzling early play *Love's Comedy* really is a comedy despite the fact that it is so lacking in humor that other critics want to call it *Love's Tragedy* instead (Moi 2006, 184).

I hasten to add that the value of a sense of humor is not such that having one becomes a sign of personal superiority. At least, the lack of a sense of humor is not a moral failing. Similarly, it's unfortunate, it's even unfair, that I always respond soberly to sarcasm and hyperbole because they sound to me, at least on a first hearing, like straightforward statements of fact. This is a failing but not a moral one. In Moi's case the humorlessness of her reading of Wilde is, if anything, an advantage. It allows her to see the thematization of idealism in Wilde's writing, which disappears in the readings of the critics who decorously maintain an unserious attitude.

The other possibility is that Moi views the aestheticism of Wilde's method as destructive to idealism. In other words, she doesn't see the value of humor, not because she is insensitive to it but because it is fundamentally an *aesthetic* value. I fear this is what she really means. If so, she is making a mistake that Trilling warns against, which is to read Wilde's aestheticism as an overture to nihilism (*Sincerity and Authenticity* 1972, 121). The preface to *Dorian Gray* can look like a research protocol for an experiment on human subjects that disregards respect for persons, benevolence, and justice, but only if you start with the assumption that art has no value. Wilde argues, on the contrary, that aesthetic values are intrinsic. The values that art upholds are in works of art and not elsewhere, and thus the morality of writing is to write well. "A beautiful thing helps by being what it is" (Wilde 1905, 16), and humorous things help by being what they are.

# The legs/of the twentieth century

"We live, as I hope you know, Mr. Worthing, in an age of ideals" (*Earnest*, 1.278–79). "We live, I regret to say, in an age of surfaces" (3.164–65). I have argued that these two propositions do not have to contradict each other. Do matters of the soul deteriorate so rapidly that the ideals of Act 1 reduce to surfaces by Act 3 ("less than twenty-four hours" later, according to Wilde's stage direction)? Not if your ideal is a beautiful surface. Self-sacrifice, the hoariest convention of nineteenth-century idealism, is a useful criterion in Wilde's case. Would you be willing to give up your position in society for the sake of maintaining an aesthetic? Would you be willing to die if the alternative were to make a statement without irony? Then irony is your ideal.

My effort has been to redescribe Moi's account of modernism using a different example (Wilde rather than Ibsen), and, more importantly, from the vantage of idealism. From this vantage, which assumes that the idealizing of reality is a necessary condition for making art, Wilde appears to idealize the aesthetic. I would be similarly inclined to interpret what Moi describes as Ibsen's turn to the ordinary as an idealization of ordinary life and things, as opposed to a turn away from ideals altogether. Although Wilde and Ibsen do not challenge the core assumption that artistic creation posits an ideal, they are hardly typical nineteenth-century idealists. They present real, lasting challenges to traditional expressions of idealism—the ongoing sign of which is the erasure of the very name of this theory of art from literary history—and set the stage for different systems of values in modern art. Moi is emphatically right to say that the first generation of modern artists, including Ibsen and Wilde, alter idealism so drastically that later literary historians forget what to call it.

What happened in the reception of idealism among later generations of artists and critics? Moi's explanation is that Ibsen murdered idealism so thoroughly that he then became unreadable.

> But when we forget all about the idealist tradition in aesthetics, we are no longer able to see that *Ghosts* is not just about family sickness and family secrets, but about aesthetic norms. Paradoxically, then, the death of idealism that Ibsen helped to bring about makes it more, not less, difficult to understand what Ibsen was doing in his modern plays.
>
> (*Ibsen and the Birth of Modernism* **2006, 93–94**)

Moi uses Ibsen's long struggle with idealism to explain his neglect in literary studies. Literary critics don't talk about Ibsen because they are neither invested in nor threatened by idealism, and therefore lack a conceptual vocabulary even for talking about his issues with it. One problem with this explanation is that it should also apply to other writers such as Wilde and Baudelaire who make idealism an explicit theme in their work but do not suffer the same neglect as Ibsen in histories of modern literature. Another problem with this explanation is that Ibsen is not a neglected playwright. As Moi says, he is a "classic of the stage" (1), and his plays are constantly read, translated, performed, adapted into movies.

Moi is well aware and even resentful of the discrepancy between popular and academic reception. Her book begins with the complaint that histories of modernism make "incessant references to Baudelaire, Flaubert, and Manet as the great founders of modernism. Why . . . was Ibsen's name not included?" (1). Although idealism may be a dead issue for the profession of literary studies, it remains very much alive in other cultural institutions. I will briefly refer to just two examples. What is the concept of heroism in Hollywood film—sympathy, beauty, frivolity, adherence to a moral code that covers both the story of the character and the life of the actor, the convention of self-sacrifice (think of the ending of *Casablanca*, or the ending of *Stella Dallas*, or think of the cliché, "Save yourself!")—if not an idealized human image?

My second example returns to the field of literary studies, where materialist criticism has long been shadowed by what Hans Robert Jauss calls the "embarrassment" that it might secretly be idealism ("The Idealist Embarrassment,"1975, 191–92). Lukacs, for example, is only a Hegelian at the start of his career, but he never gives up on the principle that art must posit an ideal. That is why he prefers Mann to Kafka: because the latter does not imagine a world in which meaningful social change could occur.

What is the legacy of idealism for modernism? Consider the case of Henry Parland, an early twentieth-century poet who wrote in Swedish. Here is the title poem, quoted in its entirety, from his 1929 collection *Ideals Clearance* (in Swedish, *Idealrealisation*), as translated by Johannes Göransson:

The Clearance Sale of Ideals
—you say it has already begun.

But I say:
Better cut the prices.

**(PARLAND 2006, 35)**

My first thought about this poem is that it is a perfect confirmation of Moi's thesis. Parland expresses the modernist hostility to idealism in the image of a price war. He will aggressively and continually lower the prices on ideals until he has put his competitors out of business and sold off the accumulated stock of platitudes from nineteenth-century art. At the same time, I have to wonder, isn't 1929 a little late, according to Moi's timeline, for a modernist poet to be struggling to divest himself of the burden of idealism? Does idealism have a particular meaning or persistence in the cultures and languages of Scandinavia that might link Ibsen to Parland and give the project of selling off ideals a traditional value?

According to Göransson, early reviewers of *Ideals Clearance* interpreted its stance as anti-idealist: "The critics unanimously attacked the book as 'nihilist'" (iii). However, there are some indications that in this collection Parland espouses a weird idealism that his critics may not have recognized. Here are the first few lines of the next poem:

> Now I know—
> it's on socks it all depends!
> Everything, erotics, aesthetics, religion,
> human values.

(37)

Huh. That's . . . different. It isn't nihilism. There are "human values" and "everything" else, but in a dependent relationship to socks. This poem almost sounds like a treatise on monist ontology, where socks are the primary substance. I have observed elsewhere that Herrick's poem "Delight in Disorder" finds erotic fulfillment in styles of dress and does not bother to verify the existence of a body under the clothes. The speaker's desire could be satisfied by looking at a body in disordered dress, or "disorder" could mean cross-dressing, or the speaker might just want to see and brush against the clothes. Parland goes further. He is more explicit: "I thought: / it was a human being, / but it was her clothes" (33). Where Herrick blurs the boundaries of the human body and its layers of dress, Parland first draws a line between them. Maybe the speaker was originally excited by the promise of a body under the clothes, but then gets a surprise—no body, just clothes—and then makes the more surprising discovery "that that's the same thing / and that clothes can be very beautiful" (33).

What makes clothes so beautiful? Maybe it's that clothes take their form from the human body and thus partake of the human potential for perfection. That would just be fetishism. Maybe it's that clothes subsume the symbolic value of human labor. That would just be commodity fetishism. (Which Parland cleverly reverses. Remember, human values depend on socks!) Parland has a different idea. Maybe clothes are the perfection at which the human body aims.

> we should be
> more clothes,
> less human,
> and the soul sewed into the cuffs.

(39)

The English expression "to wear one's heart on one's sleeve," adapted from Iago's line in *Othello*, emphasizes the risk involved in showing what one loves. Parland's line "the soul sewed into the cuffs" emphasizes the style. This revaluation of style comes at the expense of the human; it requires us to become "less human." But the consequence is not nihilism. Rather than hiding in an absent interior, soul becomes the province of a comfortable, protective, and stylish garment.

Can this attitude be assimilated to idealism? That is what Parland calls it in his manifesto "The Revolution of Things" (also translated by Göransson):

> This is about idealism. The idealism of things. The idealism of car tires, stockings. cough drops. They love life, their surface-hymn moves toward deeper connections.

There may be no precedent for a revolution of ordinary objects ("tires, stockings, cough drops") in the canons of romantic idealism. As Moi shows, the doctrine of idealism in German romanticism—the graduated improvement of the human form toward its ultimate perfection—takes advantage of the autonomy of the human as opposed to the object-world, which is governed by necessity (*Ibsen* 2006, 72). The wish to be an object would ordinarily be the longing of free beings for a condition of unfreedom, but Parland finds life and freedom in mass-produced things.

The socks on which "human values" depend are promoted from human accessories to displays in shop windows (where they appear on their own or on the limbs of mannequins), and finally to the advertisements that Parland's speaker approaches with a religious attitude: "a poster about hubcaps / the year's best / . . . I stand silent, pious / in front of its / proud, commanding / b u y !" (*Ideals* 2006, 63 [spacing in original]). "Truthfully, anyone who wanders the streets without hearing the posters' clamorous lifesong is both deaf and blind" ("The Revolution of Things"). Parland understands the images in advertisements as expressions of ideals, but not human ones. The advertisements are propaganda for a revolution that occurred in the object-world while we humans slept. Thus socks become "the legs / of the twentieth century" (41). Long live the new flesh.

When was the age of ideals? Maybe it isn't over yet. Periods have a way of turning into question marks. How do you periodize the age of ideals when, as Wilde shows, people habitually lie about their ages? (Cecily gives her age as "eighteen but admitting to twenty at evening parties" [*Earnest*, 3.245], and a sufficiently "trivial buttonhole" takes years off

Lord Goring's age [*An Ideal Husband*, 3.29–30].) But if the unfortunate effect of Moi's explanation is to limit the age of ideals to its narrowest horizon, the nineteenth century or Ibsen's career, my explanation has two potentially unfortunate effects, one of which would be to repeat the narrowing of horizons and put Wilde neatly back in his historical context as a good idealist after all, and the other of which would be to extend idealism to its ultimate horizon, which is universal, embracing the entire history of art.

The historical break that Moi identifies is undeniable. But maybe it doesn't happen exactly where Moi puts it. Maybe art doesn't give up on idealism but criticism does, first abandoning the term, and later ceasing to believe that there are values in art. I have said that literature can't give up on idealism because it has no other way of valuing. As Jauss puts it, "fictionalizing things inevitably brings with it their idealization" (Jauss 1989, 24). "That is what Fiction means," as Letitia Prism puts it. If terms such as ideal, universal, and value seem offensively pious or quaint, then let's call it desire instead, and subject it to all the confusion and ambivalence of which desires are capable. With a single exception: the desires expressed in art are fully accessible to consciousness. Anyone motivated to make something wants that thing to be in the world, and fantasizes living inside it.

# The ideal thing

Studies of the novel have maintained an antiformalist theory of character that rewrites earlier literary history so that what used to be called character has to be renamed caricature or stereotype. Alex Woloch compellingly demonstrates the chilling implications of this theory for social relations between characters in *The One vs. the Many*. The antiformalist theory works beautifully as a description of the realist novel, almost works for early novels and modernist novels, and does not work at all for other media in which characters appear.

Against this literary history in which the novel is exceptional, I propose a different literary history that includes the novel. My literary history is comic rather than tragic. It is written from the perspective of idealism. In the following sections of this chapter I am going to talk about a few familiar English novels in ways that will make them seem unfamiliar. I want to show how different the novel looks when you assume that its job is to generalize.

My history of the novel has a teleology whose name is Henry James, so let's start there. James belonged to the same modernist generation as Ibsen and Wilde, and, like them, set realism on a collision course with idealism. His tale "The Real Thing" makes a series of jokes out of the conflict. The narrator, an artist who aspires to paint portraits of wealthy clients but in the meantime supports himself by producing illustrations for novels and magazines, undertakes a commission to illustrate a deluxe edition of the collected novels of a neglected genius, "the rarest of the novelists" (James 1977, 111), who specializes in subtle studies of the manners of people in "the highest circles" of society (129). In other words, he is going to illustrate the New York Edition of the prose fiction of Henry James. His engravings come out perfectly when he uses servants and professional models to stand in for the persons of quality who populate the novels, but when he tries using an actual gentleman and a lady, Major and Mrs. Monarch, to represent a gentleman and a lady, the effect on the engravings is mysteriously indecorous.

> "I don't know—I don't like your types." This was lame for a critic who had never consented to discuss with me anything but the question of execution, the direction of strokes, and the mystery of values.
> "In the drawings you've been looking at I think my types are very handsome."
> "Oh they won't do!"
> "I've been working with new models."
> "I see you have. *They* won't do."
>
> **(127–28)**

The first joke is that the real thing is always the wrong thing. Art refers not to the world but to other works of art. The second joke is the opposite of the first. Not that artistic realism lacks a foundation in reality but rather than the effects of realist technique are inevitable. The types that you find in art are based on types that you find in the world. The engraver's tools are truth-telling mirrors that reflect whatever you put in front of them. The indecorousness of the image exposes a real flaw in the real social universe, which is that the servants possess an innate nobility that their masters lack. That is what makes them better subjects, types, for idealist art.

The lesson regarding realism seems ambiguous. One interpretation repudiates realism as wishful thinking. Another affirms it as a property inherent in any image-making practice. Still, the lesson regarding technique is the same in both interpretations. Technique is irrelevant. "The question of execution" and "the direction of the strokes" have no impact on "the mystery of values." The engraver contributes no features to the image. If technique has any meaning, it belongs only to the models who pose for the illustrations.

The treatment of portraiture in "The Real Thing" is schematic as befits the gently allegorical genre of the tale. Portraiture has the same implication in novels such as *The Tragic Muse*, where a model, an actress suggested by Sarah Siddons, rather than a plastic artist, determines the image of tragedy in a painting. Same thing in *Portrait of a Lady*, a novel that thematizes portraiture without depending on the emblem of an art object, where Isabel wishes for and receives an unusual freedom to choose the parameters of the image by which others will know her. In these major works, James offers his characters the appealing prospect of simultaneously enjoying the perfection of being a work of art and the control of being an artist.

Thus James's real subject is freedom, as Leo Bersani argues in his classic essay "The Jamesian Lie." If allowed to develop, the consequences of this freedom would erase the difference between real and ideal such that "fictional invention is neither tautological nor evasive" but "constitutes the self" (132). The meaning of the "lie" of Bersani's title is that James's characters paradoxically are incapable of lying. "Language would no longer reveal character or reveal the desires behind words; it would be the unfolding of an improvised and never completed psychological design" (Bersani 1976, 139). What one says constitutes one's self-image, and (since James assigns the powers of plastic manipulation solely to models, not artists) one's figures have no rhetorical force for the images that others project. At last the only thing to do with the other images is to appreciate them, and go, "Ah."

# The failure of portraiture

In James's fiction the creative power of portraiture shows up in a surprising place. Artists who paint, draw, sculpt, or engrave portraits can't influence their creations. Artistry belongs instead to their models. At the other end of the history of the novel, in Richardson's fiction, plastic portraiture has an emblematic failure.

There is a lot of excellent criticism of *Clarissa*. However, since critics tend to write about the same controversial passages, much of the text has escaped commentary. There are some basic facts about this novel that I know and, it seems, no one else does. I am going to share a few of them with you.

There are several paintings of Clarissa Harlowe in the house at Harlowe Place. Midway through the novel *Clarissa*, the portraits are removed from view, covered, and enclosed; at the very end, in her will, they are released and distributed outside of the Harlowe family. In Bella Harlowe's letter renouncing her sister, every image either made by or representing Clarissa is deaccessioned: "They are all taken down, and thrown into your closet, which will be nailed up as though it were not part of the house; there to perish together, for who can bear to see them?" (509).

The repeated identification of one of the paintings as "a full-length picture in the Vandyke taste" may sound overspecific, but the scale distinguishes it from a miniature done by a "famous Italian master," and the style distinguishes it from another full-length portrait commissioned by Clarissa's grandfather. As in James's fiction, the paintings do not have value as art in the usual sense. No one has an aesthetic response to the paintings; no one judges the artistry of the painters. Even the fame and mastery of the Italian master seem to have no remarkable effects. The only effect of these images is to refer to Clarissa.

The association of these paintings with Clarissa torments the Harlowes, but they do not try to get the whole-length portrait and the other things out of the house, either by sending them to their lost daughter or selling them, or, on the other hand, by destroying them. Nor do they repurpose the rooms that she used to occupy, furnishing them with new paintings and decorations. They make the images disappear by sealing them in rooms, and they make the rooms disappear by pretending that they do not exist. For the Harlowes the point is not just to avoid the unbearable sight of these images but to keep from seeing them by accident, so that, without adequate preparation, they would not suddenly find themselves staring at Clarissa's whole-length picture. For the pictures and the needlework, the plan seems to be a passive work of destruction, as though works of art would eventually perish as a consequence of not being looked at.

What motivates this neglect? What do the Harlowes imagine they can do to things, or to themselves, by not seeing? There may be some things in Richardson's universe that depend on constant surveillance in order to exist at all, and feed on particular responses, such as wonder and amazement, in order to flourish. These are the objects called, in Richardson's vocabulary, "glare," "splendor," and "blaze." The word "blaze" suggests both heraldic display and the mode of Petrarchist lyric in which Lovelace engages when, hundreds of pages into the narrative, he finally describes Clarissa's body. His conventional blazon divides her body into parts, zones, and itemizes the beauties of each one. All of these terms suggest a quality of light that aggressively demands the attention of a beholder. This light dazzles the eye, making it impossible to observe anything else.

Bella attributes this quality of light to her sister, "the celebrated, blazing Clarissa," exactly one sentence before detailing the fate of her portrait, which, removed from view, will literally starve for attention (509). Her brother James thinks that all women value this quality of light; their minds, he says, are "determined by glare and splendour" (110). (Most characters, however, associate "splendor" and "ostentation" not with Clarissa but rather with the Harlowe family as a group.) Charlotte Harlowe describes relations within the family as a competition for the highest degree of brightness, which Clarissa traditionally wins. The superiority of the favorite daughter "ornaments" the family, "reflecting honor" on it, but also causes her siblings to fall into neglect: "They confessed themselves eclipsed without envying the eclipser" (584). Anna Howe similarly distinguishes Clarissa as the "sun" of the Harlowe family, but without allowing the rest of the family the dubious compensation of reflected light; Clarissa is simply a "star" and the others are "a family of faint twinklers" (129).

Light is one of the meanings of Clarissa's name. Clarity. Transparency. Enlightenment. (This is an obvious thing to say, but I don't think any student of Richardson's novels has said it before. So obvious is this fact that characters make jokes about it. For example, Clarissa, trying to enlist her aunt to intervene on her behalf, offers to produce an "éclaircissement" of the circumstances in which she was compelled to leave home.) Her name identifies her as a figure of enlightenment. This is also the explicit theme of the poem she sets to music, the refrain of which is, "Source of Intellectual Light."

In all of her artistic endeavors, in her music, in her drawings and embroidery, in acting as a model for paintings, Clarissa is consistently a secondary rather than primary maker of culture. In creating a musical setting for a poem, she is not a poet or composer but an arranger; similarly, she is the author of a book of criticism, a collection of observations on tragedy. Here is the exact quotation. In a letter to Anna Howe, Clarissa refers to "the little book you made me write on the principal acting plays" (640). Critics should take note, because the existence of this little book is something we can be proud of. She is one of us. A critic!

Is enlightenment light all glare and splendor, like the harsh light of truth to which the inhabitants of Plato's cave unwillingly expose their eyes? (Because they do not want to be blinded, not even by the truth?) No. Clarissa's practice as a literary critic is iconoclastic. Instead of replacing the primary text with a convenient image, she illuminates it, makes it obvious. The voice in Clarissa's song carefully distinguishes between what she calls "the glittering toys" of "gems, plumes, and blooms" exposed by "the blaze" or "beam of day," and a different, gentle, "steady ray" in which all objects become available to a "clear, discerning eye" (232–34). Her goal, proclaimed in the motto "rather useful than glaring" (40), is to act as a certain quality of light. Not to be an object illuminated by light, not to produce images or to be an image, not to reflect blindingly off objects, but to be the light itself in which you see things.

# Invasion of the body snatchers

The Harlowe family's treatment of the pictures roughly parallels their usage of Clarissa. The terms of Clarissa's confinement in the first movement of the novel include the instruction to move through the house only by the "back-stairs" intended for servants, "that the sight of so perverse a young creature may not add to the pain you have given everybody" (121). When Clarissa's apartment is being disfurnished and the pictures distributed to her heirs, Colonel Morden describes his relatives tracing the same path through their house, "making use of the less convenient back-stairs, that they may avoid passing by the doors of her apartment" (1447). The novel begins with Clarissa moving so as not to be seen and ends with her family moving so as not to see.

In the essential dramatic situation of *Clarissa*, a mother regards her daughter and denies the relationship. "Is this Clarissa?" "Can this . . . be from you?" (96). The problem that Charlotte Harlowe encounters in her daughter's image is not a telling defect in iconic resemblance. She recognizes the image before her as her daughter's. It looks just like her daughter. And yet, without being able to identify any feature that seems even slightly off, she asks what she is looking at. Antony Harlowe has the same problem: "My uncle came up to me, looking up to my face, and down to my feet: And is it possible this can be you?" (307). In a once-over, from the face to the feet, the body perfectly matches its description. Nothing happens to thwart Antony Harlowe's recognition of his niece except that he refuses to identify her.

To take the measure of these scenes, I want to paraphrase Jalal Toufic's description of *Invasion of the Body Snatchers* as a scenario of failed portraiture (Toufic 2001, 209–26). I recognize my daughter. But I judge that recognition to be unsatisfactory. This is not my daughter. It is a false portrait. A perfect copy—too perfect. A changeling. A pod. The only excuse for the Harlowe family's usage of their daughter is that she is not really their daughter—because, if she were, she would be more obedient. Only if she passes every test of connoisseurship and proves herself "worthy of the name," will she be the daughter of the Harlowes (93). Conversely, their only possible excuse is that she must be their daughter, because who else would submit to this treatment?

The question is not whether she is a pod but whose pod she is. The Harlowes are certain that she is not theirs but Lovelace's, that she is "prepossessed" in his favor. For her part, Clarissa's excuse for disobeying her parents is that they are not her authentic mother and father. She owes obedience to her father and mother, not her brother and sister, who have "engaged" her parents with "leading wires" (96), and now speak both through them and through "public talk": "The authors of my disgrace within doors, the talkers of my prepossession without, and the reporters of it from abroad, were originally the same persons" (108). When you talk to me, it isn't your voice that I hear. Instead I hear my brother's voice. And he may not be my brother. At least, Clarissa is not ready to declare her recognition of her brother. She only goes this far: "I would be glad, sir . . . to understand that you are my brother" (57). She recognizes him as her brother and wants to affirm that recognition, but her judgment resists and finds him "unbrotherly" (57).

Lovelace encourages a reading in which Lovelace is the only human being in the community of the novel, and everyone else is a pod, manipulated and therefore replaced by him. "Her brother and uncle were but my pioneers, her father stormed as I directed him to storm" (517), and even Anna Howe, he says, "is herself a puppet danced upon my wires, at second or third hand" (464). Even Clarissa, on this account, may be merely an extension of Lovelace, at least in the moment when she unbolts the door to the summer-house, and, Lovelace writes, "I was sure of her," sure, that is to say, that he can get her to leave home against her will.

Sandra Macpherson's first great essay on the novel takes this reading as far as it can go. Lovelace establishes a limited liability corporation to distribute complicity so that even though he may be the only character in the novel and therefore responsible for all that happens in its pages, he is nonetheless not at fault for the consequences of the actions of this monstrous single entity. This reading even extends beyond the novel's covers. When some readers put the book down, it comes after them. For, according to Macpherson, any critic who uses the word "elopement" to refer to Lovelace's abduction of Clarissa is also a pod of Lovelace's (Macpherson 1998, 116n15).

# The Richardsonian lie

Why has no one written an essay called "The Richardsonian Lie"? The conceit of this section is that I am doing so. To my colleagues this labor may appear unnecessary. Don't the earliest and most perceptive criticisms of *Clarissa* define the achievement of this novel as a lie that, unknown to itself, tells the truth?

I will recall a few of the fine phrases from this great critical tradition. Here is Samuel Johnson: "There is always something which she prefers to truth" (Piozzi, 1.281). In a conversation reported by Hester Piozzi, Johnson notes Clarissa's habitual equivocations. He may be referring to the absurd pretexts that she invents and repeats to justify her correspondence with Lovelace, or her reluctance to claim possession of the estate left to her in her grandfather's will, or her reserve in entertaining Lovelace's proposals of marriage, or the mental contortions by which she avoids accusing herself of disobedience and her mother of callousness. Johnson views the bad faith of these statements as a character flaw and therefore as a flaw in the form of the novel, the responsibility and stated ambition of which is to posit an ideal, "an exemplar to her sex," by way of her character (Richardson 1986, xiv). Clarissa insufficiently embodies a virtue deserving of a reward.

Now here is Diderot: "He [Richardson] it is who lights the depths of the cavern with his torch; he it is who teaches you to detect the cunning, dishonest motives concealed and hidden from our sight beneath other, honest motives, which are always the first to show themselves" (Diderot 1994, 83). Diderot's interpretation does not exactly disagree with Johnson's. The difference is that Diderot judges the habit of lying as part of the structure of the novel and its supreme achievement. Richardson "lights the depths of the cavern" to reveal a violent, terrible love whose object is equally violent. The text of the letters sublimates this love, which could never survive the ascent to the level of consciousness, but is at the same time "richly menaced" by it, to borrow Bersani's phrase (Bersani 1976, 131).

To some degree this reading is inarguable. Richardson does everything possible to suggest that Clarissa unconsciously wants Lovelace. The Harlowes are all convinced that she is "prepossessed" in his favor, and maybe, just maybe, in this one instance, they are paying attention and reading her correctly. Anna teases her for "throbs," tones of admiration, language of praise, and for the funny logic of her decisions. Even Belford, when he first sees Clarissa, observes that her looks express a conflict between love and fear of Lovelace. Clarissa herself acknowledges the prepossession, although in her correspondence with Anna she frames the acknowledgment as a purely tactical measure. Nonetheless, a countertradition represented by readers such as Castle, Eagleton, and Macpherson demonstrates that the novel does not become less interesting if readers take Clarissa at her word when she says that she does not want Lovelace.

I have always felt that Richardson's real psychological insight is not the illumination of hidden motives. You know, everyone has a sense that Richardson knew something about psychology. He studied the human heart and he learned something. I feel the truth of what he learned too. Richardson understood exactly one true thing about the human heart. What he understood was a fear of rhetoric. The basic principle of psychology in his novels is a universal belief in and consequent fear of rhetorical power.

The power attributed to the gesture of kneeling will provide a convenient example. In a meeting with her family that does not come off, because, contrary to her resolution, she leaves Harlowe Place, Clarissa intends to kneel to each member of her family in turn, and, by kneeling, triumph.

> I will kneel to each, one by one, to make a friend. They have been afraid, some of them, to see me, lest they should be moved in my favour; does not this give me a reasonable hope that I may move them?

> **(361–62)**

Unbeknownst to Clarissa, her father has devised exactly the same plan:

> I will kneel to her, if nothing else will do, to prevail upon her to oblige me!

> **(504)**

When she later hears about this plan, she is struck by the probable consequences:

> A father to KNEEL to a daughter!—There would not indeed have been any bearing of that. . . . I had deserved annihilation had I suffered my father to kneel in vain.

> **(506)**

> How should I have resisted a condescending, a kneeling father?

> **(507)**

Note, on both sides, the confidence in the power of the rhetorical gesture, the fear each has of the other's power, and the intuition each has of the other's fear. The upshot is that the same gesture of submission that Clarissa believes might have released her from the obligation to obey her parents' commands, she also believes, if directed at her, would compel her to follow their commands.

But here's the thing. The characters in this novel constantly kneel to one another, and it never has any effect. Or its effect on every audience is to be viewed and scorned as an empty rhetorical gesture, a bid for power in the guise of submission. When Clarissa kneels to her mother, as she always does when in her presence, kneeling has no useful effect. Her mother sees her posture as pure rhetoric and despises her "limbs so supple" that belie a "will so stubborn" (103) or instructs her that her "heart, not the knees, must bend" (89).

Meanwhile, in the same scene, Clarissa wonders if her mother is "capable of art" (97). Each character believes herself to be unfairly manipulated by the other character's pure rhetoric. Charlotte Harlowe looks at her kneeling daughter and accuses her of playing a rhetorical trick. Clarissa looks back at her and wonders, could mother be using art?

In other scenes, Clarissa sees in Lovelace what her mother sees in her: that he has "too-ready knees" (166, 653). Lovelace is hurt, not because it isn't true that he is kneeling without feeling, but because he can't understand why the gesture doesn't have a seductive effect. Although the characters believe in the efficacy of kneeling, so that both Clarissa and Lovelace fear what might happen if one kneeled to the other, there is no evidence to suggest that it ever works on any audience.

Why are the characters afraid of devices that have exerted no influence within living memory? As Wendy Lee argues in a brilliant essay, the moral ideal for the characters in *Clarissa* seems to be a position of emotional "indifferency," stoniness. Why do they compete for a position that everyone already seems to enjoy? "Teach me, some power, the happy art of speech," Lovelace writes, transcribing lines from Rowe (736). He, like the Harlowes, wants to harness this uncanny power. Only Clarissa, "reluctant to use art," abjures it (122). Everyone fears it.

So deep does this fear run in all of Richardson's characters that it leads them to suspect their own affective responses because they may be the result of someone's unfair rhetorical manipulation. "No one could help feeling affected by your pathetic grief," Bella says in response to Clarissa's dying wish for a blessing, "but that . . . was your talent" (1322). "What was there in what was read," her brother asks of the same communication, "but the result of the talent you had of moving the passions?" (1323). I feel a raging tenderness for you. But can I be certain that this tenderness is really what I am feeling? What if this tenderness is not my feeling at all but rather something that you are doing to me with your damned art? And why won't you stop doing that?

The term "art" conjoins the failures of eloquence and the failures of portraiture. If portraiture succeeds, then it becomes rhetoric, and rhetoric becomes a new, frightening game. Art, I would say, is Richardson's lie. The threat of art in Richardson's novels is the reverse of its promise in James. Whereas James grants his characters the freedom to determine their own images, the first principle of Richardsonian portraiture is the same as the first answer in the catechism. This is the basis for Goodman Andrews's warning to his daughter not to trust that her own strength will be sufficient to resist temptation, because "you did not make yourself."

# Real or personal?

"And is this all!—Is it all of my CLARISSA'S story!" (1402). Viewing the dead body of her friend, Anna Howe apprehends it as a totality, "all," but not as a unity, because it represents less than "half" of her "excellence" (1403). After a million words exchanged in correspondence, her appetite for this story remains unsatisfied. She has outlasted even Richardson's stamina as novelist.

Terry Castle has taught us to read the question "Is this all?" as the culmination of a pattern of interruptions. Clarissa has never been able to realize her intentions in the world; someone always stands in her way, stopping her before she can complete her thoughts as speech or action. A verbal motif establishes this pattern by repeatedly cutting her in half (Castle 1982, 33–35). Her mother goes out of the room, "and I thought the better half of my heart went with her" (180). Lovelace is full, "full of tender despondency," and Clarissa is no more than half-full, "half-concerned . . . for him" (Richardson 1986, 377).

Somehow the corpse is both all and not even half. How can this be so? And what *is* the other half? The half that is worse or smaller? (Can a part that is greater or lesser can still rightly be called a half?) The half that is not "concerned" (to add a third half)? Is Clarissa's composition always the same in quantity, divided into two roughly equal parts, or does each new division imply a subdivision, reducing her to half of what she was before?

Even if Anna Howe could answer these questions, even if she had the second half and the third half, the inclusion of this information would not contribute unity to the novel. Complete representation of a person would have the opposite effect of undoing unity. All of a person is not all of a story. In fact, "all" of a story is less than "half" of Clarissa's excellence. The complaint in the form of a question "Is this all?" describes a failure of complete representation. Clarissa's corpse is formally closed; it has a form because it does not completely represent her.

Exactly the same descriptive figure applies to the entire community of the novel. Looking at her mother, Clarissa discerns "half a sigh . . . as if she would not have sighed could she have helped it" (102). Lovelace's seeming frankness in confessing his errors in conduct only indicates, Clarissa writes, "that he may think it policy to give up one half of his character to save the other" (184). She wants to know what happens to things when you cut them in half—or Richardson does, since these half-constructions are in no way limited to Clarissa's letters. "The greatest half of my wickedness is vapour," Lovelace writes, making a cut that divides a quantity into two unequal parts, both of which he persists in describing as "halves" (464).

The fragmentation of Richardson's characters is best understood as a fact about character itself. The function of incomplete form in characterization is a familiar topic in studies of the novel—think of Catherine Gallagher's "Nobodies," Franco Moretti's vortices of culture, and Kent Puckett's "social mistakes." These are all names for the fragmentary appearance of character, which takes parts for wholes. There are other, traditional names: the form of character in writing is called a sketch; the form of character in performance is called a part. Character operates by synecdoche so that one example of a kind includes the complete collection of examples.

When Overbury tries to say "what a character is," one of his suggestions is a choice between "real or personal" pictures. Maybe one of the halves of Clarissa is real and the other half is personal. A real character is a figure of absolute reality; a personal one would be merely biographical. This is the meaning that "personal" has when satirists such as Jonson, Molière, and Swift disavow any personal application, any key, to specify the historical objects they depict. They insist that their interest is in what they call the "world" or "nature," but not in any single thing. Molière has one of his characters speak on his behalf in the *Versailles impromptu*: the goal is "to paint manners without touching persons" [sans vouloir toucher aux personnes], and the artist would be "distressed" [fâché] to have "marked out" any individual (scene 4). A real character represents the totality of examples of a kind, whereas a personal character completely represents a person.

Theatrical performances drive apart the real and the personal. In the event of a performance, a single actor substitutes a unique human body for the multitude of other bodies that share the same qualities. The others come into view in the entire history of performance, in the many rehearsals and reprises that a company of actors must endure in repertory, and in the variety of actors cast in the same roles in different stagings. Performance reveals itself as performance, putting the who of the actor and the what of the character on display so as to distinguish them, in the not at all special cases that observe an uneconomical rule of performance, such as the parsimonious one that calls on one actor to play more than one character, or the extravagant one that enlists several actors to play a single character.

To take an example from a canonical play, in the long tavern scene from *1 Henry IV*, the actors playing Hal and Falstaff also play Henry IV. In the most conventional staging of this scene, both the abundance of the character and the transformation of the actor are simultaneously on display, as the actor playing Hal also plays his father, the actor playing Falstaff also plays Henry IV and Hal, and both actors collaborate on epideictic sketches of Falstaff's character.

The realist novel inverts this procedure by setting character, which posits an ideal, against portraiture, which, with its own idealism, posits a unique human image. The novel is concerned with individuation, as literary historians including Auerbach, Van Ghent, and Watt have shown. Only I would make this adjustment: the novel is concerned to see it fail. Remember the first line of Shakespeare's song: "Who is Sylvia? What is she?" Proteus's musicians move quickly to replace who with what, the personal with the real. Similarly, in place of a recognizably human image, and in place of the image of a particular member of human society, the novel substitutes character.

# Emotional fuckwittage

In Richardson's novels, portraiture spectacularly fails; in Austen's, it fails daily, mundanely, moment by moment. Austen takes the failure of portraiture from Richardson's novels and both enlarges and banalizes it into an unrelentingly bleak vision of human society. If James's characters invariably receive accurate impressions of their fellow characters and appreciate them and go, "Ah," Austen's characters invariably make mistakes. (This series of mistakes is the plot of *Emma*, for example.) Sometimes, as an adaptation, they learn to enjoy the mistakes.

I am just starting to learn how to read Austen's novels. Two other writers have helped to open them up for me. The first is the popular novelist Helen Fielding, whose book *Bridget Jones's Diary* is sort of an adaptation of *Pride and Prejudice*. Her novel is only indirectly based on Austen's and directly based on the BBC serial. The two novels don't quite touch, but they are connected by television and by the idea of a national viewership that turns Bridget on.

Fielding gets at least one thing right about Austen, and that's one more thing than I used to be able to get. Her concept of emotional fuckwittage names a form of pretend relationship. I pretend we're going out; you pretend not to notice. A pretend relationship. Or you pretend we're *not* going out; I pretend not to notice. A pretend relationship. That's not my girlfriend; that's the woman I'm sleeping with who *thinks* she's my girlfriend. Emotional fuckwittage. From watching *Pride and Prejudice* on television Bridget learns that impressions are invariably mistakes and relations are at least awkward and sometimes excruciatingly painful.

The second writer who has helped me to read Austen is D. W. Harding. Readers have sensed for a long time that there is something not very nice in Austen's novels. To put it bluntly, as Harding does in his classic essay "Regulated Hatred," Austen wrote novels to be "read and enjoyed by precisely the sort of people she disliked" (Harding 1998, 6). This claim, which he deftly unfolds for each of the six major novels, is useful in a few different ways.

First, it acknowledges the many readers who experience the schizophrenic feeling that Austen is addressing them directly. Harding both gives back this special relationship and takes it away. Yes, he affirms, Austen is writing just for you. It's because she hates you.

Second, it brings to light Austen's deep interest in hatred. How many statements in her novels begin with the phrase, "I hate." "I hate an open carriage." One might even speculate that positive feelings in her novels, including the perfect happiness that her conclusions invariably defer, are only tertiary hybrids generated out of the interaction of several fundamental bad feelings. Like the pleasure of remembering pain. Or like the "angry pleasure" that you experience when your anger makes you notice that you are still alive and have a capacity to be enraged.

Third, it accounts for Austen's unlikely conservatism. Harding writes that Austen, by her own intention, "is a literary classic of the society which attitudes like hers, held widely enough, would undermine" (Harding 1998, 6). In other words, if everyone believed what Austen believed, there would be revolution. But they don't. And there isn't. And that is her project!

In this extraordinary formulation, Harding goes beyond even Trilling, who, in a controversial passage from *Sincerity and Authenticity*, compares Austen to Robespierre (Trilling 1972, 68). The point of Trilling's comparison is to remind us that we don't exactly know what society would look like if Austen had been made its omnipotent governor. The point of Harding's description is to say frankly that we do know what it would look like, because it would look exactly like English society in her lifetime. She wouldn't change a thing. No one is more aware than Austen of the systematic and incidental unfairness of her social organization, and she supports it in every specific instance.

From Fielding I take the idea that Austen's characters get off on manipulating their emotions; from Harding I take the idea of regulation. I want to use these ideas to characterize the key terms from the title *Sense and Sensibility* and then to identify a third term, an overlooked form of emotional fuckwittage that links the first two.

Austen introduces the key terms in character sketches of Elinor and Marianne. She defines sense as a knowledge of "how to govern" strong feelings, sensibility as a condition of "no moderation" in feeling (Austen 2008, 6). The weight of historical context on both terms (in the first place, common sense, enlightenment rationalism; in the second, the romantic cult of sensibility) has sometimes obscured how they operate in the community of the novel and how they configure the characters to which they are assigned. Both are forms of sensitivity that exclude physical sensation and psychological experience. They are not feelings or even capacities for feeling. They are emotional in the way Gertrude Stein means when she says that "paragraphs are emotional; sentences are not." That is, they are emotional because they limit or regulate emotion. This psychological configuration separates person from feeling. There's the part of you that feels, but that's not you. The real you stands outside of the feeling and controls it either by repressing it or by encouraging it.

Here's how it works for Elinor.

> "I do not attempt to deny," said she, "that I think very highly of him—that I greatly esteem, that I like him." Marianne here burst forth with indignation—"Esteem him! Like him! Cold-hearted Elinor! Oh! Worse than cold-hearted! Ashamed of being otherwise."

**(14)**

This passage is both an instance of sense in action and a critique of sense by sensibility. Sense is either coldhearted (and proud of it) or deceitful (and equally proud). (Here, again, pride, a positive feeling, appears as a product of a feedback system that sets negative feelings against themselves.)

Marianne is right. The claim that Elinor "likes" and "esteems" but is not "attached" to Edward is a deliberate lie. Elinor comes close to admitting that she is lying when she invites her sister to "believe" that her feelings are "stronger than I have declared." The narrator confirms that Edward and Elinor have "mutual" feelings of "regard" and "attachment." Yet the narrator also endorses the lie as Elinor's "real opinion": "Elinor had given her real opinion to her sister" (15). How can this be? The person that Elinor really is is not the person who feels but the person who responds to the feeling and controls it.

I can be more specific about the technique of control. Elinor's first move in any situation is to lie. To her is given "the whole task of telling lies when politeness required it" (92). Her life's work is "to command herself to guard every suspicion of the truth from her mother and sisters" (104). This is the ideal Elinor projects and the mode of conduct she recommends.

There is one more layer of disingenuousness. Elinor lies about her feelings. For the purposes of ordinary conversation, she expects the rest of the world to treat her lies as statements of fact. But she also expects her friends to know that she is lying. Thus she speaks resentfully when they take her at her word. She admits her impossible expectation that others should be able to discern her carefully hidden feelings when she says that her operations on feeling are concerned only with "behavior" and are not "aimed at the subjection of the understanding" (72). Her resentment at the belief in her pretense of being unfeeling is most clearly expressed in a long confidential speech to Marianne that catalogues her sufferings and ends by describing the curious fantasy that she has yet to describe them: "Perhaps nothing could have kept me entirely . . . from openly showing that I was very unhappy" (199).

Is resentment the right word? Elinor's rhetoric may not primarily be expressive. It might be more accurately described as a transfer of the entire weight of suffering from Elinor to Marianne. Or perhaps this is best described as not a rhetoric at all but rather a kind of therapy. Maybe this is another example of what sense tries to do. Maybe the fantasy that Elinor has never acknowledged her suffering makes her effectively deaf to the paragraph of suffering that she has just spoken. Maybe this brilliant lie gives Elinor the benefit of exerting her sense while being an object of pity for her sister.

The lesson Mrs. Dashwood finally learns is not the practical knowledge to apply Elinor's techniques to her own feelings but a key to interpreting Elinor's accounts of herself. "She now found that she had erred in relying on Elinor's representations of herself" (270). The hermeneutic is to assume that Elinor is always lying.

Only Marianne seems to approach Elinor's lies as a rhetoric, or, in other words, a psychology directed outward and concerned primarily with effects on an audience. The terms that Elinor and the narrator prefer are "exertion" and "self-command," both of which indicate an imperative of personal transformation. Elinor "commands herself" (30–31). She "composes herself" (99). She "determines to subdue her feelings" (78), and she does. The governance of feeling actually means self-discipline. An inward-directed pressure that shapes, alters, and even destroys what she feels.

To put it another way, sense internalizes the techniques for composing and displaying the outermost surfaces of the person, particularly the face and clothing, that Aphra Behn calls "management." (The foil for Elinor, Lucy Steele, who functions as a negative image of sense, is called an "active, contriving manager" [271]. Elinor and Lucy are the same character in different modes. Two examples of the same type, sense.)

How deep a divide does sense make between person and feeling? Not only do the techniques of sense obfuscate what one feels but they diminish feelings to a point where they no longer feel. Sense means pretending that you have no feelings. Until you really don't.

Sensibility has the same structure. It separates the person who feels from the real person who disciplines feeling. "Her sensibility was potent enough!" (63). Which is to say that sensibility is a kind of power, like sense, a form of self-government. Her character, the ideal she projects, is neither the preformatted feeling nor the formatted feeling but rather the part that formats the feeling. One aspect of sensibility is prohibitive, making the absence of marks of feeling "shameful," "inexcusable," "disgraceful" (63); its positive, productive aspect is "indulgence of feeling," "gaining" of sadness, and "courting of misery" (63). We are not talking about an absence of regulation. For Marianne, the point is to give power to expression, a complex and difficult intervention in psychology.

The excess of feeling makes sensibility appear to be a promising site for intersubjectivity. Marianne fantasizes that her lover "must enter into all my feelings." But she always keeps in mind the impossibility of realizing the fantasy: "I am convinced that I shall never see a man whom I can really love" (14). The rejection of the possibility of intersubjectivity is related to a running joke noted by Eve Kosofsky Sedgwick in which Marianne, the figure of sensibility, is described as "insensible" to her environment (Sedgwick 1993, 119–20).

Marianne's insensibility is more than a joke; it's a definition of the work of sensibility. She actively cultivates an indifference to the feelings of her friends. When she says of Elinor that "she has not my feelings," the meaning is a little ambiguous. Maybe Elinor doesn't feel what Marianne feels. Marianne makes similar statements about Colonel Brandon and about the imaginary 27-year-old woman whose feelings "diminish" as she grows older. They have feelings, but not the kind that Marianne has. Or maybe Elinor doesn't feel—at all. That is what Marianne says about Mrs. Jennings: "She cannot feel" (150).

This is the ultimate form of sensibility: idiopathy, the claim that one's feelings are incommunicable because other people have no capacity for them. At Norwood the "happy house" and trees "will continue the same . . . but who will remain to enjoy you?" If Marianne is not present, the things that remain are houses, trees, and people who feel less than the houses and trees.

Edward teases Marianne for her insensibility to other people's feelings by imagining that, given a legacy, she would use her wealth to purchase multiple copies of her favorite books "to prevent their falling into unworthy hands" (70). Edward's "sauciness" isn't even a joke, since many scenes in the novel show Marianne doing exactly that—for example, taking Elinor's screens away from the Ferrars family because they are incapable of "admiring them as they ought to be admired" (177). Her sensibility may be defined as the belief that others have no feelings.

There is a third term between sense and sensibility, doing the work of "and" in the title. This is the mysterious idea of comfort. Unlike the other terms, comfort is unregulated. It occupies both the position of preformatted feeling and the desired result of pretending that you have no feelings or denying that other people have feelings. Thus Elinor "could not deny herself the comfort" of "exerting her sense," and Marianne indulges the "exquisite comfort" of an unrepresentable misery (106, 238).

Comfort does not individuate but holds together the entire community of the novel. It is not assigned to a solitary character or even to a family such as the Dashwoods, who monopolize the novel's allegorical energy. "How few people know what comfort is!" says Mr. Palmer. But his attempts to limit the concept of comfort to a single kind of object, a billiard room, can't be sustained in a novel where the other examples of objectified comforts include houses, silverware, china, preserved olives, dried cherries, and Constantia wine.

There are two ways to understand how the ordinary household objects on this list embody comfort. First, comfort may be the barely perceptible feeling of using or possessing an object that one takes for granted. The billiard room is where you expect to find it, in the part of the house where you built it at home. The fork is in its place setting or in its drawer, exactly where you put your hand. Second, comfort may be the impossible experience of being such an instrument or possession. In both cases comfort is different from the regulatory devices of self-command or self-indulgence. Comfort is what you command, the material mechanized by the command.

Like composure, comfort oscillates between holding and being held. "Yet when I thought of her today as really dying, it was a kind of comfort to imagine that I knew exactly how she would appear to those, who saw her last in the world" (248). To Willoughby, the image of Marianne's "sweet face white as death" is "a kind of comfort." What kind? I can specify this astonishing refinement of the concept, because Willoughby shares it with Colonel Brandon. (Only Claudia Johnson seems to have noticed the language they share [Johnson 1972, 67–68].) This vision of a dying woman's face is in fact "the greatest comfort": "That she was, to all appearance, in the last stage of a consumption," Brandon says, speaking of his first love, "yes, in such a situation it was my greatest comfort" (155).

The greatest comfort is watching someone die—if it's the person you love most in the world. The intensity of this comfort is not like the tertiary hybrid of bad feelings that you experience as a better feeling, not like the pain experienced as nostalgia, a reminder that you are alive and can still feel pain. Rather the greatest comfort is the extinction of something that can cause you the most pain because you put most of your care into it. What remains is a world of indifferent objects, and that is comfort. In fact comfort is "better than you deserve," to use the phrase that Austen typically substitutes for a happy ending in order to register the profound unfairness of a society that she nonetheless supports completely.

# Depicturing the gothic novel

Realist novels typically begin by assuming that portraiture can't succeed. They proceed by proving it. The failure of portraiture is a framing device distinguishing the novel's fiction from the human lifeworld.

The gothic subgenre is dedicated to what the character Caleb Williams, in William Godwin's novel of the same name, calls "the other side of the picture" (122). In gothic it becomes possible to make a person successfully, as in *Frankenstein*. The convention of successful portraiture is emblematized by a familiar trope in which figures in portraits step out of their frames and act and speak (*Otranto*), or characters fall in love with figures in portraits (*The Monk*), or painted images change in response to actions and events (*Melmoth*), or characters find themselves depicted in paintings and manuscripts (*The Romance of the Forest*). To name this trope, I borrow the term "depicture," which is nothing more than an old spelling of depict. A framed portrait is pictured, and a portrait stepping out of its frame is depictured.

The word "depicture" is a cornerstone in the vocabulary of Radcliffe's novels. It can simply be used to mean: make a picture, draw, represent. This is what it seems to mean in the following passage from *Udolpho*, where a "sumptuous tapestry . . . depictured scenes from the antient Provençal romances" (Radcliffe 1998, 469). The stunted ekphrasis of this passage, which develops the narrative of the Provençal romances no further than the vague word "scenes," suggests the utter conventionality of the genre. Gothic novels introduce no new ideas, but repeat the scenes depicted in earlier novels, finally pointing to ancient sources in other media.

Another passage refers to "the complacency and ease of healthy age, depictured on the countenance of La Voisin" (90), and seems to use the word in the same sense. La Voisin's face expresses what he feels and shows a picture of what he is: the idea of "healthy age" itself, and all the qualities pertaining to this idea. Applied to a tapestry, "depicture" names the defining function of the tapestry, which is a narrative picture. Applied to part of the body of La Voisin, his countenance, "depicture" aestheticizes him, reduces him to an instrument for expressing an ideal.

A third use of "depicture" has a different sense not covered by any of the ordinary definitions. Blanche, in fantasy, "represents," that is, imagines, "a very lovely prospect . . . and she stood for some time, surveying the grey obscurity and depicturing imaginary woods and mountains, vallies and rivers, on this scene of night" (471). This is strange. "Depicture," like "represent" above, has a subjective as well as an objective sense. The tapestry shows an image, and La Voisin's face shows an idea, that would be available to any observer, but the prospect that Blanche sees in the "grey obscurity" is "imaginary," visible only to her. The same could be said, in retrospect, of the other instances of depicturing. Blanche encounters the gothic tapestry in the same dim light, "too dark to distinguish" the scenes from "antient romance." How does she know that they illustrate an old story that may be the source for her conventionally predictable adventure? By depicturing, that is, imagining it to be present although not apparent.

The dual sense of "depicture" may be considered roughly the opposite of the romantic project of coalescence of subject and object. Instead of regarding a scene and imaginatively projecting oneself into it, to feel what it might be like to be a ravine or a tree, depicturing toggles anxiously between subjective and objective, so that Emily and Blanche in *Udolpho* are unable to determine whether they are looking at a mental projection or an object in the built or geographical environment.

It seems to me that "depicture" already has a specialized sense in Radcliffe's novels. Radcliffe uses "depicture" to activate a mood in which the frame separating inside and outside has been erased. I also intend "depicturing" as analogous to Marjorie Levinson's notion of "picturing": a kind of "looking that resists reading or knowing" (Levinson 2000, 195). Depicturing blurs levels of reality: inside and outside, mind and world, art and nature.

Critics have often associated Godwin's novel *Caleb Williams* with the gothic genre without being able to specify why, since this anomalous novel seems to fulfill none of the requirements of a genre whose conventions are, as Sedgwick puts it, so thoroughly "coherent" as to seem almost unvarying. Godwin's novel presents a materialist, mechanistic universe, with no room for the machinery of high spirituality (gods, devils), low spirituality (ghosts), or organized religion (monasteries). Even the psychology is based on natural causation, with the single exception of the unmotivated aversion that several characters conceive for Caleb. (One possible implication is that this aversion, too, has a cause, which Caleb is reluctant to trace, since he is doing something to provoke it.)

*Caleb Williams* also refuses the conventional foreign settings of Italy and Spain. The plot actually begins in Italy, where Falkland's early triumph reenacts an episode from *Grandison*, then returns to England as though to demonstrate that the novel occupies no single location. "Sure," says the impoverished Hawkins, "I arn't a cabbage, that if you pull it out of the ground it must die" (Godwin 2005, 120). Characters in most gothic novels are cabbages in Hawkins's sense. They are attached to plots of ground, deriving energy from fixed points in geographical and architectural space. Buildings are felicitous in that they suggest and bind certain actions.

(I take the term "felicitous" from Fritz Lang's film *Secret Beyond the Door*, where Michael Redgrave plays an architect who collects "felicitous rooms," which he defines as rooms where the design influences human behavior. He turns out to mean rooms where murders were committed. His second definition could be generic. Gothic is first a style in architecture, then a literary genre where architecture is destiny.)

Caleb, however, is surprisingly mobile. To describe the gothic element in the novel, then, critics have had to rely on tone, mood, a paranoid atmosphere. What if the convention identifying *Caleb Williams* as gothic was the trope of depicturing? Then its special problem would not be creating a unique human image, which happens without much effort, but the "other side" of the problem, which is how do you tell the difference? Assuming that you could successfully make a human image, what distinguishes that image from a human creature in life and history?

It is tempting to reply that determining the limits of the human does not seem to be a difficult problem in this novel. Grimes, for example, is "scarcely human," with "features" that are "coarse," and "strangely discordant and disjointed" (50). He is equipped with a human body, but its parts are not quite on a human scale, and not quite in the right places; they are scarcely so, which means, I guess, that they fall just within the recognized limits. Caleb describes an unnamed woman as a "witch" in whose veins "the feverous blood of savage ferocity" circulates as opposed to that of "human kindness" (222).

The characters are highly talented, even eloquent, in their efforts to exclude one another from the category of humanity.

> Mr. Tyrrel, I am ashamed of you! . . . To hear you talk gives one a loathing for the institutions and regulations of society, and would induce one to fly the very face of man! But, no! Society casts you out; man abominates you. . . . You will live deserted in the midst of your species; you will go into crowded societies, and no one will deign so much as to salute you. They will fly from your glance as they would from the gaze of a basilisk. Where do you expect to find the hearts of flint that shall sympathize with yours?
>
> (81)

Let me pause to appreciate the generosity of Godwin's novel. You don't have to press Falkland to get him to say that Tyrrel is inhuman. He relishes saying it. Godwin relishes having Falkland say it. He is almost ready to invent new words in his enthusiasm for casting Tyrrell out of human society.

A different character, the motherly Mrs. Jakeman, says exactly the same thing to Tyrell, promising that he "will be obliged to fly the very face of a human creature" (950). Falkland later reiterates the point that Tyrell is "inhuman" (98) and should consider himself lucky, "too happy that you are permitted to fly the face of man" (99) rather than be exterminated.

These passages seem to indicate a clear enough limit. Universal human nature constitutes itself through the exclusion of one individual, Tyrell, in a repeated gesture of mutual nonrecognition. On one side, all human nature, in the form of the face, the human face divine, resolutely turns away from Tyrell, who, on his side, flees the personified abstraction of the one face of all human creatures.

The qualities that exclude Tyrell from humanity are the two meanings of his name: "tyrant," a word that recurs in Caleb's judgments of his behavior. "Perhaps tyranny never exhibited a more painful memorial of the detestation in which it deserves to be held" (93). The other, less obvious meaning, a partial anagram of the name, is "illiterate," which also recurs in the narrative, somewhat less frequently. Tyrell: an illiterate spelling of "illiterate," with a y. The opposite of Falkland, a figure of enlightenment—a very type of Clarissa—Tyrell is illiterate, not in the sense that he can't read or write, but in the old sense that he doesn't speak or write well, properly, beautifully. He is "not undiscerning" (21), but also not literary. He stands for brutality rather than civilization, superstition rather than knowledge.

The stark opposition between the minds of Falkland and Tyrell becomes still more clear in their contrasting views on the constitution of the world. Falkland: "Begone! . . . I will trample you into atoms" (10). Tyrell: "I will tread you to paste!" (74). In both cases, absolute power manifests in a tendency to reduce things to their component parts. The difference is in the scale of the reduction. Falkland, the enlightenment hero, knows that the world is made of atoms, and atoms are indivisible. Tyrell's content analysis seems to refer to some folk wisdom regarding human anatomy. What holds people together? Paste!

In drawing the original limit Falkland is uncertain where to locate himself. He finally decides that "society casts out" Tyrell, but his first impulse is that he, Falkland, enlightened man of a civilized world, should "fly the very face of man," because, presumably, that face is embodied in Tyrell! The image of the "heart of flint" is also open to another interpretation. The interesting idea that a community of "hearts of flint" would "sympathize" with Tyrrel's heart confirms that Tyrell, not Falkland, embodies a human ideal. Lara Bovilsky, in a brilliant study of what she calls "mineral emotions," has taught us to read the trope of the "heart of flint" not as excluding emotion, but rather as an indication of durability. A flinty heart could withstand heavy psychological turmoil better than a fleshy heart.

Tyrell seems to concur. The story he tells is a rewriting of *Clarissa* where, rather than brutality conquering sensitivity, *even the brutal are sensitive.*

Tyrell sees himself, not Falkland, as a type of Clarissa unfairly persecuted by his ward and neighbor. He asks his ward:

> Could I ever inflict upon you such injuries as you have made me suffer? And who are you? The lives of fifty such cannot atone for an hour of my uneasiness. If you were to linger twenty years upon the rack, you would never feel what I have felt.
>
> **(57)**

This speech could be yet another instance of Tyrell's tyranny and selfishness. However, Godwin leaves open the possibility that Tyrell could be telling the truth. Maybe he is much more sensitive than his neighbors and friends, like the woman in *David Copperfield* who feels the same cold as everyone else but "feels it more," or like Mary in *Persuasion*, who suffers from the same sore throat that is going around, only her "sore throats, you know, are worse than anybody's." Tyrell's account of his psychology is idiopathic. His sensitivity is unique, causeless, and incommunicable. In this account, the dynamic of mutual nonrecognition, where humanity constitutes itself by expelling one of its members, easily flips. Tyrell may be the only human being, while the members of the society that "casts him out" and "abominates him" are the brutes.

That's what's so interesting about the trope of the "hearts of flint." The accusation that Tyrell has a heart made of flint could be used to suggest that he lacks a capacity for feelings of any kind. Or it could suggest that he belongs to a society of flint-hearted creatures who feel "sympathies" of which ordinary human beings are not capable. Falkland deaccessions Tyrell's portrait from the human gallery. Tyrell returns the favor. In a society organized by the trope of depicturing, where every image is recognizably human, everyone is desperately trying to establish limits on membership in the human community.

The same applies to Caleb, who is constantly being told that he is a "monster" (181), or that it would be "an abuse of words to consider him in the light of a human creature" (258), or that he is a "machine, not constituted . . . to be greatly useful" (321). Collins, who speaks this last line, may have a point. Caleb seems to be a poor instrument, tends to leave his work unfinished (never finishes work on the watches he is assigned to repair, never completes his dictionary of etymology, and can only write sensational stories that end with the hero being hanged). He tends to ruin the lives of everyone he meets, either by communicating an incurable depression or by somehow sending them to prison. The crime writer Patricia Highsmith calls this character type a "bungler."

The description of Caleb as a non-useful machine is particularly interesting in the light of Frances Ferguson's reading of the utilitarian ethic of the novel, where members of the human community are expected to be useful instruments for others (Ferguson 1992, 98–105). The characteristic use of Falkland, for example, is that he puts out fires. He saves a village from destruction by fire, appearing "as if in the midst of the flames" (Godwin 2005, 46), and later preserves his own house in a fire. So closely is he identified with the element of fire that he finally acquires a perpetually burned appearance, "burnt and parched by the eternal fire that burned within him" (290–91). (Yes, both burnt and burned. And parched too.)

Caleb also has a characteristic activity, although not an obviously useful one. He has an intuitive knowledge of how to release any lock (on Falkland's trunk, or on a pair of manacles), and open any door (to a room, a house, or a prison cell). I propose this skill as a possible referent for the mysterious phrase that Caleb uses to introduce himself, which identifies his characteristic quality of "mechanical inventiveness." This phrase has been a crux in recent criticism of the novel; Christian Thorne in particular has seized on it as an indicator of the passage in the early history of the realist novel from a system of causation based on decision to a system of emergent causation. In my reading, it also indicates a fluid relationship with objective reality. Caleb relates personally to things like locks and doors; that is, he treats them as persons.

The opening of Falkland's trunk has the effect of satisfying Caleb's deepest desires, even before he discovers what it contains: "All that I sought," he exclaims, "was within my reach" (138). The opening of his cell door is a strange scene of mutual satisfaction: "The door was no longer opposed to my wishes" (202). In the tales told of him, Caleb "makes his way through stone walls as if they were so many cobwebs" (246); in his own narrative, he brags of his "faculty of imitation," his capacity to pick up anyone's gait, expression, or accent. (Strangest of all, he speaks with an Irish brogue for 100 pages without referring to this fact in the narrative, or representing his speech as dialect.) On the level of plot, I would also note Caleb's tendency to insinuate himself into intimate family relations; he becomes the adopted son and heir of four different characters in the novel. (This serial family attachment may correspond to Falkland's tendency to be pregnant without giving birth to a child; his face is constantly "pregnant with meaning.")

Caleb is a member of all families, a brother even to inanimate objects, a key that fits any lock. He matches all descriptions. He can be arrested on a principle of "sufficient resemblance" even if "the description tallied neither as to height or to complexion." The description of the criminal refers to an Irishman, which Caleb is not; and to a shorter person than Caleb, "a circumstance of all others the least capable of being counterfeited" (252). Nonetheless, the bailiffs who arrest Caleb are satisfied that the description "tallies to the minutest tittle" (250), and the justice sees no need to "squabble about trifles" (251), and has "a kind of notion that he had seen my face" (253). What allows the law to identify Caleb with a particular person? Any resemblance is sufficient. The law is looking for anyone with an Irish accent. Any portrait is good enough.

Despite his "imitative faculty," despite his "mechanical inventiveness," no matter how Caleb alters his appearance or voice, he is always instantly recognizable to everyone as the protagonist of the miraculously efficacious halfpenny pamphlet "Adventures of Caleb Williams." Any reader can see that he matches the description in the pamphlet even though he has told no one his history and has stopped using his given name. The distribution of the pamphlet is described as an "infectious disease" (306), and it has the effect of associating him with the disease. People shun him as though he were a carrier. Humanity turns its back. If it were true, if Caleb were a carrier, then humanity might be right to ostracize him, like Typhoid Mary. Caleb himself considers this possibility. He even recognizes himself in the pamphlet: "I found it to contain a greater number of circumstances than could have been expected in this species of publication" (279).

In the novel's canceled ending, Caleb, confined to a mental hospital, is unable to distinguish between himself and the chair he sits on. "I sit in a chair in the corner, and never move hand or foot—I am like a log . . . I wonder which is the man, I or my chair?" (346). This coalescence of subject and object in the act of sitting is an extreme example of the personal quality of mechanical inventiveness, Caleb's fluid relationship with objective reality. What is the difference between "the door was no longer opposed to my wishes" and "I wonder which is the man, I or my chair?" The difference between recognizing a door as a sort of person and recognizing a chair as oneself is the precise difference between sanity and madness in a community where portraiture succeeds.

# 4 THE WISH TO BE AN OBJECT

## Nature's shyness

Plotinus once asked Nature why she made things. Nature said nothing in reply, but Plotinus understood what she meant to say.

First, she would have said that she was not used to talking, "for I am a silent one, and to talk is not my custom" (Nature, quoted by Plotinus, in Dodds 1980, 34). If he had remembered the correct way to address her, Plotinus would have used silent meditation rather than speech. For him the habit of speech was second nature, but Nature's shyness, like her other habits, was simply nature.

She would have said that her silence was better than his speech: "It were more seemly not to question, but like me to understand in silence." She did not need to express herself in speech. Instead she communicated through the things of this world, which she made by meditating. "That which meditates in me creates its own object, as the geometers when they meditate draw lines." Nature does not talk, but she meditates, and the peculiar feature of her meditation is that when she thinks about a thing, the outline of its body comes into being.

This imaginary conversation (to be clear, Plotinus imagined it; I did not) suggests a difference between Plotinus and Nature more basic than that between custom and nature. The difference between them can be described as a gift and a deficiency on both sides.

What was Plotinus's gift? Plotinus had imagination. This image-producing faculty allowed him to think about Nature, to imagine her speaking, without creating every object in the world all over again. Nature could not do that. She could not think about Plotinus without creating him again.

Nature's gift, on the other hand, was that she could make any object just by thinking. Plotinus could not do that. His thoughts did not automatically come into the world as objects. His imagination dealt in the world of objects by dematerializing them, then replacing them with images, so they could be reproduced in other objects, such as his book, the *Enniads*.

The whole exchange between Plotinus and Nature is based on a distinction between images and objects. Nature's thoughts are objects. They don't just correspond to objects in the world; they are the same objects. She doesn't need to talk because communication isn't much of a problem for her. None of her thoughts is private. She doesn't have any motives hidden deeper than the world that you see. Plotinus's thoughts are images. They have no physical extension in space. In order to communicate them, he needs some kind of objective support. A book, a painting, a monument. He can think them without participating in Nature's world of objects. In fact they are basically destructive to the objects they represent. Marvell said they "annihilate all that's made / To a green thought in a green shade."

Maybe you don't believe that the encounter between Plotinus and Nature ever happened. Or maybe you don't believe in the distinction that this story is intended to illustrate. I think it's a useful distinction, and it isn't made often enough. When people talk about objects, they sometimes mean images. The reverse can also happen.

Marvell was interested in this distinction, and he understood it in the terms that he received from Plotinus. Whether you believe in it or not, I think it will clarify what Marvell thought he was doing in his experiment in characteristic writing "The Gallery."

> Clora, come view my soul, and tell
> Whether I have contrived it well.
> Now all its several lodgings lie
> Composed into one gallery;
> And the great arras-hangings, made
> Of various faces, by are laid;
> That for all furniture you'll find
> Only your picture in my mind.

Marvell modeled "The Gallery" on seventeenth-century books of Theophrastan characters. His poem also presents a challenge to the genre. The poem is not just one sketch but an entire gallery of sketches. A collection of collections.

Space in "The Gallery" is a paradox. "Gallery" should mean an indoor space. Only this space has no divisions: "Now all its several lodgings lie / Composed into one gallery." Which means that there are no doors. Not even subspaces marked by invisible boundaries for different uses. This is a space that has an inside but no outside; thus a paradox. As the voice-over says in Jørgen Leth's film *The Perfect Human*, "We are in a room," in other words, indoors, but "here are no boundaries," in other words, no walls or doors, "here is nothing."

Marvell takes advantage of the paradoxical organization of this imaginary space to incorporate an entire society of beings—a "people," a "numerous colony." He emphasizes the paradox by having the speaker point to the "various faces" of the deaccessioned arras, as though the paintings, each of which shows the same woman's face, formed a single continuous surface. But the speaker also describes the paintings as having three dimensions, in some cases bearing images on both front and back. Some of the paintings face one another, so that the same image seems to be looking at itself.

The gallery space is an attempt to depict what I have been calling the unthinkable space of character, a space that collects different examples of the same character. Well, that isn't quite right. Maybe the gallery used to show different examples of types when it displayed arras "made of various faces." Now the speaker has discarded all of those different examples and replaced them with a single image repeated more than one thousand times. (Note that the poem does not cover every painting in the collection; one of the virtues of this gallery, like any well-organized archive, is that you are not forced to look at the entire collection every time you open it up. You have the option of viewing only the one that you want.)

There is an anomaly here that I have not found in any other character sketch from the period. This gallery doesn't collect every example of a character. Instead it collects one example of each character—the one that looks like Clora. The gallery is like the ideal future world envisioned in Shakespeare's sonnets, where every object bears the image of the same beautiful face.

Strange as it may seem, the poem does not sketch the character of Clora, the addressee, despite the fact that the gallery includes only images of her face. It might help to think of Clora as an actor, and the gallery as a resume of the different roles she plays in the course of a life in the theater. Clora gives her image to a variety of characters, each of which appears in a painting, which corresponds to precisely one stanza of description.

There is another anomaly. The first stanza makes clear that each depiction of Clora is a fantasy of the speaker's. The poem is an invitation to inspect this private fantasy. "Clora, come view my soul." We are dealing with pure imagination, not the objective world of nature. "For all furniture, you'll find / Only your picture in my mind." "My soul," "my mind," "your picture": the speaker addresses Clora from within the image-producing faculty itself, an interior contiguous with no identifiable exterior.

Based on such unmistakable cues as these, critics have interpreted "The Gallery" as a poem about idealization. The moral is supposed to be the failure of an ideal to satisfy aesthetic criteria. For Rosalie Colie, a brilliant reader of Marvell, the important feature of this poem is the absence of Clora, who is no more available as a real person living in the world than the mistress of "To His Coy Mistress," whose body is pointedly not described—and if she were described, it would be in uninspired, conventional, idealized terms. Clora is actually described in those terms. She is described according to the terms of several different sets of conventions: as a Petrarchist fantasy; as two different goddesses, Aurora and Venus; as a witch; and as a shepherdess. In short, "All the forms thou canst invent / Either to please me, or torment."

Each character is introduced as a part that Clora plays in the speaker's fantasy. Pointedly not Clora's fantasy, pointedly not Clora's body. What you get instead is Clora's image as she appears in the speaker's mind "in the dress of" or "like" a fantasy image with either a positive (pleasing) or negative (tormenting) value. The implication may be that the characters represent changes and possibilities in Clora's life. Or they may have nothing to do with her history, merely representing ways of thinking about her. In either case, Clora, a person, not a character, lives outside of the speaker.

The thoroughgoing conventionality of the entire gallery of characters is not a problem for Colie, who understands the archiving of conventions as an operation of "Marvell's poetry of criticism." Her chiastic formula should be understood transitively. That is to say, a critic criticizes poetry; Marvell poetizes criticism, opening up the conventions of a genre in order to close them down, so that they can never be used again. Each poem will be the summation and last of its kind. Donald Friedman, like Colie, finds the conventions unsatisfying in themselves, and appreciates them as "ironic courtly compliment" (Friedman 1970, 9). The crowning irony in both interpretations is the final image of Clora, which promises to show her as a unique individual, and pointedly fails, describing her as that old warhorse of Elizabethan pastoral, "a tender shepherdess." I will give the last word on this interpretation to Colie: "It doesn't matter who the lady is, or whether she is real or not" (Colie 1970, 109).

Colie's formulation is somewhat overstated. To test it, you might ask yourself whether your fantasies would mean as much to you without at least what Spinoza called "the *idea* of an external cause." Yes, the independent existence of Clora matters. Further, there is something special about the final image. Not that it isn't a convention. It's a conventional image of sovereignty, uniting the positive and negative strains of the speaker's praise. As Friedman suggests, this shepherdess, like the shepherdesses in the old Elizabethan poems, is an image of Elizabeth, a queen who wears the symbol of her office, "Transplanting flowers from the green hill / To *crown* her head, and bosom fill."

What readers have missed in the last image is that it's also the first image, the one "at the entrance," the one "with which I first was took." I missed it too. I see it now only because I recently read Michael Clune's book *Writing against Time*. Clune studies a set of problems following from the ambition of Romantic poetry and post-Romantic literature to stop time, which, unlike poetry in the Classical tradition, attempts to immortalize not just the names and qualities of persons, but personal experience. The modernist version of this ambition is defamiliarization, which attempts to turn back the clock of perception so that an object, on its ten thousandth viewing, can be experienced as though for the first time.

In the elements of the Classical tradition, Marvell has found the Romantic problem and the modernist solution. The image of the tender shepherdess "likes him best" (note the passive construction) because it is first. Even after being seen more than "a thousand" times, it's still first.

The conceit of "The Gallery" is the reverse of Haywood's novel "Fantomina," where a woman takes on different characters in an effort to hold the attention of a fickle man who never penetrates her disguises. The speaker in "The Gallery" sees the same face in every character. If he never recognizes the face, it's only because he has never seen her before and is now seeing her for the first time.

Why is the first image of Clora not the only one?

The reorganization of the gallery, which the speaker refers to as his "contrivance," describes a seemingly unnecessary movement. First, there are many different images. The speaker reduces them to just one image. Then he collects many reproductions of that one image.

Why more than one painting? If they are all doing the same job, showing the same image, more than one seems excessive. Maybe it's because they don't really do the job? (Maybe the existence of the poem requires that they fail, in the same way that poetry of seduction requires that the relationship not be consummated.) Or maybe it's because they stop working after a while. Maybe they start to disappear after the first viewing, as in the Romantic paradigm that Clune studies.

But that isn't right. The pictures in the gallery are doing the job. They are acting on the speaker, giving him the exact experience that he wants, pleasure and torment.

For thou alone to people me
Art grown a numerous colony.

**(MARVELL 1952)**

The images do not colonize Clora. Instead, they live in the speaker, the object who bears this gallery of images in his soul. He doesn't want to make her into an art object. He wants to turn her into an image, and he does. He wants to be an object himself.

Although critics have traditionally interpreted the poem as a work of idealization, it is finally a work of objectification in the terms of the distinction that Plotinus, in collaboration with Nature, makes between image and object. The poem's central conceit is that the speaker has been reduced to an object, a gallery of paintings, and thus a platform for the images to which Clora has been reduced. The speaker has turned his soul, a factory where images are made, into an object, the gallery, which he offers up for judgment. "Have I contrived it well?"

(Is a soul a thing that one uses to contrive, in the way that birds "contrive" a nest [Marvell, "Upon Appleton House"]? Yes, if by "contrive" you mean "imagine." Creating images is the business of the soul.)

## Adrian's footstool

All throughout this book I have been studying ways in which characters are meaningful to other characters, and I have been ignoring questions about what writers and readers do with characters. Poems don't give detailed information about the experiences of poets and readers. But they do give some information. They tell you something about what poets want.

Marvell's poems tell you what he wanted to see in a poem. Many readers have noticed a pattern where Marvell seems to find enjoyment in representing various kinds of unfreedom. His poems put people in boxes, use them as building materials, treat them as wall-hangings and furniture. In "The Gallery," Clora tortures the speaker with "keen engines," kills him, and mutilates his corpse. The speaker acts mainly as a platform for someone else's image. He inserts his self-image only in the scenes of "torment" and never in the scenes of "pleasure," suggesting a secondary kind of pleasure in fantasizing about torment if not in the sensation itself.

The poem tells you that Marvell wanted to see these images in a poem. It doesn't tell you what he was getting from these images. What desire was he gratifying? Maybe he liked to imagine himself as the corpse. Maybe he liked to imagine himself as the torturer. Maybe he thought that he was denouncing an inhumane practice. Maybe he was interested in these conventional images as conventions.

In this final chapter of the book, I am studying human examples of characters who are treated as objects, and ordinary household objects that are examples of character types. Contrary to my usual procedure, I intend to use these examples to suggest an answer to the questions I have been avoiding. What do authors and readers do with characters? Why do we have characters at all?

My examples might sound like special cases. I don't think so. I think they are examples of what art usually does. One of the powers of art is to turn people into objects. Art replaces people with objects, such as poems. Why would anyone want to do that?

In talking about "The Gallery," I took care to make a precise distinction between objects and images. The poem turns Clora into an image, and the speaker into an object. The speaker becomes a platform for someone else's image. He is the gallery that houses all of the images of Clora.

Here is another, much simpler way of wanting to see people as objects. Marlowe was fascinated by the image of a man stepping on another man's back to climb into a chair. This image is a remarkable motif in his plays. The following passage is from *Doctor Faustus*.

—Cast down our footstool.
—Saxon Bruno, stoop,
    Whilst on thy back his holiness ascends
    Saint Peter's chair and state pontifical.

—Proud Lucifer, that state belongs to me!
But thus I fall to Peter, not to thee.

—To me and Peter shalt thou groveling lie
And crouch before the papal dignity.
Sound trumpets then, for thus Saint Peter's heir
From Bruno's back ascends Saint Peter's chair.

(*Doctor Faustus*, B-TEXT, **3.1.88–97**)

Pope Bruno, the footstool, has to be "cast down," because he wasn't originally in the down position. He has to "stoop" from an upright position, and—because, left to his own devices, he wouldn't always be waiting by the throne to be used—for that to happen, someone has to tell him to stoop. Pope Adrian can't tell him. An elaborate chain of command separates Adrian from direct communication with the furniture. The chain of command links elite political operators: Adrian, a spiritual power, gives the command to Raymond, King of Hungary, a temporal power, who passes it to Bruno, a rival spiritual power. Here the chain breaks. The footstool resists. He thinks he is the Pope; he says so distinctly and eloquently.

From a design perspective Bruno's service as footstool is impractical. His use could never be ordinary and is, on the contrary, ritualistic. Surely some clever engineer could imagine a smoother, more comfortable path to the throne. Bruno's ritual function is something more important than comfort, which is the opposite of comfort. Adrian sacrifices his own comfort to enhance Bruno's discomfort.

I deliberately use the word discomfort rather than dehumanization. The footstool in this scene has everything in common with human form, because Bruno's is a human body, living and whole. His other human attributes include a gender (masculine), a name (Bruno), and an ambition (to enjoy the state of the papacy) and its verbal expression: "That state belongs to me!"

(Some readers think that he might be Giordano Bruno. I would like to think so too, because this identification would give him the additional human attribute of participation in intellectual history. Giordano Bruno, victim of the persecution of Clement VIII, and a sort of animist thinker, might have appreciated the image of a defiant stool talking back to the Pope. However, since the character is called Saxon Bruno rather than Nolan Bruno, I doubt it.)

This list of attributes is overspecific if I am merely trying to establish Bruno's humanity, and that is the point: this footstool is overspecific. Note that there are *two* Popes, but only *one* footstool. Common and proper nouns have traded places. When Adrian intones, "Cast down our footstool," he refers to one footstool only. No other article of furniture in the Vatican collection, no matter how convenient or luxurious, will do.

# Tamburlaine's footstool, part 1

The short scene from *Faustus* revises and condenses a relationship that Marlowe explores more thoroughly in two acts of *Tamburlaine the Great, Part 1*. Here is a relevant sample.

—Bring out my footstool.

. . .

Fall prostrate on the low, disdainful earth
And be the footstool of great Tamburlaine,
That I may rise into my royal throne.

—First thou shalt rip my bowels with thy sword
And sacrifice my heart to death and hell
Before I yield to such a slavery.

—Base villain, vassal, slave to Tamburlaine,
Unworthy to embrace or touch the ground
That bears the honor of my royal weight,
Stoop, villain, stoop, stoop, for so he bids
That may command thee piecemeal to be torn
Or scattered like the lofty cedar trees
Struck with the voice of thund'ring Jupiter.

—Then, as I look down to the damnèd fiends,
Fiends, look on me, and, thou dread god of hell,
With ebon scepter strike this hateful earth
And make it swallow both of us at once!

—Now clear the triple region of the air
And let the majesty of heaven behold
Their scourge and terror tread on emperors.

(*Tamburlaine, Part 1*, **4.2.1–32**)

Adrian's footstool and Tamburlaine's footstool are the only footstools in Marlowe's theater. This means that they are, in a sense, normal. Marlowe never writes about stools made of wood—neither discrete pieces nailed to one another by a carpenter, nor interlocking pieces fitted together by a joiner, nor a single piece shaped on a turner's lathe. Instead a great ruler, a pope or a king, makes a footstool out of another great ruler, a pope or a king. He does it with his voice.

Think of it this way. When Adrian calls for his footstool he wants a unique object, Bruno. When Tamburlaine calls for his footstool he wants a unique object, Bajazeth. Comparing the two passages I learn something about footstools as a species. When Marlowe calls for a footstool he wants a living man's body.

Why would he want this? Elias Canetti suggests one explanation. In the volume on "Aspects of Power" in *Crowds and Power*, Canetti discerns a hidden meaning in the careers of all soft chairs.

> An upholstered chair is not only soft, but also obscurely gives the sitter the feeling that he is sitting on something *living*. The give of the cushions, their springiness and tension, has something of the quality of living flesh and may conceivably be the cause both of the aversion which many people feel for chairs that are too soft, and of the extraordinary importance which others, not generally self-indulgent, attach to this form of comfort.
>
> **(CANETTI 1984, 390)**

When you sit in a chair, you are sitting on a person. You can pretend that this is not so by sitting in a hard chair. Or you can remind yourself of this relationship, luxuriate in your power over others, by using an especially comfy chair. Or you can make the point clear to everyone by making use of a person's actual body. Even the body of an extraordinary person, such as the Ottoman Emperor!

If Canetti is right, everyone wants to do what Tamburlaine does to Bajazeth. Tamburlaine's footstool is an unnecessarily graphic representation of what people want from furniture. Tamburlaine seems to agree that his treatment (he calls it his "handling") of Bajazeth responds to a basic, universal, unspoken desire. At first he is uncharacteristically laconic in announcing what he is going to do with Bajazeth after defeating him, inevitably, in battle: "I will not tell thee," he tells Bajazeth, "how I'll handle thee" (3.3.84), because the idea is so good that he doesn't want to ruin it by anticipation. Everyone will appreciate it, though. They will "smile to see thy miserable state" (3.3.86). Even the stars in the sky will "Smile . . ./ And dim the brightness of their neighbor lamps" (4.1.33–34). Tamburlaine's soldiers and the stars above are smiling because they have now satisfied a desire they did not know they had. They wouldn't have imagined it, but when they see it, they like it. Maybe the spectators in Marlowe's theater wear the same smile.

Canetti's account of the power of sitting is inadequate to Tamburlaine's handling of his footstool in at least one way. Tamburlaine talks to his footstool. What's more, the footstool talks back. It does not consent to its use as a footstool. Canetti could not have imagined that.

> The thing sat on is no longer even animate. Its function is settled forever and it has less volition even than a slave; its state is the quintessence of slavery. Its user is free to do exactly as he likes with it. He can come and sit down and remain sitting for as long as he pleases, or he can get up and go away without giving it a thought.
>
> **(CANETTI 1984, 389)**

There is some trouble in this account even before I test it against the example from *Tamburlaine*. A chair has "less volition than a slave," but is nonetheless "the quintessence of slavery." These two forceful statements do not go together. Canetti seems to say that the chair typifies slavery—that is its symbolic meaning, which the sitter either unconsciously relishes or unconsciously avoids—without being an example of slavery. Because it's impossible to enslave a piece of wood. You can't even enslave a horse. The wood can be property, and the horse can be tamed, but enslavement only happens when people are treated as property.

According to Canetti, people are naturally free. They have a special gift of self-transformation, which "is clearly expressed in the mobility of the face. . . . It is inconceivable how many changes a face can undergo in the course of a single hour" (374). Objects, on the other hand, are governed by necessity. Treating a person as property, a slave, violates human freedom. Treating a person as an object cancels human freedom entirely.

(Since he does not particularly value human freedom, Canetti does not seem to be disturbed by its loss. Both enslavement and objectification appear as relatively benign forms of violence in an account of human civilization in which power relationships more frequently look like one person eating another. For example, Canetti defines "family" not in terms of genealogy, but rather as an occasional, exceptional grouping: people eating together, but not eating one another [221].)

The first thing Canetti notices about a chair is that it is "not even animate." By contrast, Julia Reinhard Lupton views mobility as the essential fact in a chair's existence. She is commenting on a passage from Shakespeare's *Taming of the Shrew*.

—I knew you at the first
 You were a movable.
—Why, what's a movable?
—A joint-stool.
—Thou hast hit it. Come, sit on me.

**(2.1. 192–96)**

Kate calls Petruchio "a movable" (a piece of furniture, or *meuble*), which she then specifies as a "joint-stool," the lowest form of seating in medieval and Renaissance houses. Denying him the dignity of a chair, she reduces him to an object designed to bear the rump of anyone in the house, and to be moved about at will for the frequent rezonings of shared space that characterized the minimalist choreography of Renaissance furnishing. Joint-stools afford sitting; they also afford rapid transport from one space to another; and they can, under certain circumstances, afford hurling.

**(LUPTON 2011, 55)**

So. Another stool. A joint-stool, to be precise, but not interlocking pieces of wood: rather, Petruchio's human limbs. Like all furniture, as Lupton shows, this footstool with human joints is a "movable," and therefore not attached to a place as a house or a rooted tree would be. It moves around the room, and into other rooms, and can be carted away to other buildings. Different people can sit on it, step from it to a higher seat, play cards on it, lay out tomorrow's shirt on it.

Lupton calls these various options "affordances." The term, which comes from design, is strategic. Designers talk about the affordances of objects and environments, whereas engineers talk about uses and abuses. A tool has a use, which is the activity for which an engineer intended it. The stool's use is sitting, and anything else, such as hurling, would be tool abuse. (On tool abuse, see Luke Wilson; his examples are limited to tools used as weapons, but the concept has a broader application.) But designers don't necessarily intend just one use. They design for living, which is to say, for freedom.

Affordances are the measure of freedom available to furniture. You can't restrict the possible uses of a piece of furniture any more than you can design a perfectly safe piece of furniture. Anything a footstool can do is an affordance. Because it has options, the footstool is not entirely subject to necessity.

What about Bajazeth? He does not have "less volition than a slave." While acting as a footstool, he still wants to rule his empire. His volition is exactly that of a slave. He wants something, and meanwhile he is being used for what someone else wants. "Slavery" is his name for this condition, and "slave" is one of Tamburlaine's names for him, along with "villain," "vassal," and "footstool."

Maybe he would rather have less volition. Unlike Petruchio, who declares a wish to be used as an object, he does not say, with obscene suggestion, "Sit on me." Instead he says, "Rip my bowels with thy sword / And sacrifice my heart to death and hell." In other words: kill me and make furniture out of my skeleton. The bowels and heart are crucial elements of a human organism that have no purpose in a footstool. In asking to have them eliminated, Bajazeth, who really wants to be Emperor, prefers objecthood to slavery.

Should he prefer it? There is some question as to whether being "the footstool of great Tamburlaine" is an honor or a degradation. The very ground that he walks on is honored to receive Tamburlaine's "royal weight." Tamburlaine calls the same ground "the low, disdainful earth," and Bajazeth calls it "this hateful earth," which I take to be names for the same feeling at greater and lesser degrees of intensity. The disdain that the ground feels for Bajazeth may be compared to that of the washroom attendant who notes the unfashionable appearance and poor fit of your clothes, and icily calls you "Ma'am."

The ground's affordances include bearing Tamburlaine's weight and receiving Bajazeth's embrace, but it experiences the former as an honor and the latter as a kind of abuse. Bajazeth does not even deserve the ground's support, and is therefore doubly unworthy of the honor of stooping to insert his body between the ground and Tamburlaine's foot.

If Bajazeth's nomination as footstool—but royal footstool—is simultaneously insult and honorific, Tamburlaine's position is similarly ambivalent. I do not so much mean that his glory in this exchange depends on the neck of the emperor on which he treads. Rather, that his power derives from a different source of which he is the honored but undeserving instrument. In the formula that he repeats obsessively throughout both five-act plays, he is the "scourge of heaven" or "scourge of God."

Isn't the Pope also conceived as a similar kind of instrument? In the traditional formula, "Servant of the servants of God"? "Of all titles ever assumed by prince or potentate," as Henry Adams observes, "the proudest" (Adams 2008, 101).

# Tamburlaine's footstool, part 2

"Stoop, villain, stoop, stoop" (*Tamburlaine, Part 1*, 4.2.22–23). Marlowe liked the sound of the vowel in "stoop" so much that he wanted to hear Tamburlaine say it three times. Then he wanted to hear it again in *Faustus*: "Saxon Bruno, stoop" (*Doctor Faustus*, B-Text, 3.1.89). But this was not enough! Adrian says the word another time—a fifth repetition—just seventy lines later: "Then thou and he and all the world shall stoop" 3.1.158).

Maybe it was the final "p," the only sound that "stoop" doesn't share with "stool," that Marlowe really wanted to hear. In any case the frequent returns of the simple command to stoop suggest a frustration of someone's desire. No matter how many times you indulge this desire, it's still not enough. Maybe the command simply isn't working except as a sound effect. (You might say that Tamburlaine has to give the command a third time because Bajazeth hasn't carried it out after the second.)

The fact that Tamburlaine is talking at all is somewhat gratuitous. The entire exchange could be replaced by a short stage direction: "Bajazeth kneels before the throne. Tamburlaine steps on his back and climbs into the seat." The scene doesn't go like that. Instead, they command, reply, curse, and wrangle, for thirty-two lines. Marlowe wanted to hear all of the words. The king and the footstool have to be talking the entire time.

Tamburlaine's counselors observe the inefficiency of the play's language and try to correct it. "You must devise some torment worse, my lord," Techelles offers, "to make these captives rein their lavish tongues" (*Tamburlaine, Part* 1, 4.2.66–67). Techelles has a point. The efficient political solution would be the destruction of Tamburlaine's enemies. Recall Bajazeth's preferred solution: "First thou shalt rip my bowels with thy sword . . ." (4.1.16). He will be a footstool only when Tamburlaine has him killed and fabricates a useful object from his skeleton.

Tamburlaine ordinarily has no scruples about resorting to this kind of solution. In *Part 1*, Marlowe dramatizes this solution in Tamburlaine's unflinching destruction of the city of Damascus, starting with the slaughter of four virgins ("O, pity us!" "Away with them, I say, and show them Death!" [5.1.119–20]); in *Part 2*, in Tamburlaine's murder of his son Calyphas.

That would be one way of handling the problem of Bajazeth. A less efficient but equally effective solution would be to use brute strength to enforce Bajazeth's unfree status. Punish his body. Take away his voice. Teach him the consequences of disobedience. Curiously, Tamburlaine is far less disciplined in handling his enemy emperor than in handling enemy towns. For although he threatens to have Bajazeth torn to pieces, which he fancifully compares to shavings from a cedar tree struck by a thunderbolt, the threat is empty. He has no intention of doing any such thing. Why does he make so many allowances for the eccentricities of his furniture? "My lord," Queen Zenocrate wonders, "how can you suffer these outrageous curses by these slaves of yours?" (*Part 1*, 4.4.26–27).

Tamburlaine's answer is instructive. "I glory in the curses of my foes" (4.4.29). He wants the footstool to be a living, conscious, willful man. He wants him to have a voice. He wants to hear his curses. He wants to step on his back—an emperor's back—while he resists. The political point of the command was never to conquer the object's resistance. The point is for the object and the speaker to hear the command and the curse over and over.

For the same reason, Adrian and Raymond do not conspire to strip Bruno of his individuality or his human attributes. They refer to him as a footstool, but they also address him as Bruno and allow him some freedom to express his views. They even listen and respond to what he says. (Adrian studiously refuses to give Bruno direct commands, but he does address him directly.) They never dispute Bruno's human dignity. They only disagree on the political question of whether he should also enjoy "papal dignity."

Thus the primary audience for their performance is Bruno, whom they treat as a negligible utility but never take for granted. They want to convince him that he is not the Pope. To a lesser degree Adrian may be his own audience. He may need to hear himself declare his ascension so that he can remember that he is actually the Pope—because it's confusing when someone else makes the same claim. Bruno's short speech has the same logic. He wants Adrian to hear that he does not acquiesce, and he wants to hear it too, particularly in circumstances that are destructive to his self-image.

There is another audience within the scene. This third audience is an anomalous figure. It has no lines—an extraordinary omission for a character in a play by Marlowe. Others talk to it and about it, but it does not talk, although it does have a human identity, a gender, and a name. I am referring to St. Peter's chair. In the setting designed by Bernini several decades after Marlowe's death, the chair has become almost inaccessible. To ascend to its seat, you would need something more than a footstool; you might have to stand on the shoulders of both John Chrysostom and Augustine, the church fathers who stand to the right of the chair, and who are made of the same materials.

Christopher Wood and Alexander Nagel have studied the logic by which St. Peter's basilica retains its identity during a period in which it is being destroyed and rebuilt (Wood and Nagel 2010, 313–19). Their account ends before Bernini intervenes, but the "chain of substitutions" they uncover is useful for understanding the association of the chair with Peter. The gilded bronze chair that Bernini designed encloses a much older chair that Peter may or may not have actually sat in. Or the older chair may include wood fragments from a chair that Peter once sat in. However old the older chair may be, it takes its chronology not from the epoch of its origin but from the ancient epoch to which it refers.

By synecdoche the chair refers to its traditional sitter in the ancient epoch, Peter, who is the antitype of the two rival popes. Bruno clarifies that he "falls" only "to Peter," and thus to himself, because Peter is his model; while Adrian further clarifies that Bruno, in falling to Peter, can't help falling "to Peter's heir" as well, meaning himself, Adrian. The chair has no lines because it has nothing to add to this exchange. Links on the same chain of substitutions, each of the rival popes refers to the same type as the chair.

There is a fine symmetry in the composition of this scene. A man acting as a footstool declares his submission to a chair acting as a man.

# Neither inside nor outside

How do you talk to a dishtowel?

> I told you to stop crying. How long are you going to cry? You have to be strong. You're so limp and shapeless, look at you. I'll help you. [Wrings dishtowel three times.] There. Isn't that more comfy?

Cop 663 uses a special tone in this scene from Wong's film *Chungking Express*. This is not the cool, polite voice that he uses when ordering coffee. Nor do I hear the doubtful tone that creeps into his voice when he flirts with the woman who pours his coffee. Nor is this the private voice of his numerous voice-overs, where he narrates his actions and thoughts to himself.

In the conversation with the towel, the twang that Cop 663 puts at the end of each phrase may be a feature of Cantonese pronunciation. In Cantonese, words have their tones built in, and someone who does not speak the language would be a fool to try to distinguish the part of tone that belongs to standard pronunciation from the part that belongs to the speaker's attitude. The folly of trying to decipher tone in a foreign language, particularly one in which diction governs tone, puts me not in the position of the cop but rather that of his towel, which, like me, does not speak Cantonese. My original mistake in identifying myself with the human figure rather than the cleaning utensil tells me something, finally, about the cop's attitude. Maybe this is a way of talking to someone who does not speak your language. You might use a similar cadence when talking to an infant or a pet, for example.

Or a big white teddy bear. The teddy bear is a toy, and when Cop 663 talks to it, he is playing with it. Because he uses the same tone with the other sad things in the apartment, I might identify that tone, provisionally, as a playful one. The other things are useful household objects. But Cop 663 isn't using them to dry the dishes, to clean or clothe his body, or for any other practical purpose. He uses them as toys too.

How do you talk to a towel? No one has to be told. Every child knows. You talk to your towel in the same voice that you use to talk to your doll.

When you play with a toy, what happens, according to the cartoonist Lynda Barry, is that it lives. "There is something brought alive during play, and this something, when played with, seems to play back" (Barry 2008, 51). This means that play does not always succeed. Sometimes you play with a toy that does not come to life. For Barry there is nothing ambiguous about the distinction between failed play and successful play: "A fake imaginary friend is still you. A real imaginary friend feels like someone else" (199).

Barry extends D. W. Winnicott's insight in *Playing and Reality* that toys are points of contact, transitions, between inside and outside. Although playing uses psychic material from inside the person, and although it may project this material onto the toy, it can't happen at all unless there is something that isn't inside. Does play occur inside the person or outside? Winnicott approaches this question on practically every page of his book, but he declines to give an answer more detailed than "neither inside nor outside." In fact, he adds, the success of play may depend on not disturbing or resolving the paradox.

Of the transitional object it can be said that it is a matter of agreement between us and the baby that we will never ask the question: "Did you conceive of this or was it presented to you from without?" The important point is that no decision on this point is to be expected. The question is not to be formulated.

**(WINNICOTT 2005, 17)**

Thus almost anything can be used as a toy, as long as it is "neither inside nor outside" the person (129).

Does the towel live? Does it play back? Maybe not. It would be easy to say that the towel is merely an extension of Cop 663 rather than a real imaginary friend. The things in the apartment aren't lonely. They don't miss the flight attendant who used to live there, because she wasn't their girlfriend. They never had a girlfriend. The cop misses the flight attendant, projects the feeling onto the things in his apartment, and, in a nightly bedtime ritual, comforts himself with the alibi that he is comforting them. Just as in a dream, every object in the apartment is a version of the cop. He might as well be talking to his image in a mirror. The toy merely provides a convenient receptacle for his feelings, allowing him to say things that would be too painful if he thought he were only talking to himself.

Cop 663 would disagree with this interpretation. For one thing, he isn't talking to a mirror image. The bar of soap looks nothing like him. Also, he has different words of advice for different objects, and his observations are specific to their careers. The bar of soap gradually loses its substance. The towel absorbs and releases water. Each object misses the flight attendant in its own way. Tony Leung, the actor who plays the cop, makes a space for these unique responses in his delivery. I mean, he doesn't give them time to say anything—why should he, since they don't speak his language? But he does pause and give them room to do the kinds of things that towels do, like flop on the counter and release a few drops of water.

For a moment, at the start of the scene, Cop 663 might be addressing his routines to himself. When he says, "You've lost a lot of weight, you know," the screen shows a dark wall in his apartment. Then the camera pans left to reveal that he is talking to the depleted bar of soap that he holds in his hand. By recording the soap's reaction, the camerawork objectively confirms the cop's sense that he is talking to something that not only might receive the communication but might also answer him. The cinematographer Christopher Doyle, in whose Hong Kong apartment this scene was shot—and whose personal hand soap, I imagine, Cop 663 might be addressing—also seems to think that the objects in the household have responses, and that film can capture them.

The towel is alone on screen three times. It probably has more screen time by itself than the face and soulful eyes of the handsome male lead. The exchange with the shirt is a shot / reverse-shot setup: first Cop 663 addresses the shirt in a close-up; then the shirt, alone on the screen, appears to meet his gaze without saying anything. The scene culminates in a mastershot that finally brings the cop and shirt together over an ironing board—not to maintain the shirt's creases, but to heat it up, compensating for the warm body of the woman who used to wear it.

Some viewers will insist that these seeming toys are mere props, extensions of Cop 663, in a different sense. Doesn't he anthropomorphize them? It is true that the teddy bear has a number of key features in common with the human body, that the soap and the towel are designed to accommodate the human hand, and that the shirt alludes to the torso that it used to clothe. It is also true that all of these objects are products of human civilization. But these references to human form are how the dolls and utensils were designed, not assumptions that the cop is projecting onto them. If the things have been anthropomorphized, this process occurred long ago, in their production.

Maybe, by focusing on the relationship between the cop and the towel, I'm missing the point. Even if the cop isn't imposing human form on the towel, the film might be. I don't think so. In general, in a film, it's easy to tell whether something has human form or not. If a human actor were cast in the role of the towel, that would give the towel human form. Instead the towel is played by a towel or a reasonable approximation. This towel may even be ragged from use in the cinematographer's kitchen.

It would make sense to say that the cop anthropomorphizes the towel only if you think that the human mind alone is capable of retaining the image of an absent person. But I don't think that. To those who say that regardless of whether a towel can miss a person, the towel in question, surely, does not miss the person in question, I would point out that the same can be said, with equal justice, of the actor Tony Leung. I would add that the towel is better equipped to cry on demand, whenever the scene happens to require it, than most human actors.

For Leung, this scene is a performance of play. Not being an expert on play like Barry or Winnicott, I am not qualified to evaluate the success or failure of his playfulness. What I study is character. I have said that the truth of character becomes visible in a performance of performance—one in which either several actors play one character, or one actor plays several characters. This is such a scene. Not, however, for Leung. For the towel, rather.

—You know, I have to tell you, you've totally changed. You can't just change personality like that. Her walking out is no excuse. I want you to think about that.

[Voice-over.] It was a relief when I saw it crying. It may look different on the outside, but it's still true to itself. It's still a very emotional towel.

This scene helps to clarify what it means for an object such as a towel to be a character. The towel does not have to be an agent. It doesn't need human form or emotional depth. (Whether you agree or disagree with Cop 663 that the towel does have emotional depth is not important.) For the performance of character, the key word in "still a very emotional towel" is not "emotional" but "still." What makes the towel a character is the fact that it remains "true to itself" even after it has been replaced by a different object. Cop 663 views two towels as a single object because they are the playing the same character.

There is no confusion here. Viewers of the film see two towels and one character. The cop sees exactly the same thing. We would see the same thing if the second towel were played by another object, such as a Coke can (with condensation on the outside to represent tears), or by a human being, such as Maggie Cheung.

It seems significant to me that there has never been any confusion regarding the performances in Buñuel's *That Obscure Object of Desire* either. Some viewers have proposed dubious interpretations of this film; they see, for example, Angela Molina and Carole Bouquet as sensual and frigid, respectively. Or they see other patterns in which the two performers represent different aspects of the character Conchita. However, no viewer has ever proposed that they are two different characters.

Buñuel himself was almost surprised to discover "that audiences have accepted the constant change of actresses. . . . So you see that cinema is like a kind of hypnosis. There is no way you could confuse the two women in real life; they look very different" (*Objects of Desire* 1993, 226). Buñuel thought that his film put viewers in a trance, subjecting them to the same obsessions as the lovestruck Matteo. I have a different explanation: character type. The character Conchita collects many different examples. The fact that two women play Conchita in this film is not different from the fact that another woman plays Conchita in the 1929 film *La femme et le pantin*, or that the same character also appears in the novel by Pierre Louÿs on which the two films are based. The extravagant rule that Buñuel's production exploits has as its basis the character's collection of examples.

If *Chungking Express* suggests that we apply the same typologies to the things we use in daily life, where a certain blindness to the home environment allows us to replace worn out objects with new ones that we treat with total familiarity, it goes a step further still and suggests that we do the same thing with people in romantic relationships.

I've become more observant. I notice things I used to take for granted. The taste of sardines, for instance.

The scene in which Cop 663 discovers a new vitality in the things in his apartment is open to an ironic reading. Sardines taste different to him because they are not sardines but swordfish: Faye, the woman who serves his coffee at Midnight Express, has been breaking into the apartment during the day and switching the labels on all the canned goods. She has also replaced many of the worn out utensils with new ones. Cop 663 attributes the changes that he observes to a new stage in the grieving process that the apartment is going through. What looks to him like a relation to his ex-girlfriend is actually a relation to the woman who is going to be his girlfriend, and whom he is going to treat in exactly the same way. In a scene near the end of the film, he massages her legs, just as he used to do for his ex-girlfriend after a hard day at work, remarking in a voice-over that this is a part of a woman's body that he especially likes. She, for her part, will get a new job as a flight attendant, the same job held by the ex-girlfriend.

The characters treat each other as types, as does the film. Cop 663 is known only by his number on the Hong Kong police force, which suggests a typology of profession. He and Cop 223 are examples of the same type. Other character names suggest a similar typology. For example, Cop 223 considers asking out a woman who works at Midnight Express who has the same name as his ex-girlfriend May; her successor working at the counter of Midnight Express is a rhyme, Faye.

The lesson is clear. In erotic life, as in home life, people make use of types, and are even attracted to types. The "gift of the magi" is real. It happens all the time. Consciously or not, people accommodate each another by exchanging and diminishing the qualities to which they are adapting, until the original qualities are gone, and only the adaptations remain.

This insight from *Chungking Express* suggests in turn a new, although no less dubious, interpretation of *That Obscure Object of Desire*. Isn't this the story of serial monogamy, which is a kind of polygamy? I have been saying that *That Obscure Object* owes its intelligibility to typologies of character. The film should additionally be intelligible to anyone who has spoken the same words to different lovers, taken different lovers to the same place, told them the same stories, had the same kind of sex. Or anyone who has accidentally used the name of an old lover for a current one.

Maybe it's just me? But I doubt it. I think that I am talking about a basic human desire. Hitchcock thought so too, which is why he celebrated the logic of this desire in a film, *Vertigo*. Turning people into objects one of the reasons why we make art. No one says you have to like this desire, any more than you have to like art.

The other side of this desire is even more interesting, and it is a real human possibility. Why would anyone want to be an object?

What about Faye? In her seduction of Cop 663, she deploys the powers of cuteness, among which are indirection and cunning. But how can I be certain that seduction is Faye's intended goal? Maybe, by entering the cop's apartment while he is away, she is practicing a kind of flirtation that would deny anything so deep as an erotic relationship. Or maybe she wants to fast forward to a point in the relationship where he would take her for granted, and she would enjoy the closeness (or blindness) of the utensils that he lives with. (On flirtation, see Moi 2008, 145–67; for the suggestion that being taken for granted is the best kind of love, see François.)

Here is a paradox worthy of Winnicott. Although Faye seems to embody the spirit of play, she does not seem to be playing with these utensils when she visits the apartment. She isn't even using the Mary Poppins method of turning dreary chores into a game. No, she's cleaning the things. Like in a hotel, where cleaning the room means replacing the sheets, towels, and soaps with different sheets, towels, and soaps.

## Toys and spoons

Winnicott's writing is useful for identifying instances of playing, but less useful for identifying activities that are not instances of playing. He sometimes says that all cultural activity is play. He sometimes seems to think that any relationship is a kind of play—when wind blows through the curtains, he says the wind is playing with the curtains (132). Perhaps playing was Winnicott's method of analysis. Certainly playing is what he did when he met with the children who were his patients. But at this point in my account I need to reintroduce some distinctions that Winnicott, in his effort to maintain a strong middle ground between inside and outside, is reluctant to make.

In the captions to her cartoon "Magic Lanterns," Barry follows Winnicott in expanding the field of play to include all cultural activities.

> How does a story come so alive? . . . When we finish a good book, why do we hold it in both hands and gaze at it as if it were somehow alive? What happened to my yellow blanket?
>
> **(BARRY 2002, 154)**

Drawing a cartoon history of the loss of a transitional object, a yellow blanket, from her early childhood, Barry seems to treat the story she tells as the same kind of object. She does not use Winnicott's term, but, as Hillary Chute has shown, the piece is an extended meditation on his ideas about playing (Chute 2010, 127). However, the exclusion of his term may be deliberate, because the term does not accurately describe what Barry does in her cartoons.

There is already a suggestion of something added to Winnicott in Barry's impatience with "fake imaginary friends" as opposed to real ones. The difference between real and fake imaginary friends—a difference between playing and playing at playing?—is obvious to Barry but would not be to Winnicott. The difference becomes crystal clear in "Magic Lanterns," which is only incidentally about her lost yellow blanket, and predominantly concerned with a stuffed panda toy that she picks up in an airport and imagines as the precious lost transitional object of some child.

—You're throwing this out?
—You want it?
—It should go to lost and found.
—They only gonna toss it. Airport's too big to keep everything. Some kid's gonna cry tonight.

**(BARRY 2002, 155)**

When Barry plays with her blanket, it's neither inside nor outside. When she saves another child's toy from the trash, the toy is unambiguously outside. When she draws a cartoon story about her blanket and the other child's toy and sends it into the world, the cartoon is definitely outside.

Similarly, Lewis Carroll liked playing with young girls, and he also wrote two novels for a particular girl. These activities were not unrelated, but the novels have a frame that makes them the product of a very different kind of activity. They are works of art, and therefore outside.

In 2013 I went to the Museum of Childhood in East London to look at the eighteenth-century dollhouse restored by Denton Welch in the 1940s. The funny thing about the Museum of Childhood is that people bring their children there. The displays are uneasily addressed to an audience that might include adult patrons and children. But the children have little interest in some of the displays, particularly of the museum's older holdings. They might like to play with some of the toys, but they don't particularly want to look at toys that they can't play with. They don't even want to play with the eighteenth-century toys, which don't look like toys to them. But I didn't go there to play, and I don't usually want to get too close to pieces in museums. I was doing research.

What was Welch doing with the old dollhouse? Not playing with dolls. But not studying it either. He did some things that were kind of like playing. For example, he slowly filled the house with toy furniture and miniature cups and dishes. At one point he wrote in his journal that "slowly the house is coming to life again" (March 26, 1945). That sounds like Barry's language: Welch interacts with the dollhouse in a way that brings it to life. Some of what he did sounds like the work of scholars in museums—stripping the outer layer of paint to reveal older painted lines that represented brickwork, and trying to match the rooms to period-correct furnishings. Welch himself seems to have been at a loss to account for the motives behind his activity, mainly repeating the word "again" as though going in circles: "I suddenly had a passion for it again, unaccountable, unless it was just looking at it in its ruined condition and seeing again how lovely it could be." A purely aesthetic motive: wanting to see the house lovely rather than ruined.

Welch was doing with the dollhouse the same thing that he does with the bottles, combs, and other handheld things that are, along with himself, the main and recurring characters in his books. In a scene that recurs in all three of his novels, the protagonist drinks tea in an institutional setting such as a hospital, hotel, or school, and notices that some beautiful old pieces of silverware have been incorporated into the regular rotation for everyday use. The following is taken from his first novel *Maiden Voyage*:

> I stopped at the table and looked down. Most of the things were electro-plate but two spoons had caught my eye. They had large hall-marks on the thin part of the stem and I knew that they were early Georgian. They belonged to Sister, I supposed, and had got muddled with the others. I thought how easy it would be to steal them. I would like to have had them for myself very much.
>
> **(WELCH 1968, 38)**

What is he looking for? Not something to sweeten his tea. The spoons themselves fix his attention. He examines the pieces and learns everything about them. He is able to read the marks that announce their age, manufacture, and provenance. He also guesses the identity of the current owner and why the valuable pieces are on the table with the ordinary ones.

The climax of this scene is the imagined act of taking the spoons. The fantasy of stealing could be described as a temptation, but the narrator might not think that it would be wrong. Stealing the spoons might be better for the spoons. (In another scene, touring the home of the Duke of Devonshire, he is offended by a guide who asks that he "not touch the things," and nurses his wounded pride with the reflection "that I could appreciate and take care of the things better than the whole lot of them put together!" [55].) At least, unlike the Sister, he isn't going to lose track of the spoons.

There is a surprise at the end of the passage. "I would like," the narrator says, "to have had them for myself." He does not say, "I would have liked." He still wants them! In narrating this scene, he reaches back through memory and longs to hold them. The tone suggests regret for not taking them when he had the chance. That is the meaning of the last sentence: he would like to have stolen them very much.

He wanted them so much that he wrote about them in several places. Here is a version of the same scene from his second novel *In Youth Is Pleasure*:

> Orvill remembered with pleasure the low dining-room in the desolate house . . . the kitchen cups large as babies' chambers, and the thin delicate old spoons quite lost in their rude saucers.

> Orvill remembered the spoons particularly, for they were beautiful early Victorian ones with bowls shaped like scallop shells and crests on the handles. How he wanted one of the spoons! But he had not the strength of mind to steal the one which lay so near on his saucer.

**(WELCH 1946, 14–15)**

This passage delivers some of the "pleasure" advertised in the title. For once the word is not used ironically; Orvil experiences pleasure in remembering a set of Victorian spoons, mixed with regret for not stealing a spoon. Here the act of theft is not even implicitly criminalized but fully heroized. Only a kind of moral weakness stops Orvil from seizing the opportunity: he lacks "strength of mind," which means that he is not attentive enough to see that he could steal a spoon, not clever enough to plan the theft, or not courageous enough to carry it out.

By this point you will not be surprised to learn that Welch actually stole some spoons. He writes about doing so in a journal of a walking tour in Sussex. In a youth hostel, another traveler steals the spoon that Welch had previously stolen at school, "the George IV spoon with the Prince of Wales feathers on it, which I had found amongst the greasy base-metal cutlery at school, and which I had appropriated to myself with such satisfaction" (Welch 1994, 167). Later, at a different hostel, he steals someone else's spoon as compensation: "I found a silver spoon there. It seemed to be sent specially to compensate me for the one I'd lost at Midhurst" (214). What makes the spoon a character is not the detail and the sensitivity of the descriptions, but the substitution. Various pieces of silverware play the singular role of "spoon." Welch replaces the spoon with a different object, and treats it as the same object.

I'm isolating the spoons because they are a theme in Welch's writing. But I could do similar work with other things, even bits of detritus. In *Maiden Voyage*, the protagonist spies on a man waiting for his lover, and notices him throwing his cigarette "impatiently, so that it fell like a small rocket" (96). Later he returns to the same spot, finds "the shape their two bodies had made in the snow" and "the sickly yellow patch of his cigarette," the sodden remains of which he gathers and saves. In his journals, after a picnic with Eric Oliver, he writes about the eggshells left on the ground, and two months later, he takes Oliver back to the same spot in the forest to view "those blessed eggshells, lying there still" (April 2, 1944).

My examples have been taken indiscriminately from Welch's journals and novels. The fictional status of the novels is not easy to establish; the fictional guise is thin at best. *In Youth Is Pleasure* was to have been subtitled, "a fragment of life story with changed names." The printed book finally did not carry this subtitle only because the publisher feared lawsuits (De-la-Noy 1987, 47). Like Barry, Welch is an artist who champions imagination but works entirely from memory, as though the work of imagination were not to add new objects to the world but to invest existing objects with fantasy and anxiety, so that "the best tea-table" becomes "endowed with nightmarish possibilities" in the words of Auden's review of *Maiden Voyage* (Auden 2002, 252).

Or perhaps the fictional element in Welch's novels is the uncanny knowledge of other minds that the narrator consistently has. The attribute of heightened sensitivity gives these books, which are essentially first-person memoirs, the traditional advantage of third-person novels: no private thoughts. Perhaps this feature fictionalizes the memoirs enough to turn them into novels. However, Welch's knowledge of other minds may not have been a fiction. So skilled was Welch at reading minds that, according to Eric Oliver, "the only way of keeping a secret from him (and even that was not always effective) was to force oneself to think only of other matters in his presence" (Welch 1951, 7).

There are no indifferent objects in Welch's writing, neither in the fiction nor in the nonfiction. In his review, Auden describes the unrelieved differentiation of each object as a "Hitchcock lighting" effect under which "both persons and things stand out with startling and sinister sharpness" (Auden 2002, 252). The spoons reward attention with pleasure, but everything else on the tea table demands the same attention. The narrator of *Voyage* notices the modern plated pieces as well as the solid silver eighteenth-century spoons, and Orvil in *Pleasure* can't help noticing the "rude saucers" since they practically swallow the "thin delicate old spoons." Even the "hateful" school uniform attracts a special kind of attention: "Although I had always hated their tightness and blackness, I had never felt so conscious of myself as I had in them. To wear clothes you hate makes you concentrate inside yourself" (Welch 1968, 74).

Welch's readers have proposed two psychological explanations for this obsessive sensitivity. Both explanations replace the things with a person. Either Welch's attention to things compensates for the early loss of his mother, or it registers the fragility of his injured body. (Michael De-la-Noy's critical biography develops both explanations fully. For a different view of the influence of Welch's accident on his development as a writer, see Waters 2010, 178–84.) Why does the narrator of *Voyage* take such an interest in pieces of silverware? "Because they were my mother's," obviously, and "if she were alive, she'd give them all to me!" (Welch 1968, 280). Why do the opening pages of *A Voice* linger over the "creamy white ivory comb" that has been "carefully wrapped up . . . and stowed" in a traveling case (Welch 1966, 9)? Why, when the narrator stops for tea on the road, do the decayed or absent "beautiful little brass handles" on the windows of the tea shop seem to him emblems of "universal damage and loss"? Because a car is about to run into him, leading to spinal tuberculosis and years of suffering.

Both explanations are obviously true, but insufficient. Note that the narrator does not say, "If mother were alive, I wouldn't need the silverware!" He wants his mother to be alive, and he also wants the silver. It is not clear that he even wants his father to be alive. In an astonishing journal entry that records the news of his father's death, he speculates about items that he might inherit, and is careful to state that he wants his father's cufflinks "chiefly for what they are and only a very little because they were his" (July 12, 1942). Anyone else would be careful to say the opposite.

No one else in Welch's books is like Welch. For the waiter at the hotel, for the Sister in the infirmary, the place settings are "a nest of forks and spoons melted together" (November 13, 1942). One spoon is as good as another if you are looking for an instrument to stir milk and sugar into your tea. The narrators in the novels are frequently shocked by the failures of their companions to recognize that they are in the presence of rare beauty. "'I thought that there was nothing you would like.' I was startled. I had never been in a house where I had liked so much" (Welch 1968, 94). "I thought nobody could miss such obvious beauty" (133). In journal entries, Welch characterizes the neglect of old things as "another form of cruelty," and the human agents of this cruelty as themselves degraded to a bad form of objecthood, lacking the human features of "eyes, nose, mouth, ears, limbs. They are trunks of wood always repudiating, though they have already been deprived of all sense and movement" (January 31, 1946).

At the same time, Welch doesn't seem to enjoy the effects of his greater sensitivity. Unlike Barry, if he had a choice, he would not give life to inanimate matter. "I have had the horrible sensation that the tables, chairs, lamps, and confusion of books near me were writhing into life" (January 28, 1947). Similarly, Orvil in *Youth* resents the "evil souls" of "the wardrobe, the chest of drawers," and "the chairs . . . even the eiderdown stored evil knowledge" (Welch 1946, 144). His sensitivity gives life to the things, but he would rather be insensible among inanimate things. Elsewhere he complains about conventions of speech that attribute human qualities, such as gender, to things, "calling an inanimate object, like a boat or a car, she" (December 7, 1942). The root of his dislike for this language, which he puzzlingly calls "vulgar," appears to be a helpless sense of the vividness of conventional phrases:

> Hackneyed images and phrases have always had the power to jump suddenly alive for me. There is a click and I see the needle in the bottle of hay, the stupid one crying over the spilt milk, the stitch in time saving nine.
>
> **(WELCH 1966, 212)**

You get a different sense of what the things mean to Welch from passages where he imagines what it would be like to be an ordinary household object whose usefulness is taken for granted and whose other qualities barely register. In fact, he consistently discovers this condition of objecthood would be desirable but impossible to experience. His term for this condition from which consciousness has been deleted, for this "never-happening happening," is "acceptance." "His pleasure lay chiefly in the fact that the man seemed to have accepted him as completely as the tables and chairs in the hut" (Welch 1946, 117). "I suppose deep down she accepted me placidly, did not necessarily understand, but did not question; so this acceptance flowed out to me and I was warmed" (Welch 1966, 171). It might be bad for you to take things for granted, but it might not be so bad to be taken for granted. How pleasant, how warm it would be to be ordinary. To be accepted without question, to be used without attention. To be acceptable.

Welch's sensitivity is automatic. He can't turn it off. One name for this condition of total, excruciating awareness might be grief; another might be stupid physical pain; a third might be art. From this point of view, the opposing condition of indifference (to put it negatively) or comfort (to put it positively) looks increasingly alluring. It looks like the cure of his spinal injury, the end of mourning and of his career as an artist: "One day you will want dullness and no help from outside—for only in dullness can your heart and mind grow" (Welch 1966, 139). The condition of objecthood is impossible for Welch, the one thing he can't have, but at the same time utterly desirable. That is the best explanation for his sensitivity to things. He is waiting for them to recede into the background. He is waiting to follow them.

# Sofas, chairs, desks, footstools

I propose to call the stories that I have been discussing—Plotinus's anecdote, Marvell's poem, Marlowe's plays, Wong's film, Barry's cartoon, Welch's novels—it-narratives. Critics recently invented this term to classify a genre in the early European novel in which ordinary household objects such as shoes, corkscrews, wheels, and coins are heroes and tell their own stories. In current usage the name of this genre has several problems. For one thing, it is supposed to name an eighteenth-century genre, but it is a new term, not in use in the eighteenth century. The neutrality of "it" is a problem in that the objects at the center of the stories, although they have no sexual parts, usually have a gender. A shoe, for example, is usually masculine or feminine. "Narrative" is a problem in that these novels foreground setting at the expense of action and causation. The narratives, such as they are, tend to be circular rather than linear.

The term has some virtues insofar as the same problems are often built into the novels. In Crébillon's *Le sopha*, the narrative element threatens to undo the work of objectification. The sofa tells his own story, and positively enjoys his contact with persons; he (for this sofa is occupied by a masculine soul) even communicates his love to a particular person. Here is a sort of kiss between a sofa cushion and a human face: "My soul transferred itself to the padding, and so close to Zeinida's mouth that at length it succeeded in adhering wholly to it" (Crébillon 1927, 275). Crébillon gets around the problem through metempsychosis. The narrator, presently a man, was a sofa in a previous existence, which a god mysteriously allows him to recall. In this way, "narrative" is in a relation of productive tension with "it."

Critics have suggested numerous ingenious explanations for the existence of this genre, finding in it-narratives allegories of reification (Lynch), imperialism (Festa), and slavery (Lamb). My interpretation of Welch's tortured relationship with silverware suggests a different reading. What if these books are about exactly what they say they are about? That is to say, an impossible desire to delete consciousness and recede into the background, like a sofa cushion.

Readers in the eighteenth century understood Crébillon's novel as a work of pornography whose final perversion was to describe itself, with an attitude that might be irony or hypocrisy, as a "moral tale." In *Les liaisons dangereuses*, this moral tale is a constant presence on the bookshelves of various characters who use it to inspire themselves or corrupt younger readers. The conceit of the amorous sofa provides the inspiration for Valmont's virtuoso letter with double meanings, written to seduce its addressee, but using the back of a different sexual partner as a writing-desk (Laclos, Letter XLVIII). (This letter may be, indirectly, Crébillon's most important contribution to literature.) In this scene, Crébillon's novel inspires its readers to imitate its exact mode of intimate relation. The meaning of the book, for Valmont and Émilie, is that it would be sexy to be a writing-desk, or to treat another person as a writing-desk.

In the twentieth century, *Le sopha* may also have inspired Edogawa Rampo's story "The Human Chair," in which a carpenter creates a superlatively comfortable chair and spends several years living inside it. The key to this story is the multiplication of motives. Why does the narrator conceal himself in the chair he has made? Here are some of his explanations.

Because he is hideously ugly, "ugly beyond description," and can hope for no other mode of human contact (Rampo 1956, 31).

Because he is so proud of his work that he can't bear to part with it (31).

Because he wants to possess the chair himself, but he can't, and living inside the chair is a dismal compromise. "At first, no doubt, the idea found its seed in my secret yearning to keep the chair for myself. Realizing, however, that this was totally out of the question, I next longed to accompany it wherever it went" (34). "No doubt" is a nice touch.

Because he wants to hide in the Western-style hotel and steal jewels from the guests. "You may have guessed long ago," he presumes, that theft was his motive all along (35).

Because he enjoys physical contact with people who sit in the chair (35).

Because he especially enjoys the different weights and smells of the bodies, "the feel of flesh, the sound of the voice, and body odor" (38). (Note that this part of the story is indifferent to the sexes of the people sitting in the chair. The narrator's "love in a chair" is a sexual preference in that it's sexually gratifying, but not a preference for one of the sexes. It's more like a preference in the sense that a chair has human scale, and prefers the bodies for which it was designed.)

Because he prefers the extraordinary bodies of foreign dancers. "On this occasion, instead of my carnal instincts being aroused, I simply felt like a gifted artist caressed by the magic wand of a fairy" (40).

Because, in a fit of nationalism, he wants a Japanese body to sit in the chair: "As a Japanese, I really preferred a lover of my own kind."

The narrator, the human chair, is as ingenious in proposing motives as critics have been in their interpretations of it-narratives. These things are all good things to want, and the narrator clearly wants them. But the most eloquent passages in the story are the ones where the narrator does not offer a motive, but describes what it feels like to live in the chair.

> I felt that I had buried myself in a lonely grave. Upon careful
> reflection I realized that it was indeed a grave. As soon as I entered
> the chair I was swallowed up in complete darkness, and to everyone
> else in the world I no longer existed!
>
> . . .
>
> What was it about this mystic hole that fascinated me so? I
> somehow felt like an animal living in a totally new world.
>
> **(35, 37)**

(Scenes in which a man seals himself inside a piece of furniture and experiences unanticipated joy seem to have a special meaning for Rampo, and recur in his fiction. Compare "The Apparition of Osei," where the hero climbs inside a bridal chest: "The pitch-black confines of the chest, which smelled strongly of camphor, were strangely comfortable. Kakutaro was suddenly overcome with fond memories of his childhood" [Rampo 2008, 23].)

"The Human Chair" is finally about what happens in the story: wanting to be a chair, while at the same time retaining human consciousness, and thus adding experience to the chair's existence. Rampo wrote an essay on this subject later in his career, where he considers the wish to be an inanimate object as a subcategory of a universal human desire for transformation. "Under the right conditions, human beings will even want to become wooden planks" (Rampo 2008, 214).

It would be moving too quickly to identify this wish with masochism, although there is probably an element of that in the stories by Rampo and Crébillon. (My own opinion is that masochism should be understood in an almost philosophical sense, and restricted to pain experienced as pleasure, but the term is commonly used to refer to eroticized humiliation.) In masochism, the fantasy is simple abuse: treating a human being as an object. Ritualistic degradation, as in Sade, where the libertines use their victims as tables or candelabra; and Sacher-Masoch, where Wanda uses Gregor as a footstool. In the latter scene, dehumanization becomes contractual, as Deleuze observes (Deleuze 1989, 91–102). In both scenes there is a pretense of forgetting that the object is a human being. The lure, potentially on both sides, is the violation of the categorical imperative. Neither sadist nor masochist ever forgets that it's wrong to treat someone as a means, not an end. And that imperative, always in the foreground, is what makes the scene sexy.

Now imagine that part of this transaction is unknown. (The distinction may seem unremarkable or academic, but not if the quality of your sexual experience depends on it.) Imagine, for example, Wanda resting her foot on Gregor's body without first addressing him as a footstool. To call someone a footstool is not the same as treating a person as a footstool, since ordinarily it isn't necessary to have conversations with the furniture. The contractual relationship couldn't be sustained, or it would become an obstacle, if Gregor wanted to be a useful household object (in other words, to disappear), and Wanda actually forgot about his existence as she relaxed. This is more or less the kind of scene that Crébillon and Rampo describe.

Now imagine that the transaction is unknown on both sides. The concepts of sadism and masochism become inadequate at this point, as both person and object disappear into habitual existence. Neither person nor object has any awareness; the most intense feeling that such a scene could generate is comfort. Pornography also becomes an inadequate term, insofar as a description of such a scene would be innocuous. A person lounging on a sofa. This is the impossible desire that Welch calls "acceptance."

There are not many pornographic images that would answer to such a description, but there is a market for them, and a subgenre called "forniphilia." Jeff Gord, who maintained the website "House of Gord" until his recent death, specialized in this subgenre. His vision of the human body is as spectacular and thorough in its commitment to objectification as Busby Berkeley's. He defines forniphilia as "the ultimate in artistic expression" because it uses "the ultimate material." By this he means that he uses women's bodies as furniture (chairs, lamps, chandeliers, hood ornaments) and takes pictures of them. Because he uses real bodies and never forgets it, Gord's work should properly be called sadism. His work is instructive in that it shows how difficult the approach to objecthood would be for most persons, and what existence is really like for most objects.

The longest and most instructive page on his website is a list of admonitions addressed to readers who think they would like to try using living human bodies as materials for art. Plaster, he warns, should be used with caution:

> I have seen plaster molds so hot they were steaming and could not be touched without asbestos gloves. Think about that before you pour it around the woman you love.

Urethane foam is a volatile material:

> NEVER, EVER get this stuff around the head region unless you wanna lose your loved one.

Indifference can be simulated in play but is forbidden in fact:

> NEVER leave an inverted person gagged. In fact, NEVER leave them anyway.

The care that people require when they are used as furniture is a strange reminder of the care they ordinarily require in human society, as well as the care that furniture requires if you don't want it to go completely to hell. Furniture can take care of itself, and is superior to human furniture, only to this extent: it is in no danger of suffocating if you leave it alone. Otherwise, just like a human body, a piece of furniture will fall apart if you concentrate too much weight on its back. If it falls over, furniture has no way of protecting itself, just like a human body.

However, Gord writes, this defenselessness, this need for protection, makes furniture "not an object of ridicule but an object of immense power." In fact we do not treat furniture with contempt. Instead we take care of it, arrange it, cover it, clean it. Or (better) we aren't supposed to treat furniture with contempt. No doubt we *do* sometimes talk to furniture.

# ACKNOWLEDGMENTS

David Scher provided the images.

My intellectual debts to Michael Clune are staggering to contemplate.

Joanna Picciotto helped me to see what this book could be when I was having trouble seeing it.

Ian Moyer once bought me lunch and shared with me his extraordinary knowledge of ancient anecdotes about Timon the misanthrope.

Anna Moschovakis and Johannes Göransson graciously permitted me to reproduce quotations from Johannes's translations of poems by Henry Parland.

Many other people shared helpful thoughts, questions, and suggestions while I was working on different parts of this book. I will name as many of them as I can remember but I'm probably forgetting some important ones. Thanks go to Charles Altieri, Dina Al-Kasim, Ayal Amiran, Amanda Anderson, Emily Anderson, Jennifer Ashton, J. K. Barret, Stephen Best, Brian Blanchfield, Stephen Booth, Lara Bovilsky, Anne Boyer, Marshall Brown, Kyle Buckley, Andrew Carlson, Anne Cheng, Michael Clody, Emily-Jane Cohen, Rose Comaduran, Drew Daniel, Theo Davis, Anthony Dawson, Kevin Dettmar, Helen Deutsch, Jeff Dolven, Thom Donovan, Hunter Dukes, Oona Eisenstadt, Meredith Evans, Andy Fitch, Stephen Foley, Robert Folkenflik, Anne-Lise François, Adam Frank, Marcie Frank, Dan Gil, Peter Gizzi, David Glimp, Mark Goble, Jonathan Goldberg, Judith Goldman, CJ Gordon, Andrew Griffin, Jonathan Hall, Corrinne Harol, Lucy Ives, Noel Jackson, Joe Jeon, Victoria Kahn, Sarah Kareem, Eleanor Kaufman, Heather Keenlyside, Alex Klein, Wayne Koestenbaum, Jonathan Kramnick, James Kuzner, Aliza Lalji, David Landreth, David Larsen, Grace Lavery, Ben Lerner, Jayne Lewis, Daniel Lipson, Christina Lupton, Julia Reinhard Lupton, Jeff Masten, Anthony McCann, Mark McGurl, Gage McWheeney, Michael Moon, Sawako Nakayasu, Chris Nealon, Maggie Nelson, Karen Newman, Sianne Ngai, Sharon O'Dair, Julie Orlemanski, Mark Owens, Simon Palfrey, Julie Park, Brad Pasanek, Kevin Pask, Adam Plunkett, Robert Polito, Kirsten Poole, Christopher Pye, Claudia Rankine,

Bernie Rhie, Jessica Rosenberg, Colleen Rosenfeld, Paul Saint-Amour, Wolfram Schmidgen, Sarah Schwartz, Laurie Shannon, Mark Simpson, Bennett Sims, Vivasvan Soni, Brian Kim Stefans, Elisa Tamarkin, Rei Terada, Christian Thorne, Daniel Tiffany, Kyla Wazana Tompkins, Douglas Trevor, Irene Tucker, Henry Turner, Peggy Waller, Kenneth Warren, Joshua Marie Wilkinson, Lynn Xu, Elizabeth Marie Young, Magdalena Zurawski, and several anonymous readers.

Parts of this book first appeared elsewhere in an altered form. A version of "Confession" titled "Question and Answer" appeared in *Poets on Teaching*, edited by Joshua Marie Wilkinson (Iowa City: University of Iowa Press, 2010). A short version of my reading of *The Five Obstructions* appeared as "The Riddle of Style" in *Postmedieval* 6:4 (1999). An early version of the first section, "Many Is Not More Than One," appeared as "Characters Lounge," with brilliant but severe edits by Marshall Brown, in *Modern Language Quarterly* 70: 3 (2009). Some of my ideas about misanthropes appeared in "Banish the World," a transcript of a lecture given at the Mandrake Bar in 2009, in *Contra Mundum*, edited by Alex Klein and Mark Owens (Los Angeles: Oslo Editions, 2010, 93–123). A much longer version of my reading of the footstools in Marlowe's plays appeared as "Marlowe's Footstools" in *This Distracted Globe*, edited by Marcie Frank, Jonathan Goldberg, and Karen Newman (New York: Fordham University Press, 2016). The last three chapters appeared more or less as they do here in *Liberalism and Literary History*, edited by Corrinne Harol and Mark Simpson (Toronto: University of Toronto Press, 2017).

This book is for Michael Kunin and Linda Schwalen.

# WORKS CITED

Adams, Henry. *Democracy: An American Novel*. New York: Penguin, 2008. Print.

Allen, Doug. *Steven*. Four vols., unpaginated. Princeton, WI: Kitchen Sink, 1989–91. Print.

Arendt, Hannah. *The Human Condition*. Chicago: Chicago University Press, 1958. Print.

Aristotle. *Poetics*. James Hutton, trans. New York: Norton, 1982. Print.

Arnold, Jack, dir. *The Incredible Shrinking Man*. 1957. Film.

Ashford, Daisy. *The Young Visiters, or, Mr. Salteena's Plan*. J. M. Barrie, intr. New York: Doran, 1919. Print.

Auden, Wystan. *Prose, Volume Two: 1939–1948*. Edward Mendelson, ed. Princeton: Princeton University Press, 2002. Print.

Auerbach, Erich. "Figura." In *Scenes from the Drama of European Literature*. Ralph Manheim, trans. Minneapolis: University of Minnesota Press, 1984. Print.

Auerbach, Erich. *Mimesis: The Representation of Reality in Western Literature*. Willard R. Trask, trans. Princeton: Princeton University Press, 1953. Print.

Austen, Jane. *Sense and Sensibility*. James Kinsley, ed. Oxford: Oxford University Press, 2008. Print.

Balzac, Honoré de. *La comédie humaine*, vol. 1. Pierre-Georges Castex, ed. Paris: Gallimard, 1976. Print.

Balzac, Honoré de. *Le père Goriot*. Phillippe Berthier, ed. Paris: Flammarion, 1995. Print.

Barber, Ceasar L. *Shakespeare's Festive Comedy: A Study of Dramatic Form and Its Relation to Social Custom*. Princeton: Princeton University Press, 1972. Print.

Barry, Lynda. *One! Hundred! Demons!* Seattle: Sasquatch Books, 2002. Print.

Barry, Lynda. *What It Is*. Montreal: Drawn and Quarterly, 2008. Print.

Barthes, Roland. "La Bruyère." In *Critical Essays*. Richard Howard, trans. Evanston: Northwestern University Press, 1972. Print.

Bellow, Saul. *Novels 1956–1964*. James Wood, ed. New York: Library of America, 2007. Print.

Berger, Harry. *Second World and Green World: Studies in Renaissance Fiction-Making*. Berkeley: University of California Press, 1992. Print.

Bersani, Leo. *A Future for Astyanax: Character and Desire in Literature*. Boston: Little, Brown, 1976. Print.

Boswell, James. *Life of Johnson*. Robert W. Chapman, ed. Oxford: Oxford University Press, 1980. Print.

Brecht, Bertolt. *Brecht on Theatre: The Development of an Aesthetic*. New York: Hill and Wang, 1964. Print.

Brewer, David. *The Afterlife of Character, 1726–1825*. Philadelphia: University of Pennsylvania Press, 2005. Print.

Buñuel, Luis, dir. *That Obscure Object of Desire*. 1977. Film.

Buñuel, Luis, *Objects of Desire: Conversations with Luis Buñuel*. Paul Lenti, ed. and trans. New York: Marsilio, 1993. Print.

Burton, Robert. *The Anatomy of Melancholy*. Holbrook Jackson, ed. New York: New York Review Books, 2001. Print.

Butler, Samuel. (1612–1680). *Characters*. A. R. Waller, ed. Cambridge: Cambridge University Press, 1908. Print.

Butler, Samuel. (1835–1902). *The Way of All Flesh*. Richard Hoggart, ed. New York: Penguin, 1966. Print.

Canetti, Elias. *Crowds and Power*. Carol Stewart, trans. New York: Farrar Straus Giroux, 1984. Print.

Castle, Terry. *Clarissa's Cyphers: Meaning and Disruption in Richardson's Clarissa*. Ithaca: Cornell University Press, 1982. Print.

Cavell, Stanley. "A Cover Letter to Molière's *Misanthrope*." *Themes out of School: Effects and Causes*. Chicago: University of Chicago Press, 1988, 97–105. Print.

Christensen, Jerome. *America's Corporate Art: The Studio Authorship of Hollywood Motion Pictures*. Stanford: Stanford University Press, 2012. Print.

Chute, Hillary. *Graphic Women: Life Narrative and Contemporary Comics*. New York: Columbia University Press, 2010. Print.

Clune, Michael. *Writing Against Time*. Stanford: Stanford University Press, 2013. Print.

Cohn, Dorrit. *The Distinction of Fiction*. Baltimore: Johns Hopkins University Press, 1999. Print.

Colie, Rosalie. *"My Ecchoing Song": Andrew Marvell's Poetry of Criticism*. Princeton: Princeton University Press, 1970. Print.

Colie, Rosalie. *Shakespeare's Living Art*. Princeton: Princeton University Press, 1974. Print.

Corneille, Pierre. *Oeuvres complètes*. Paris: Gallimard, 1970. Print.

Corneille, Pierre. *Three Plays: The Cid, Cinna, The Theatrical Illusion*. John Cairncross, trans. New York: Penguin, 1975. Print.

Crébillon, Claude Prosper Jolyot, fils. *The Sofa: A Moral Tale*. Bonamy Dobrée, trans. London: Routledge, 1927. Print.

Cromwell, John, dir. *Algiers*. 1938. Film.

Curtius, Ernst Robert. *European Literature and the Latin Middle Ages*. Willard Trask, trans. Princeton: Princeton University Press, 1991. Print.

Curtiz, Michael, dir. *Casablanca*. 1942. Film.

Dassin, Jules, dir. *Never on Sunday*. 1960. Film.

Dawson, Anthony. "Is Timon a Character?" *Shakespeare and Character: Theory, History, Performance, and Theatrical Persons*. Jessica Sights and Paul Yachnin eds. New York: Palgrave Macmillan, 2009. Print.

De-la-Noy, Michael. *Denton Welch: The Making of a Writer*. New York: Penguin, 1987. Print.

Del Ruth, Roy, dir. *Folies Bergères de Paris*. 1935. Film.

Deleuze, Gilles. *Masochism: Coldness and Cruelty*. Jean McNeil, trans. New York: Zone Books, 1989. Print.

Demetz, Peter. "Balzac and the Zoologists: A Concept of the Type." In *The Disciplines of Criticism: Essays in Literary Theory, Interpretation, and History*. Demetz, Thomas Greene, and Lowry Nelson, Jr., eds. New Haven: Yale University Press, 1968. Print.

Dickens, Charles. *Great Expectations*. New York: Dutton, 1950. Print.

Dickens, Charles. *Our Mutual Friend*. Monroe Engel, ed. New York: Modern Library, 1960. Print.

Diderot, Denis. *Selected Writings on Literature and Art*. Geoffrey Bremner, ed. and trans. New York: Penguin, 1994. Print.

Dimock, Wai Chee. "Nonbiological Clock: Literary History against Newtonian Mechanics." *South Atlantic Quarterly* 102:1 (2003), 153–77. Print.

Dimock, Wai Chee. *Through Other Continents: American Literature across Deep Time*. Princeton: Princeton University Press, 2006. Print.

Dodds, Eric R., ed. and trans. *Select Passages Illustrating Neoplatonism*. Chicago: Ares, 1980. Print.

Duvivier, Julien, dir. *Pépé le Moko*. 1937. Film.

Eagleton, Terry. *The Rape of Clarissa: Writing, Sexuality, and Class Struggle in Samuel Richardson*. Minneapolis: University of Minnesota Press, 1982. Print.

Earle, John. *Microcosmography*. Alfred S. West, ed. Cambridge: Cambridge University Press, 1897. Print.

Empson, William. *The Structure of Complex Words*. London: Chatto and Windus, 1951. Print.

Fantuzzi, Marco, and Richard Hunter. *Tradition and Innovation in Hellenistic Poetry*. Cambridge: Cambridge University Press, 2005. Print.

Faust, Joan. *Andrew Marvell's Liminal Lyrics: The Space Between*. Lanham: University of Delaware Press, 2014. Print.

Ferguson, Frances. "Austen, *Emma*, and the Impact of Form." *Modern Language Quarterly* 61:1 (2000), 157–80. Print.

Ferguson, Frances. "Envy Rising." *ELH* 69 (2002), 889–905. Print.

Ferguson, Frances. *Solitude and the Sublime: Romanticism and the Aesthetics of Individuation*. New York: Routledge, 1992. Print.

Fernandez, Ramon. *Molière: The Man Seen through the Plays*. Wilson Follett, trans. New York: Hill and Wang, 1958. Print.

Festa, Lynn. *Sentimental Figures of Empire in Eighteenth-Century Britain and France*. Baltimore: Johns Hopkins University Press, 2006. Print.

Fielding, Helen. *Bridget Jones's Diary*. New York: Penguin, 1996. Print.

Fineman, Joel. *The Subjectivity Effect in Western Literary Tradition: Notes Toward the Release of Shakespeare's Will*. Cambridge, MA: MIT Press, 1991. Print.

Forster, Marc, dir. *Stranger Than Fiction*. 2006. Film.

Fowler, Elizabeth. *Literary Character: The Human Figure in Early English Writing*. Ithaca: Cornell University Press, 2003. Print.

Fowler, Elizabeth. "Shylock's Virtual Injuries." *Shakespeare Studies* 34 (2006), 56–64. Print.

François, Anne-Lise. "'Not Thinking of You as Left Behind': Virgil and the Missing of Love in Hardy's *Poems of 1912–13.*" *English Literary History* 75:1 (2008), 63–88. Print.

Freeman, Lisa. *Character's Theater: Genre and Identity on the Eighteenth-Century English Stage*. Philadelphia: University of Pennsylvania Press, 2002. Print.

Friedman, Donald. *Marvell's Pastoral Art*. Berkeley: University of California Press, 1970. Print.

Friedman, Stanley. "The Motif of Reading in *Our Mutual Friend*." *Nineteenth-Century Fiction* 28:1 (1973), 38–61. Print.

Gallagher, Catherine. *Nobody's Story: The Vanishing Acts of Women Writers in the Marketplace, 1670–1820*. Berkeley: University of California Press, 1995. Print.

Ginzburg, Carlo. *Clues, Myths, and Historical Method*. John Tedeschi and Ann Tedeschi, eds. and trans. Baltimore: Johns Hopkins University Press, 1989. Print.

Godard, Jean-Luc. *Godard on Godard*. Tom Milne, trans. Cambridge: Da Capo Books, 1986. Print.

Godwin, William. *Caleb Williams*. Maurice Hindle, ed. New York: Penguin, 2005. Print.

Goffman, Erving. *Asylums: Essays on the Social Situation of Mental Patients and Other Inmates*. New York: Anchor Books, 1961. Print.

Goffman, Erving. *Relations in Public: Microstudies of the Public Order*. New York: Harper and Row, 1971. Print.

Goldberg, Jonathan. *Shakespeare's Hand*. Minneapolis: University of Minnesota Press, 2003. Print.

Gord, Jeff. "Frequently Asked Questions." *House of Gord*. <houseofgord.com> March 13, 2014. Digital.

Gorey, Edward, with Jane Merrill Fillstrup. "An Interview with Edward Gorey at the Gotham Book Mart." *The Lion and the Unicorn* 2:1 (1978), 17–37. Print.

Gossman, Lionel. *Men and Masks: A Study of Molière*. Baltimore: Johns Hopkins University Press, 1963. Print.

Grossman, Allen. "*Summa Lyrica.*" In *The Sighted Singer: Two Works on Poetry for Readers and Writers*. With Mark Halliday. Baltimore: Johns Hopkins University Press. 1991. Print.

Harding, Denys W. *Regulated Hatred and Other Essays on Jane Austen*. Monica Lawler, ed. London: Athlone Press, 1998. Print.

Harman, Graham. *Prince of Networks: Bruno Latour and Metaphysics*. Melbourne: re.press, 2009. Print.

Harman, Graham. *Weird Realism: Lovecraft and Philosophy*. Alresford: Zero Books, 2012. Print.

Hartley, Hal, dir. *Flirt*. 1995. Film.

Hartley, Hal. *Flirt* (screenplay). London: Faber and Faber, 1996. Print.

Hartley, Hal. *True Fiction Pictures and Possible Films: Hal Hartley in Conversation with Kenneth Kaleta*. New York: Soft Skull Press, 2008. Print.

Hartley, Hal, dir. *The Unbelievable Truth*. 1989. Film.

Hamer, Robert, dir. *Kind Hearts and Coronets*. 1948. Film.

Haynes, Todd, dir. *I'm Not There*. 2007. Film.

Heerman, Victor, dir. *Animal Crackers*. 1930. Film.

Heisler, Stuart, dir. *Blue Skies*. 1946. Film.

Henley, Hobart, dir. *The Big Pond*. 1930. Film.

Hitchcock, Alfred, dir. *Vertigo*. 1958. Film.

Hitchcock, Alfred, with François Truffaut. *Hitchcock*. New York: Simon and Schuster, 1985. Print.

Hume, David. *Essays: Moral, Political, and Literary*. Eugene F. Miller, ed. Indianapolis: Liberty Fund, 1987. Print.

Iser, Wolfgang. "The Dramatization of Double Meaning in Shakespeare's 'As You Like It.'" *Theatre Journal* 35:3 (1983), 307–32. Print.

James, Henry. *Daumier: Caricaturist*. Emmaus: Rodale Books, 1954. Print.

James, Henry. *The Portable Henry James*. Morton Dauwen Zabel, ed. New York: Penguin, 1977. Print.

James, Henry. *Selected Letters, Vol. 1*. Percy Lubbock, ed. London: Macmillan, 1920. Print.

James, William. *Writings 1878–1899*. Gerald E. Myers, ed. New York: Library of America, 1992. Print.

Jarmusch, Jim, dir. *Mystery Train*. 1989. Film.

Jauss, Hans Robert. "The Idealist Embarrassment: Observations on Marxist Aesthetics." *New Literary History* 7:1 (1975), 191–208. Print.

Jauss, Hans Robert. "The Paradox of the Misanthrope." *Comparative Literature* 35:4 (1983), 305–22. Print.

Jauss, Hans Robert. *Question and Answer: Forms of Dialogic Understanding*. Michael Hays, trans. Minneapolis: University of Minnesota Press, 1989. Print.

Johnson, Claudia. *Jane Austen: Women, Politics, and the Novel*. Chicago: Chicago University Press, 1972. Print.

Jones, Chuck, dir. *The Cat's Bah*. 1954. Film.

Jones, Chuck, dir. *For Scent-imental Reasons*. 1949. Film.

Jones, Chuck, dir. *Little Beau Pépé*. 1952, Film.

Jones, Kent. "Hal Hartley: The Book I Read in Your Eyes." *Film Comment* 32:4 (1996), 68–72. Print.

Jonson, Ben. *Major Works*. Ian Donaldson, ed. Oxford: Oxford University Press, 1985. Print.

Kauffman, Stanley. Review of *Flirt*. *The New Republic* 215 (September 2, 1996), 24. Print.

Kieslowski, Krystof. *Three Colors: Blue, White, Red*. 1993–94. Film.

Klawans, Stuart. "Review of *Henry Fool*." *The Nation* 267:2 (1998), 35–36. Print.

Knight, G. Wilson. *The Wheel of Fire: Interpretations of Shakespearean Tragedy*. London: Methuen, 1949. Print.

Ko, Young Nam, dir. *Sonagi*. 1979. Film.

Koestenbaum, Wayne. *The Anatomy of Harpo Marx*. Berkeley: University of California Press, 2012. Print.

Kubler, George. *The Shape of Time: Remarks on the History of Things*. New Haven: Yale University Press, 1962. Print.

Kubler, George. "Style and the Representation of Historical Time." In *Studies in Ancient American and European Art*, ed. Thomas F. Reese. New Haven: Yale University Press, 1985. Print.

Kurnick, David. "What Does Jamesian Style Want?" *The Henry James Review* 28: (2007), 213–22. Print.

Kwak, Jae-Young, dir. *Yeopgi Girl*. 2001. Film.

La Bruyère, Jean de. *Oeuvres complètes*. Julien Benda, ed. Paris: Gallimard, 1951. Print.

Laclos, Pierre Choderlos de. *Les liaisons dangereuses*. René Pomeau, ed. Paris: Flammarion, 1964. Print.

Lamb, Jonathan. *The Things Things Say*. Princeton: Princeton University Press, 2011. Print.

Lang, Fritz, dir. *Secret Beyond the Door*. 1947. Film.

Latour, Bruno. *The Pasteurization of France*. John Law and Alan Sheridan, trans. Cambridge: Harvard University Press, 1993. Print.

Latour, Bruno. *Reassembling the Social: An Introduction to Actor-Network Theory*. Oxford: Oxford University Press, 2005. Print.

Latour, Bruno. "Why Has Critique Run Out of Steam? From Matters of Fact to Matters of Concern." *Critical Inquiry* 30:2 (2004), 225–48. Print.

Latour, Bruno, and Michel Callon. "Unscrewing the Big Leviathan: How Actors Macro-structure Reality and How Sociologists Help Them to Do So." In *Advances in Social Theory and Methodology*. Karin Knorr-Cetina and Aaron Cicourel, eds. London: Routledge, 1981, 277–303. Print.

Latour, Bruno, and Peter Weibel, eds. *Making Things Public: Atmospheres of Democracy*. Cambridge, MA: MIT Press, 2005. Print.

Lee, Ang, dir. *Sense and Sensibility*. 1995. Film.

Lee, Wendy. "A Case for Hard-Heartedness: *Clarissa*, Indifferency, Impersonality." *Eighteenth-Century Fiction* 26:1 (2013), 33–65.

Lermontov, Mikhail. *A Hero of Our Own Times*. Eden and Cedar Paul, trans. Oxford: Oxford University Press, 1958. Print.

Levinson, Marjorie. "Picturing Pleasure: Some Poems by Elizabeth Bishop." In *What's Left of Theory?: New Work on the Politics of Literary Theory*. London: Routledge, 2000, 192–239. Print.

Levinson, Marjorie. "What Is New Formalism?" *PMLA* 122:2 (2007), 558–69. Print.

Lichtenberg, Georg. *The Waste Books*. Reginald J. Hollingdale, trans. New York: New York Review Books, 2000. Print.

Lupton, Julia Reinhard. *Citizen-Saints: Shakespeare and Political Theology*. Chicago: Chicago University Press, 2005. Print.

Lupton, Julia Reinhard. "Forms of Life in *Timon of Athens*." Paper delivered at the Huntington Library, San Marino, April 2008. Lecture.

Lupton, Julia Reinhard. "Shylock between Exception and Emancipation: Shakespeare, Schmitt, Arendt." *Journal for Cultural and Religious Theory* 8:3 (2007), 42–53. Print.

Lupton, Julia Reinhard. *Thinking with Shakespeare: Essays on Politics and Life*. Chicago: University of Chicago Press, 2011. Print.

Lynch, Deidre Shauna. *The Economy of Character: Novels, Market Culture, and the Business of Inner Meaning*. Chicago: University of Chicago Press, 1998. Print.

Lynch, Deidre Shauna. "Review of Alex Woloch, *The One vs. the Many*." *Victorian Studies* 47:2 (2005), 281–82. Print.

Mac Low, Jackson, with Kevin Bezner. "Jackson Mac Low, Interviewed by Kevin Bezner." *New American Writing* 11 (1993), 109–24.

Macpherson, Sandra. "Lovelace, Ltd." *ELH* 65:1 (1998), 99–121. Print.

McCarey, Leo, dir. *Duck Soup*. 1933. Film.

McCoy, Jennifer and Kevin. *Every Anvil*. 2001. Video installation.

McCoy, Jennifer and Kevin *Every Shot, Every Episode*. 2000. Video installation.

McLeod, Norman Z., dir. *Monkey Business*. 1931. Film.

McLeod, Randall. "'The Very Names of the Persons': Editing and the Invention of Dramatick Character." In *Staging the Renaissance: Reinterpretations of Elizabethan and Jacobean Drama*. David Scott Kastan and Peter Stallybrass, eds. New York: Routledge, 1991. Print.

McMaster, Juliet. "What Daisy Knew: The Epistemology of the Child Writer." In *The Child Writer from Austen to Woolf*. McMaster and Christine Alexander, eds. Cambridge: Cambridge University Press, 2005, 51–69. Print.

Mamoulian, Rouben, dir. *Love Me Tonight*. 1932. Film.

Mansfield, Katherine. *Novels and Novelists*. J. Middleton Murray, ed. New York: Knopf, 1930. Print.

Marcus, Sharon. "Comparative Sapphism." In *The Literary Channel: The Inter-National Invention of the Novel*. Margaret Cohen and Carolyn Dever, eds. Princeton: Princeton University Press, 2002. Print.

Marlowe, Christopher. *Doctor Faustus and Other Plays*. David Bevington and Eric Rasmussen, eds. Oxford: Oxford University Press, 1995. Print.

Marshall, Cynthia. "The Doubled Jaques and Constructions of Negation in *As You Like It*." *Shakespeare Quarterly* 49:4 (1986), 375–92. Print.

Marvell, Andrew. *Poems and Letters*. Herschel M. Margoliouth, ed. Oxford: Clarendon, 1952. Print.

Matheson, Richard. *The Shrinking Man*. London: Gollancz, 1994. Print.

Meredith, George. *The Amazing Marriage*. New York: Scribner's, 1923. Print.

Meredith, George. *Diana of the Crossways*. New York: Scribner's, 1906. Print.

Meredith, George. *The Egoist*. Robert M. Adams, ed. New York: Norton, 1979. Print.

Meredith, George. *On the Idea of Comedy and the Uses of the Comic Spirit*. New York: Charles Scribner's Sons, 1906. Print.

Meredith, George. *The Ordeal of Richard Feverel: A History of Father and Son*. New York: Modern Library, 1950. Print.

Miller, J. Hillis. *Ariadne's Thread: Story Lines*. New Haven: Yale University Press, 1992. Print.

Miller, David A. *Jane Austen, or The Secret of Style*. Princeton: Princeton University Press, 2003. Print.

Miller, David A.. *The Novel and the Police*. Berkeley: University of California Press, 1989 Print.

Milton, John. *Complete Poems and Major Prose*. Merritt Y. Hughes, ed. New York: Odyssey, 1957. Print.

Milton, John. *Major Works*. Jonathan Goldberg and Stephen Orgel, eds. Oxford: Oxford University Press, 1991. Print.

Minnelli, Vincente. *Singin' in the Rain*. 1952. Film.

Moi, Toril. *Henrik Ibsen and the Birth of Modernism: Art, Theater, Philosophy*. Oxford: Oxford University Press, 2006. Print.

Moi, Toril. *Simone de Beauvoir: The Making of an Intellectual Woman*, 2nd edition. New York: Oxford University Press, 2008. Print.

Molière. *Don Juan and Other Plays*. George Graveley and Ian Maclean, trans. Oxford: Oxford University Press, 2008. Print.

Molière. *Oeuvres*. Maurice Rat, ed. Paris: Gallimard, 1965. Print.

Molière. *The Misanthrope and Other Plays*. David Coward and John Wood, trans. London: Penguin Books, 2000. Print.

Montaigne, Michel. *Essays*. Michael A. Screech, trans. New York: Penguin, 2003. Print.

Montrose, Louis Adrian. "The Place of a Brother in *As You Like It*: Social Process and Comic Form." *Shakespeare Quarterly* 32:1 (1981), 28–54. Print.

Montrose, Louis Adrian. "The Purpose of Playing: Reflections on a Shakespearean Anthropology." *Helios* 7 (1980), 51–74. Print.

Montrose, Louis Adrian. *The Purpose of Playing: Shakespeare and the Cultural Politics of the Elizabethan Theatre*. Chicago: University of Chicago Press, 1996. Print.

Moretti, Franco. "Conjectures on World Literature." *New Left Review* 1 (2000), 54–68. Print.

Moretti, Franco. *Graphs, Maps, Trees: Abstract Models for a Literary History*. London: Verso, 2005. Print.

Moretti, Franco. "Planet Hollywood." *New Left Review* 9 (2001), 90–101. Print.

Moretti, Franco. *The Way of the World: The Bildungsroman in European Culture*. Alberto Sbragia, trans. London: Verso, 1987. Print.

Morris, William. *News from Nowhere and Other Writings*. Clive Wilmer, ed. New York: Penguin, 1993. Print.

Newell, Mike, dir. *Bridget Jones's Diary*. 2001. Film.

Norman, Larry. *The Public Mirror: Molière and the Social Commerce of Description*. Chicago: University of Chicago Press, 1999. Print.

Nunokawa, Jeff. *Tame Passions of Wilde: Styles of Manageable Desire*. Princeton: Princeton University Press, 2003. Print.

Overbury, Thomas, and others. *The Overburian Characters*. Wilfrid J. Paylor, ed. Oxford: Blackwell, 1936. Print.

Parland, Henry. *Ideals Clearance*. Johannes Göransson, trans. New York: Ugly Duckling Presse, 2006. Print.

Parland, Henry. "The Revolution of Things." Johannes Göransson, trans. *Typo* 7. <typomag.com> Digital.

Phillips, Adam. *On Flirtation*. Cambridge: Harvard University Press, 1996. Print.

Piozzi, Hester Lynch. "*Anecdotes of the Late Samuel Johnson*." In *Johnsonian Miscellanies*. George Birkbeck Hill, ed. Oxford: Clarendon Press, 1897. Print.

Planinc, Zdravko. "Reading *The Merchant of Venice* through Adorno." *Journal for Cultural and Religious Theory* 8:3 (2007), 20–42. Print.

Plutarch. *Lives*. Bernadotte Perrin, trans. Cambridge: Harvard University Press, 1920. Print.

Puckett, Kent. *Bad Form: Social Mistakes and the Nineteenth-Century Novel*. Oxford: Oxford University Press, 2008. Print.

Puttenham, George. *The Art of English Poesy*. Wayne Rebhorn and Frank Wigham, eds. Ithaca: Cornell University Press, 2007. Print.

Racine, Jean. *Oeuvres complètes*. Georges Forestier, ed. Paris: Gallimard, 1999. Print.

Radcliffe, Ann. *The Mysteries of Udolpho*. Bonamy Dobrée, ed. Oxford: Oxford University Press, 1998. Print.

Rampo, Edogawa. *The Edogawa Rampo Reader*. Seth Jacobowitz, trans. Fukuoka: Kurodahan Press, 2008. Print.

Rampo, Edogawa. *Japanese Tales of Mystery and Imagination*. James B. Harris, trans. Boston: Tuttle, 1956. Print.

Reiner, Rob, dir. *When Harry Met Sally*. 1988. Film.

Richardson, Samuel. *Clarissa*. Angus Ross, ed. New York: Penguin, 1986. Print.

Roger, Jacques. *Buffon: A Life in Natural History*. Sarah Lucille Bonnefoi, trans. Ithaca: Cornell University Press, 1997. Print.

Ross, Herbert, dir. *Play It Again, Sam*. 1972. Film.

Rouch, Jean, dir. *The Mad Masters*. 1955. Film.

Rousseau, Jean. "Lettre à Monsieur d'Alembert." *Oeuvres complètes*, vol. 1. Paris: Hachette, 1909. Print.

Ruiz, Raul, dir. *Trois vies et une seule mort*. 1995. Film.

Sandrich, Mark, dir. *Top Hat*. 1935. Film.

Sautet, Claude, dir. *Un coeur en hiver*. 1992. Film.

Sautet, Claude, dir. *Nelly et Monsieur Annaud*. 1995. Film.

Sautet, Claude, dir. *Quelques jours avec moi*. 1988. Film.

Schopenhauer, Arthur. *The World as Will and Representation*. Richard B. Haldane and John Kemp, trans. London: Kegan Paul, 1907. Print.

Schor, Naomi. *George Sand and Idealism*. New York: Columbia University Press, 1993. Print.

Sedgwick, Eve Kosofsky. *Tendencies*. Durham: Duke University Press, 1993. Print.

Sedgwick, Eve Kosofsky. *Touching Feeling: Affect, Pedagogy, Performativity*. Durham: Duke University Press, 2003. Print.

Sedita, Scott. *The Eight Characters of Comedy*. Los Angeles: Atides, 2005. Print.

Serres, Michel, with Bruno Latour. *Conversations on Science, Culture, and Time*. Roxanne Lapidus, trans. Ann Arbor: University of Michigan Press, 1995. Print.

Shakespeare, William. *The Arden Shakespeare Complete Works*. David Scott Kastan, Richard Proudfoot, and Ann Thompson, eds. London: Bloomsbury, 2011. Print.

Shelley, Mary. *Frankenstein*. Maurice Hindle, ed. New York: Penguin, 1992. Print.

Shklovsky, Viktor. *Theory of Prose*. Benjamin Sher, trans. Normal: Dalkey Archive, 1990. Print.

Smith, Barbara Herrnstein. *Poetic Closure: A Study of How Poems End*. Chicago: University of Chicago Press, 2007. Print.

Smith, David Nichol. *Characters from the Histories and Memoirs of the Seventeenth Century*. Oxford: Clarendon, 1936. Print.

Sontag, Susan. *Against Interpretation and Other Essays*. New York: Farrar, Strauss and Giroux, 1966. Print.

Spinoza, Baruch. *Ethics*. Samuel Shirley, trans. Indianapolis: Hackett, 1991. Print.

Spitzer, Leo. "Saint-Simon's Portrait of Louis XIV." In *Essays on Seventeenth-Century French Literature*. David Bellos, ed. Cambridge: Cambridge University Press, 1983. Print.

Stanislavski, Constantin. *An Actor Prepares*. Elizabeth R. Hapgood, trans. New York: Routledge, 1989. Print.

Stanislavski, Constantin. *My Life in Art*. Jack J. Robbins, trans. Boston: Little, Brown, and Company, 1933. Print.

Stevenson, Robert, dir. *Jane Eyre*. 1943. Film.

Sturges, Preston, dir. *The Palm Beach Story*. 1942. Film.

Tarantino, Quentin, dir. *Pulp Fiction*. 1994. Film.

Toufic, Jalal. *Forthcoming*. Berkeley: Atelos, 2001. Print.

Trilling, Lionel. *Sincerity and Authenticity*. Cambridge: Harvard University Press, 1972. Print.

Turner, Henry S. "Lessons from Literature for the Historian of Science (and Vice Versa): Reflections on 'Form.'" *Isis* 101:3 (2010), 578–89. Print.

Turner, Henry S. "The Problem of the More-than-One: Friendship, Calculation, and Political Association in *The Merchant of Venice*," *Shakespeare Quarterly* 57:4 (2006), 413–42. Print.

Tuve, Rosemond. *Images and Themes in Five Poems by Milton*. Cambridge, MA: Harvard University Press, 1957. Print.

Tzara, Tristan. *Seven Dada Manifestos and Lampisteries*. Barbara Wright, ed. and trans. New York: Riverrun Press, 1977. Print.

Van Ghent, Dorothy. *The English Novel: Form and Function*. New York: Harper and Row, 1967. Print.

Vermeule, Blakey. *Why Do We Care about Literary Characters?* Baltimore: Johns Hopkins University Press, 2010. Print.

Walsh, Raoul, dir. *Me and My Gal*. 1932. Print.

Waters, John. *Role Models*. New York: Farrar, Straus, and Giroux, 2010. Print.

Watt, Ian. *The Rise of the Novel: Studies in Defoe, Richardson*, and *Fielding*. London: Chatto and Windus, 1957. Print.

Welch, Denton. "I Left My Grandfather's House." In *In Youth Is Pleasure*. Cambridge: Exact Change, 1994. Print.

Welch, Denton. *In Youth Is Pleasure*. New York: L.B. Fischer, 1946. Print.

Welch, Denton. *The Journals of Denton Welch*. Michael De-la-Noy, ed. New York: E.P. Dutton, 1986. Print.

Welch, Denton. *A Last Sheaf*. Eric Oliver, ed. London: John Lehmann, 1951. Print.

Welch, Denton. *Maiden Voyage*. New York: E.P. Dutton, 1968. Print.

Welch, Denton. *A Voice through a Cloud*. New York: E.P. Dutton, 1966. Print.

Whitehead, Alfred North. *Adventures of Ideas*. New York: Macmillan, 1933. Print.

Wilde, Oscar. *The Major Works*. Isobel Murray, ed. Oxford: Oxford University Press, 1989. Print.

Wilde, Oscar. *Plays*. Peter Raby, ed. Oxford: Oxford University Press, 1995. Print.

Wilde, Oscar. *The Soul of Man Under Socialism*. Portland: Mosher, 1905. Print.

Wilson, Luke. "Renaissance Tool Abuse and the Legal History of the Sudden." In *Literature, Politics, and Law in Renaissance England*. Erica Sheen and Lorna Hutson, eds. Basingstoke: Palgrave, 2005, 121–45. Print.

Winnicott, Donald W. *Playing and Reality*. London: Routledge, 2005. Print.

Woloch, Alex. *The One vs. the Many: Minor Characters and the Space of the Protagonist in the Novel*. Princeton: Princeton University Press, 2003. Print.

Wong, Kar Wai, dir. *Chungking Express*. 1994. Film.

Wood, Christopher, and Alexander Nagel. *Anachronic Renaissance*. Cambridge, MA: MI Press, 2010. Print.

Woolf, Virginia. "On Re-reading Meredith." *The Essays of Virginia Woolf, Vol. 2: 1912-1918*. Andrew McNeillie, ed. New York: Harcourt Brace Jovanovich, 1987. Print.

Wycherly, William. *Complete Plays*. Gerald Weales, ed. New York: Anchor Books, 1966. Print.

Yeats, William Butler. *Selected Poems and Four Plays*. Macha L. Rosenthal, ed. New York: Scribner, 1996. Print.

Zizek, Slavoj. "There Is No Sexual Relationship." In *Gaze and Voice as Love Objects*. Renata Saleci and Slavoj Zizek, eds. Durham: Duke University Press, 1996. Print.

# INDEX

as form   63, 73
gender of   79
generalizing from   11, 78
in gothic novels   175
iconic resemblance distinguished
     from   71–2
identity and   70–1
incomplete form in
     characterization in
     novels   166
individuality and   7, 8, 9, 67,
     70, 73
justice for   82–7
Meredith's understanding of   11
migration of   54–5, 56
minor   6, 8, 74, 75, 77, 80–1, 82
misanthrope as
     paradigmatic   106
names of   53–4, 147
objects and places as   79–80,
     187–213
omniscient narrators and   19–22
Overbury on writing and   48–9
price of   63–6
in realist novels   167
resources of   63, 65
sketches   11, 25, 27, 44, 47–8,
     68, 79, 166, 167, 169, 182, 183
solitude at heart of   49–50
stock   114–15
style distinguished from   72–3
twofold truth of character in
     performance   66–70
types   25–7, 38–42, 55, 68–9,
     187, 200–1
unity in   47
unthinkable space of   26, 50,
     183
vocal characterization   58
wealth of   56–9
what a character is   37–8, 42–4
what are they for   56–7
what other characters do with
     them   56–9

what they can't do   70–3
when they get together   73–7
whole societies in   8
"Character of a Small Poet"
     (Butler)   47–8
*Characters* (Theophrastus)   37–8
Chevalier, Maurice
     in *The Big Pond*   57, 64, 65
     in *Love Me Tonight*   62–3, 73
     in *Monkey Business*   57–66, 69–73
     straw hat associated with   60
chorus (tragic)   136, 137–8
Christensen, Jerome   63–4
*Chungking Express* (film)   196–202
Chute, Hillary   203
*Clarissa* (Richardson)   157–66,
     177–8
clichés
     in Ashford's *The Young
          Visiters*   12–15
     in Chevalier's character   66
     in Hartley's *Flirt*   101
     in Overbury's book of
          characters   42
close reading   9
Clune, Michael   4, 185
Cohn, Dorrit   19–20
Colie, Rosalie   4, 114, 184
collage   17
*La collectionneuse* (film)   27
comedy
     becomes deathly   139
     comic reading of tragedy   90–1,
          136–42, 149
     idealism and   148–50
     Meredith and   11
     musical   6
     Shakespeare's *The Merchant of
          Venice* as pure   38
     situation   35
     stock characters from   114–15
     tragic reading of   98, 139
     Wilde's *The Importance of Being
          Earnest* as   131, 132, 134–5